CHARTERED INSTITUTE FOR
SECURITIES & INVESTMENT

C000060018

UK Financial Regulation

Edition 22, January 2015

This learning manual relates to syllabus
version 22.0 and will cover examinations from
21 April 2015 to 20 December 2015

APPROVED WORKBOOK

Welcome to the Chartered Institute for Securities & Investment's UK Financial Regulation study material written to prepare you for the following CISI Level 3 examinations:

- Capital Markets Programme – Certificate in Derivatives, Financial Derivatives and Securities.
- Investment Operations Certificate (IOC) Programme.
- Certificate Programme – Combating Financial Crime, Corporate Finance, Global Financial Compliance and Risk in Financial Services.

Published by:
Chartered Institute for Securities & Investment
© Chartered Institute for Securities & Investment 2015
8 Eastcheap
London
EC3M 1AE
Tel: +44 20 7645 0600
Fax: +44 20 7645 0601

Email: customersupport@cisi.org
www.cisi.org/qualifications

Author:
Stephen Holt, MCSI

Reviewers:
Lesley Chester, Chartered FCSI
Keith Maner, FCSI REN

This is an educational manual only and the Chartered Institute for Securities & Investment accepts no responsibility for persons undertaking trading or investments in whatever form.

While every effort has been made to ensure its accuracy, no responsibility for loss occasioned to any person acting or refraining from action as a result of any material in this publication can be accepted by the publisher or authors.

A learning map, which contains the full syllabus, appears at the end of this manual. The syllabus can also be viewed on cisi.org and is also available by contacting the Customer Support Centre on +44 20 7645 0777. Please note that the examination is based upon the syllabus. Candidates are reminded to check the Candidate Update area details (cisi.org/candidateupdate) on a regular basis for updates as a result of industry change(s) that could affect their examination.

The questions contained in this manual are designed as an aid to revision of different areas of the syllabus and to help you consolidate your learning chapter by chapter.

Learning manual version: 22.2 (April 2015)

Learning and Professional Development with the CISI

The Chartered Institute for Securities & Investment is the leading professional body for those who work in, or aspire to work in, the investment sector, and we are passionately committed to enhancing knowledge, skills and integrity – the three pillars of professionalism at the heart of our Chartered body.

CISI examinations are used extensively by firms to meet the requirements of government regulators. Besides the regulators in the UK, where the CISI head office is based, CISI examinations are recognised by a wide range of governments and their regulators, from Singapore to Dubai and the US. Around 50,000 examinations are taken each year, and it is compulsory for candidates to use CISI learning manuals to prepare for CISI examinations so that they have the best chance of success. Our learning manuals are normally revised every year by experts who themselves work in the industry and also by our Accredited Training Providers, who offer training and elearning to help prepare candidates for the examinations. Information for candidates is also posted on a special area of our website: cisi.org/candidateupdate.

This learning manual not only provides a thorough preparation for the examination it refers to, it is also a valuable desktop reference for practitioners, and studying from it counts towards your Continuing Professional Development (CPD). Mock examination papers, for most of our titles, will be made available on our website, as an additional revision tool.

CISI examination candidates are automatically registered, without additional charge, as student members for one year (should they not be members of the CISI already), and this enables you to use a vast range of online resources, including CISI TV, free of any additional charge. The CISI has more than 40,000 members, and nearly half of them have already completed relevant qualifications and transferred to a core membership grade. You will find more information about the next steps for this at the end of this manual.

With best wishes for your studies.

Lydia Romero, Director of Learning

It is estimated that this manual will require approximately 75 hours of study time.

What next?
See the back of this book for details of CISI membership.

Need more support to pass your exam?
See our section on Accredited Training Providers.

Want to leave feedback?
Please email your comments to learningresources@cisi.org

Chapter One
The Regulatory Environment

This syllabus area will provide approximately 7 of the 75 examination questions

1. The Regulatory Infrastructure

Learning Objective

Understand the wider structure of UK financial regulation including the responsibilities of the main regulating bodies and the relationship between them

1.2.1   Market regulators: the Financial Conduct Authority and the Prudential Regulation Authority

1.1   The Financial Services and Markets Act (FSMA) 2000

The Financial Services and Markets Act (FSMA) came into effect on 30 November 2001.

It introduced a new structure for the regulation of the financial services industry in the United Kingdom (UK). The purpose of FSMA was to provide stronger protection for consumers of financial services than had been the case under the previous regulatory framework. Subsequently it has been amended, in particular with the Financial Services Act 2012 that introduced two new regulatory bodies – the **Financial Conduct Authority (FCA)** and the **Prudential Regulation Authority (PRA).** The regulatory framework now also comprises the **Financial Policy Committee (FPC)**. A combination of these three bodies has replaced the single regulator, the Financial Services Authority (FSA).

FSMA established:

- Regulators – the Financial Services Authority (FSA) – replaced all the existing self-regulatory organisations (SROs). From 1 April 2013, the FSA was replaced by the FCA and the PRA.
- A single ombudsman service (the Financial Ombudsman Service (FOS)) to provide for the resolution of consumer disputes.
- A single compensation scheme (the Financial Services Compensation Scheme (FSCS)) to provide a fund for consumer compensation if failed firms are unable to meet their liabilities.
- Penalties for the new crime of market abuse.
- The UK listings regime (UK Listing Authority (UKLA)), which replaced the London Stock Exchange (LSE) powers.

The FCA is solely responsible for the authorisation and supervision of all financial institutions not regulated by the PRA, including intermediaries and investment exchanges. The FCA's role is to ensure that the UK's financial markets function well and it will continue the FSA's work of consumer protection, maintaining the integrity of the financial system and promoting competition.

The FCA inherited the FSA's powers to investigate and prosecute insider dealing and market abuse and has taken over as the UKLA. It oversees the FOS, the Money Advice Service and (jointly with the PRA) the FSCS. The FCA and the PRA each set the fees and make rules in respect of the activities under their remit.

This new regulatory framework has become known as **twin peaks** regulation. This means that the supervision of deposit takers, insurers and investment banks is undertaken by two different supervisors; the PRA focuses on prudential issues and the FCA focuses on conduct and market related issues.

The FSMA is defining legislation; it applies to all persons within the UK and sets out the scope for the conduct of regulated activity. 'Persons' in this context – and throughout this workbook – means natural persons and all other types of legal person, such as incorporated bodies, partnerships, trusts and other types of unincorporated associations. It is a criminal offence to conduct regulated activity by way of business in the UK unless a person is either authorised to do so, or is an exempt person. This is known as the **general prohibition** and it is set out in Section 19 of FSMA.

Contravention of the general prohibition is punishable by a maximum sentence of two years' imprisonment and/or an unlimited fine. Agreements entered into are likely to be unenforceable. It is a defence to show that a person has taken all reasonable precautions and exercised all due diligence to avoid committing the offence. FSMA provides for attaining authorised status or for conducting regulated activity under exemption.

Authorised persons are:

- those who have been given permission to conduct regulated activity by the FSA up to 31 March 2013, and by either the FCA or the PRA subsequently (Part 4A FSMA);
- certain overseas firms that qualify for authorisation under special provisions (European Economic Area (EEA), treaty firms and Undertakings for Collective Investment in Transferable Securities (UCITS) qualifiers);
- investment companies with variable capital (ICVCs) established under open-ended investment company (OEIC) Regulations 2001;
- the Society of Lloyd's (s.315 FSMA).

Part 4A of FSMA (as amended) enables businesses to apply directly either to the FCA or the PRA for permission to conduct regulated activity in the UK. When one of the regulators grants this permission, the business becomes an authorised person under FSMA and has a **Part 4A permission** to conduct regulated activities. The firm has entered into a legally binding relationship with the relevant regulator. We shall look at the process for applying for Part 4A permission in Chapter 2.

Exempt persons attain this status by way of specific sections within the FSMA and/or by way of **exemption orders** made by the Treasury. The Treasury can create orders to make certain persons fully exempt for all regulated activity, or to make the activity exempt when it is conducted in a certain way. This distinction is significant because the way in which a firm has attained exempt status determines the way in which legal provisions will apply.

Examples of exempt persons are:

- appointed representatives of authorised persons (s.39 FSMA and the FSMA (Appointed Representatives) Regulations 2001);
- recognised investment exchanges (RIEs) and recognised clearing houses (RCHs) (s.285 FSMA);
- the Bank of England and other central banks (FSMA Exemption Order 2001);
- operators of multilateral trading systems exercising certain rights (s.312A FSMA).

A person cannot be both authorised and exempt at the same time. For example, a firm cannot conduct some regulated activities as an authorised person and others in the capacity of an appointed representative of another firm. We shall look further at exemptions in Chapter 2.

In addition to the most recent Financial Services Act of 2012, the FSMA has been amended and expanded a number of times, since it was first enacted, in order to accommodate changes in the regulatory landscape and to give effect to European Union (EU) directives in the UK.

1.2   The Regulatory Framework: the Financial Conduct Authority (FCA), the Prudential Regulation Authority (PRA) and the Financial Policy Committee (FPC)

The FCA replaces the FSA which was established by the FSMA. The PRA is a subsidiary of the Bank of England (BoE) and was given its responsibilities via the Financial Services Act 2012 amendments to the FSMA. Both the FCA and the PRA are private companies that have been given special dispensation allowing them not to use the word **limited** as part of their names.

FSMA (as amended by the Financial Services Act of 2012) gives the FCA and the PRA certain duties and objectives in relation to their roles as financial services regulators and establishes the legal powers to enable them to fulfil their roles.

Broadly, the FCA is responsible for ensuring that financial markets work well, so that consumers get a fair deal, whilst the focus of the PRA is on stability – the safety and soundness of deposit-taking firms, insurers and systemically important investment firms.

The regulators' powers are over firms carrying on regulated activities, the exchanges that are used by many of those firms, and individuals carrying out particular functions for firms. In some cases, they also extend to those not currently authorised, for example, formerly authorised firms, or firms which ought to have had authorisation, but which have been doing business without it.

The FCA and the PRA are funded entirely from fees paid by the firms which they regulate.

The FCA is accountable to the government on how it carries out its functions, via HM Treasury; the PRA is accountable to the Bank of England.

The FPC is an official committee of the Bank of England. It focuses on the macro-economic and financial issues that may threaten long-term growth prospects.

1.3   HM Treasury

Her Majesty's (HM) Treasury (or just 'the Treasury') has overall responsibility for the UK's financial system, including the institutional structure and the legislation that governs it.

The FCA is directly accountable to the Treasury through a variety of mechanisms.

Firstly, the Treasury has the power to appoint or dismiss the FCA's board and chairman.

Secondly, the FCA (like the FSA) is required to submit a report to the Treasury at least once a year – covering matters such as the way in which it has discharged its functions, the extent to which its objectives have been met and any other matters the Treasury may direct. This report is accompanied by a report from the FCA's non-executive directors and is laid before Parliament.

Thirdly, the Treasury has the power to commission reviews and inquiries into aspects of the FCA's operations. Reviews are conducted by someone the Treasury feels is independent of the FCA, and are restricted to considering the economy, efficiency and effectiveness with which the FCA has used its resources in discharging its functions. Such inquiries may relate to specific, exceptional events occurring within the FCA's range of regulatory responsibilities.

1.4   The Bank of England (BoE)

The Bank of England (BoE) has two core purposes – monetary stability and financial stability.

Monetary stability means stable prices and confidence in the currency. Stable prices are defined by the Government's inflation target, which the Bank seeks to meet through the decisions delegated to the Monetary Policy Committee (MPC), explaining those decisions transparently and implementing them effectively in the money markets.

Financial stability entails detecting and reducing threats to the financial system as a whole. It is in the area of financial stability that the PRA operates.

The PRA is responsible for promoting the safety and soundness of banks and other deposit-taking firms (building societies and credit unions), insurers and systemically important investment firms. The PRA is responsible for prudential supervision – in essence making sure that the firms it supervises hold adequate levels of capital. The PRA works closely with the Financial Policy Committee (FPC) at the BoE. The FPC has responsibility for reducing risks to the financial system as a whole.

The diagram below illustrates how the FPC contributes to the overall picture of the regulation of financial services in the UK, as well as the relative responsibilities of the PRA and FCA.

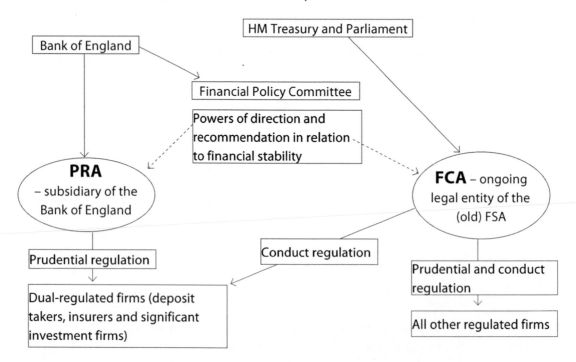

2. The FCA and the PRA and their Statutory Objectives

Learning Objective

1.1.1 Know the FCA's and PRA's statutory objectives and rule-making powers in respect of authorisation, supervision, enforcement, sanctions and disciplinary action [FSMA]

1.1.7 Know the FCA's and PRA's supervisory approach to regulation including outcome-based, early intervention and conduct risk

---

2.1 The Statutory Objectives of the FCA and the PRA

The **FCA** has been given a single strategic objective and three operational objectives within the Financial Services Act of 2012. These are:

- **Strategic objective** – ensuring that the relevant markets function well.
- **Operational objectives:**
  - **The consumer protection objective** – securing an appropriate degree of protection for consumers. This does not necessarily mean preventing all risk of loss to consumers. In considering what is the appropriate degree of protection, the FCA should have regard to the different degrees of risk involved in different kinds of investment, the differing levels of experience and expertise of consumers, the needs of the consumers for advice and accurate information and the general principle that consumers should take responsibility for their decisions.
  - **The integrity objective** – protecting and enhancing the integrity of the UK financial system. The integrity of the financial system includes the following:
    - soundness, stability and resilience;
    - not being used for a purpose connected with financial crime;
    - not being affected by behaviour that amounts to market abuse;
    - the orderly operation of the financial markets;
    - the reliability and transparency of the price formation process in those markets; and
    - the suitability of the listing rules.
  - **The competition objective** – promoting effective competition in the interests of consumers in the markets for regulated financial services or services provided by a Recognised Investment Exchange (RIE) in carrying on regulated activities in respect of which it is exempt from the general prohibition. The FCA may have regard to matters including:
    - the needs of different consumers who use or may use those services, including their need for information that enables them to make informed choices;
    - the ease with which consumers who obtain those services can change the person from whom they obtain them;
    - the ease with which new entrants can enter the market;
    - how far competition is encouraging innovation.

The **PRA** has been given a single **general objective** of *promoting the safety and soundness of PRA-authorised persons.*

The PRA's general objective is to be advanced primarily by:

- seeking to ensure that the business of PRA-authorised persons is carried on in a way which avoids any adverse effect on the stability of the UK financial system; and
- seeking to minimise the adverse effect that the failure of a PRA-authorised person could be expected to have on the stability of the UK financial system.

The PRA has also been given an **insurance objective** that only relates to the effecting or carrying out of contracts of insurance as principal to the extent it is a PRA-regulated activity. The objective is *contributing to the securing of an appropriate degree of protection for those who are or may become policyholders.*

The FCA's objectives also provide for a degree of accountability:

- **Annual report** – the FCA's annual report to the Treasury (as mentioned in Section 1.3) contains an assessment of how well or otherwise the FCA has met its statutory objectives. The report is scrutinised by various Parliamentary committees.
- **Rules** – the FCA has to show how the rules it makes relate to the statutory objectives.
- **Judicial review** – if the FCA fails to consider the objectives, or incorrectly interprets the objectives, it can be challenged in the courts.
- **Regulatory failure** - the FCA and PRA will be held accountable if breaches of the objectives occurred or were made worse because of a serious failure on the part of the regulator.

Under FSMA, the relevant regulator (the FCA and/or the PRA) is required to maintain arrangements to supervise compliance with the requirements imposed on authorised persons. The supervisory approach has to work to ensure the statutory objectives are met.

The FCA's supervision efforts focus on the conduct of both FCA-authorised and PRA-authorised firms, plus prudential regulation for those authorised firms that are not authorised by the PRA. The PRA supervises the prudential aspects of those firms that it authorises. A structured approach to supervision is adopted which is outlined in more detail in Chapter 2, Section 4.

The former regulator, the FSA, extensively reviewed its supervisory process following the collapse of Northern Rock in 2008, and concluded that, although its core supervisory principles were supported by the recent financial crisis, changes were nevertheless required, involving a move to outcomes-focused supervision and drawing upon the lessons from the global credit crisis.

The FCA implemented these changes through its supervisory enhancement programme and refers to the resulting enhanced process as 'intensive supervision'.

The intended outcomes of the supervisory enhancement programme are for better, more effective and consistent supervision as defined by:

- an integrated and consistent supervisory process across all relationship-managed firms;
- a focus on big-picture risks: business models and strategy;
- a balanced approach to prudential and conduct risks;
- an increased focus on macro-prudential and cross-sector risks;
- an effective relationship management capability;
- a willingness to make judgments on the future risks and to require firms to mitigate them in advance of them crystallising.

2.1.1 Delivering Effective, On-the-Ground, Intensive Supervision and Credible Deterrence

The FCA has radically changed the way it operates, compared with the FSA. In particular it has revised both the regulatory philosophy and the operating model which enables its delivery. The underlying principle of the old-style FSA was that it would not intervene until something went wrong. This was well supported by society and the City at the time. The new model of supervision requires the FCA to intervene in a proactive way when it believes that the results of a firm's actions will pose a risk to the FCA's statutory objectives. This, therefore, requires the FCA to adopt a more intrusive, confrontational and direct regulatory style than before and to make judgements that are undoubtedly more difficult, and may be disputed by firms (and in some cases found to be wrong).

The outcomes-focused intensive supervision model has two key features.

- Firstly, a **significant enhanced analysis and risk identification capacity** which focuses on business model risk and interacts with macro-prudential analysis. For this, the FCA requires more and better quality people and more sophisticated systems and analysis. A comprehensive conduct business model analysis is being undertaken by FCA supervisors, supported by sector teams and conduct specialists, who also contribute wider market knowledge and horizon risk scanning. This is combined with mystery shopping and on-site visits, to increase the probability of identifying issues before they gain an industry-wide hold.
- Secondly, there is a greater focus on **outcome testing**, rather than ensuring that firms have the appropriate systems and controls. This approach also requires earlier and more direct regulatory intervention.

2.1.2 The UK Regulatory Environment

Underpinning both of these is a greater scrutiny of senior management competence where, historically, the FSA only judged probity. The FCA now seeks to assess both technical competence and the ability of individuals to contribute to effective governance. As with other aspects of the new approach, this requires the FCA to make judgements that at times will be at variance with those of the firms.

A final aspect of the new supervisory approach is the aim to deliver credible deterrence, including a consistent and more transparent framework for calculating financial penalties.

2.1.3 Risk-Based Approach

The risk-based approach discussed above means that the FCA assesses individual firms for the risk each one presents to the FCA's objectives. This then helps the FCA determine what level of supervisory attention should be directed at each firm.

The starting point for this process begins with the categorisation of the regulated firm. The FCA has split this into four categories:

- **C1** – banking and insurance groups with a very large number of retail customers and universal/ investment banks with very large client asset and trading operations.
- **C2** – firms across all sectors with a substantial number of retail customers and/or large wholesale firms.

- **C3** – firms across all sectors with retail customers and/or a significant wholesale presence.
- **C4** – smaller firms, including almost all intermediaries.

Until recently, C1 and C2 firms were classed as **fixed portfolio**, which means they have a nominated supervisor. The vast majority of firms will be C3 and C4 firms and classed as **flexible portfolio**, which means they are supervised by a team of sector specialists and no nominated supervisor. FCA supervisors are allocated to firms with the greatest potential to cause risks to consumers or market integrity.

Reflective of the FCA's supervisory focus, the FCA released its updated approach to Firm Supervision in March 2014 entitled *'Our Approach to Supervision'*. The following is a high level summary of regulatory conduct supervision for C1, C2, C3 and C4 firms going forward:

C1 Firms:

- Business model and strategy analysis every two years, reviewed at the halfway stage.
- Regular meetings between FCA supervisors, senior management, board members, key control functions and external auditors, with further meetings to maintain an understanding of the business as changes happen or risks emerge.
- Regular reviews of management information. This can include board and executive committee packs and performance information.
- Annual strategy meeting between FCA senior management and the CEO and executives.
- One or two 'deep dive' assessments during each annual assessment cycle.
- Annual firm evaluation, explained in a letter to the firm and a presentation to the board.
- Regular baseline monitoring of regulatory returns.
- Routine and other activities such as transfers, acquisitions and permission changes.
- Participation in thematic reviews and market studies.

C2 Firms:

- Annual peer group business model and strategy analysis.
- Regular meetings between FCA supervisors, senior management and board members, with further meetings to maintain an understanding of the business as changes happen or risks emerge.
- Regular reviews of management information. This can include board and executive committee packs and performance information.
- Annual strategy meeting between FCA senior management and the firms' executives.
- One or two 'deep dive' assessments during each two-year assessment cycle.
- Firm evaluation every two years, explained in a letter to the firm and presentation to the board.
- Regular baseline monitoring of regulatory returns.
- Routine and other activities such as transfers, acquisitions and permission changes.
- Participation in thematic reviews and market studies.

C3 Firms:

- Annual peer group business model and strategy analysis.
- Routine interaction with the FCA via the Firm Contact Centre.
- Other interaction via trade body events and round table discussions.
- Regular baseline monitoring of regulatory returns.
- Occasional routine tasks, such as transfers, acquisitions and permission changes.
- Participation in thematic reviews and market studies.
- Periodic assessment at least once every four years.

- Additional assessments where necessary (for example, as a follow up to the main assessment, or where there have been significant changes in a firm's business model).
- Potential inclusion in issues and products work or competition market studies.

C4 Firms:

- Ongoing supervision by sectoral analysis and thematic reviews.
- Regular baseline monitoring of regulatory returns.
- Occasional routine tasks, such as transfers, acquisitions and permission changes.
- Four-yearly assessment via a phone or face-to-face interview, an online assessment, or a combination of these.
- The FCA will do further firm-specific work where risks need to be addressed.
- The FCA will also follow up with a random sample of firms that have completed the online assessment, to verify the information provided.

This updated approach is reflective of the main theme of its regulatory remit.

2.1.4   Conduct Risk

What is Conduct Risk?

The Financial Conduct Authority (FCA) has not provided a precise definition of the expression **'conduct risk'**. There are, however, a number of different ways in which the term can be viewed.

A good starting point is to consider conduct risk as the latest in a series of regulatory thinking that began with **treating customers fairly (TCF)**, which then progressed through **principles-based regulation**, and then on to **outcomes-focused regulation**, before becoming **conduct risk**. All of these expressions have at their heart the same basic idea, namely that **regulation through the creation of rules alone is not enough to protect consumers or markets**. As far back as 2006, the then regulator, the Financial Services Authority (FSA), said in the context of treating customers fairly and principles-based regulation:

'The aim is to improve industry behaviour and so reduce unfair outcomes for consumers without providing new prescriptive requirements.'

(Source: FSA Discussion Paper 06/4)

Conduct risk, along with its predecessors, is concerned with the **outcome for consumers, rather than the detail of the rules**; the FCA is concerned with the spirit, rather than the detail, of the rules. Rather than conclude that the rules do not matter, a better approach is to see that the FCA takes a balanced approach. The **rules do matter, but outcomes for consumers and markets are the principal focus of regulatory concern**. In reality, many of the detailed rules are, themselves, aimed at the conduct of firms.

Compliance with rules is generally a backward-looking philosophy. The question tends to be *'Did the firm comply?'* Certainly that is the way that firms have operated in the past, with compliance monitoring activity devoted to uncovering incidences of historic rules breaches.

The conduct risk approach, on the other hand, has a more forward-looking emphasis. *'Will the actions of the firm lead to poor outcomes for consumers or not?'*

The FCA's regulatory approach to conduct risk is, however, not a matter of making rules. The relevant powers for this approach are found in Section 55B and Schedule 6 to the Act. This deals with the **threshold conditions**. Whenever the FCA gives or varies permission to a firm to carry on one or more of the regulated activities, the FCA and PRA *'must ensure that the person concerned will satisfy, and continue to satisfy, in relation to all of the regulated activities for which the person has or will have permission, the threshold condition for which that regulator is responsible'*.

The threshold conditions themselves are set out in an order made by the Treasury under the Act. They are important because it is here that the FCA derives its authority to consider what a firm's capacity is to meet the stated threshold conditions on an on-going basis.

The threshold conditions deal with the following matters:

a. **Location of offices** – generally speaking, a regulated firm that is incorporated in the UK must have its head office in the UK also.
b. **Effective supervision** – under this condition, the firm *'must be capable of being effectively supervised by the FCA'*. There are a number of additional circumstances to consider, such as the complexity of the firm's business or products, the way in which the business is organised, the firm's membership of a group of companies, and the links the firm may have with other persons.
c. **Appropriate resources** – the firm must have appropriate resources, as judged by the FCA, to carry on the regulated activities that the firm carries on. Relevant considerations include the nature and scale of the business and the skills and experience of the firm's managers.
d. **Suitability** – the condition here is that the firm *'must be a fit and proper person having regard to all the circumstances'*. Considerations include:
    • the nature and complexity of the business;
    • whether the firm *'is complying with requirements imposed by the FCA in the exercise of its functions, or requests made by the FCA, relating to the provision of information to the FCA, and where [the firm] has complied or is so complying, the manner of that compliance'*;
    • whether those who manage the firm's affairs *'have adequate skills and experience and have acted and may be expected to act with probity'*;
    • *'whether [the firm's] business is being, or is to be, managed in such a way as to ensure that its affairs will be conducted in a sound and prudent manner'*;
    • the need to minimise the use of the firm *'for a purpose connected with financial crime'*.
e. **Business model** – the firm's strategy for business *'must be suitable for a person carrying on the regulated activities that [the firm] carries on or seeks to carry on'*. In assessing the business model, the FCA's consideration must include:
    • whether the business model is compatible with the firm's affairs being conducted soundly and prudently;
    • the interests of consumers;
    • the integrity of the UK financial system.

It is evident that the threshold conditions give the FCA significant powers to assess the firm's future behaviours. If the conclusions are adverse to the firm, the FCA has the power to vary the firm's permissions on its own initiative, or indeed to remove permissions altogether from the firm.

Now that the FCA is operating on both a rules-based and forward-looking basis, it is useful to compare the two approaches and the effects they have:

- **Rules-based approach:**
  - based on generic standard setting;
  - rules and guidance powers are used;
  - supervision assesses compliance with rules;
  - formal consultation process exists;
  - the approach leads to judgement about the firm.
- **Forward-looking approach:**
  - based on subjective judgement of the firm;
  - threshold conditions powers are used;
  - supervision challenges the firm about behaviour;
  - there is no consultation;
  - the approach leads to standard setting for the firm.

Large firms are already used to the concept of **risk management**. The risks to manage depend very much on the nature of the firm; a bank, for example, must manage its credit risk, market risk and operational risk, among others. Conduct risk seems to have the greatest affinity with operational risk, which is a risk that affects all financial firms, not just banks.

The Basel Committee defines operational risk as:

'The risk of loss resulting from inadequate or failed internal processes, people and systems or from external events.'

Regulatory or **compliance risk** has often been seen as no more than a category of operational risk. Although there is fundamentally no right answer to the categorisation of conduct risk, most risk management within firms is aimed at detecting risks to the firm. Conduct risk could be viewed in the same way, considering the question of what would happen to the firm if it failed to meet the FCA's conduct risk expectations, it is perhaps better to consider conduct risk differently as risks arising to consumers (whether retail or otherwise), or to markets arising from the behaviour of the firm's employees, or of the firm as a person in its own right.

In its Peer Review Report on Risk Governance, published in February 2013, the Financial Stability Board (FSB) identified business conduct as a new risk category, and said:

'One of the key lessons from the crisis was that reputational risk was severely underestimated; hence, there is more focus on business conduct and the suitability of products, eg, the type of products sold and to whom they are sold. As the crisis showed, consumer products such as residential mortgage loans could become a source of financial instability.'

To embed conduct risk issues fully within an organisation, the board needs to consider the conduct implications of the firm's strategy and put in place policies and procedures to support this throughout the organisation. This could be achieved by introducing an appropriate conduct risk policy that can be communicated throughout the organisation, and for which training can be devised. Key to this policy will be to define what conduct risk means to that particular organisation, to establish a meaningful strategic direction for conduct in a firm and to determine the behaviours that the firm wishes to demonstrate when fulfilling that strategy. Board involvement and the tone at the top are critical to the successful implementation and embedding of appropriate approaches to conduct risk issues.

In order to manage conduct risk, the firm must first of all understand what risks it is facing. These will vary from firm to firm, and firms in different sectors will face different conduct risks. Although it is crucial for the firm to understand its own risks, the FCA helpfully publishes an annual *Risk Outlook* publication which sets out how the FCA views the distribution of risks across its regulated sector.

It is vital that firms pay attention to *Risk Outlook* and the business plan. *Risk Outlook* provides food for thought in the detection of the firm's own risks; the business plan presents an opportunity to prepare for the FCA's own work. A firm that fails to prepare in this way risks being needlessly unsighted on the FCA's own work.

2.1.5   Main Steps in Risk Assessment

In changing the former Advanced, Risk-Responsive Operating FrameWork (ARROW) approach, the FCA has changed its model of supervision. The main steps in the FCA's risk assessment process are as follows:

- **Firm systematic framework (FSF)** – preventative work through structured conduct assessment of firms.
- **Event-driven work** – dealing faster and more decisively with problems that are emerging or have happened, and securing customer redress or other remedial work where necessary. This covers issues that occur outside the firm assessment cycle, and uses better data monitoring and intelligence.
- **Issues and products** – fast, intensive campaigns on sectors of the market or products within a sector that are putting or may put consumers at risk. This approach is driven by what we call sector risk assessment, which looks at what is currently and prospectively causing poor outcomes for consumers and market participants. It uses data analysis, market intelligence and input from the firm assessment process.

The Firm Systematic Framework (FSF)

This is designed to assess a firm's conduct risk, and aims to answer the question: *Are the interests of customers and market integrity at the heart of how the firm is run?* It does this by using a common framework across all sectors, which is targeted to the type of firm.

The common features involve:

- **Business model and strategy analysis (BMSA)** – to give a view on how sustainable the business is in respect of conduct, and of where future risks may lie.
- **Assessment** of how the firm embeds fair treatment of customers and ensures market integrity in the way it conducts its business. The assessment has four modules:
  - **governance and culture** – to assess how effectively a firm identifies, manages and reduces conduct risks;
  - **product design** – to determine whether a firm's products or services meet customer needs and are targeted accordingly;
  - **sales or transaction processes** – to assess firms' systems and controls; and
  - **post-sales/services and transaction handling** – to assess how effectively a firm ensures its customers are treated fairly after the point-of-sale, service or transaction, including complaints handling.

Deciding What Actions are Required by the Firm to Address Issues Identified

1. **Communication** to the firm, setting out the assessment and actions required.
2. **Event-driven work** – having fewer supervisors allocated to specific firms means more flexibility to devote resources to situations in firms where there is heightened risk to consumers, or where consumers have experienced some loss and quick action is required to stop the situation from worsening.
3. **Issues and products** – being more flexible in how the FCA deploys supervisors means it can react promptly to emerging issues, and carry out more reviews on products and issues across a sector or market. The FCA uses a sector risk assessment (SRA) to drive this issue and product work. This provides an assessment of the conduct risks across a sector (such as the investment intermediary sector, or the retail banking sector). This complements firm-specific work, so together they identify risks, whether they are cross-firm issues, firm-specific issues or product issues. The FCA also uses a range of data, information and intelligence from firms, consumers and trade bodies to identify the biggest risks and to prioritise its work.

The key questions that the FCA would use an SRA to answer are:

- What are the cross-firm and product issues that are behind poor outcomes for consumers or endanger market integrity?
- What is the degree of potential harm?
- What is the discovery or mitigation work proposed?

Specialist sector teams work together to deliver these assessments, making appropriate use of external data and market intelligence.

2.2 Rule-Making Powers

Part 9A of FSMA empowers the FCA to make rules that are legally binding on authorised firms concerning regulated activity and also activity that is not regulated. Such rules must appear to the FCA to be necessary or expedient for the purpose of advancing one or more of its operational objectives.

The PRA has similar rule-making powers; however the powers only extend to PRA-authorised persons.

In addition to rule-making powers, the FSMA empowers either regulator to:

- grant authorisation to persons applying for Part 4A permission, vary a firm's permission and cancel authorisation;
- supervise authorised persons on an ongoing basis to ensure that they continue to meet the regulators' authorisation requirements and that they comply with the Handbook rules and other regulatory obligations;
- employ a range of disciplinary measures and sanctions, to punish or limit the activities of firms that fail to comply;
- enforce the regulatory framework – the general approach is one of credible deterrence, using enforcement strategy as a tool to change behaviour in the industry.

2.3   Applications of EU Legislation and Guidance

Learning Objective

1.2.6   Understand the direct applications of EU legislation and guidance [EC & ESAs]

On 15 December 2010, the Government announced Guiding Principles for EU legislation generally. For financial services, the **European System of Financial Supervision** is the framework of financial supervision in the EU in operation since 2011 and it replaced the Committees of Supervisors with **European Supervisory Authorities** (ESAs) complemented by the European Systemic Risk Board (ESRB), under the responsibility of the European Central Bank (ECB).

At a global level, the FCA and PRA are actively involved in the work of the Financial Stability Board, the Basel Committee on Banking Supervision (BCBS), the International Association of Insurance supervisors, and the Joint Forum. It uses these fora to advance its safety and soundness, and policyholder protection objectives.

As a consequence of the UK's role as an international financial centre, a key responsibility of the PRA and FCA is the supervision of overseas firms operating in the UK, as well as UK groups operating abroad. The regulators engage actively with their overseas counterparts in supervising cross-border firms. To support this, the regulators maintain co-operation agreements, including memoranda of understanding with overseas counterparts to enable the sharing of confidential information on cross-border firms and they participate in 'supervisory colleges' for firms with operations in the UK.

2.3.1   European Engagement and Legislation

The policy standards agreed internationally are implemented in Europe through directives or directly applicable regulations. The UK regulators engage actively with relevant European institutions and EU regulators and are involved in the on-going development and implementation of the single market in financial services. This involves a comprehensive legislative programme, which must be implemented in the UK.

The regulation of financial services across Europe is overseen by a European System of Financial Supervision (ESFS). This is comprised of three ESAs:

- The European Banking Authority (EBA).
- The European Securities and Markets Authority (ESMA).
- The European Insurance and Occupational Pensions Authority (EIOPA).

The European Systemic Risk Board (ESRB) is an independent EU body responsible for macro-prudential oversight of the EU financial system.

Part of the role of the ESAs is to improve coordination between national supervisory authorities in the EU. They have significant powers to propose draft rules and to take decisions binding on national supervisors.

3. The FCA's Principles for Businesses and the Wider Obligations of Fair Treatment

---

Learning Objective

1.1.2 Understand the Principles for Businesses [PRIN 1.1.2 (FCA), 1.1.7, 2.1.1 (FCA/PRA)] and the requirement to act honestly, fairly and professionally and to treat customers fairly [COBS 2.1]

3.1 The Principles for Businesses

If a firm breaches any of the Principles for Businesses it will be liable to disciplinary sanctions as they are legally binding on firms.

The 11 Principles for Businesses are:

1. **Integrity** – a firm must conduct its business with integrity.
2. **Skill, care and diligence** – a firm must conduct its business with due skill, care and diligence.
3. **Management and control** – a firm must take reasonable care to organise and control its affairs responsibly and effectively, with adequate risk management systems.
4. **Financial prudence** – a firm must maintain adequate financial resources.
5. **Market conduct** – a firm must observe proper standards of market conduct.
6. **Customers' interests** – a firm must pay due regard to the interests of its customers and treat them fairly.
7. **Communications with clients** – a firm must pay due regard to the information needs of its clients and communicate information to them in a way which is clear, fair and not misleading.
8. **Conflicts of interest** – a firm must manage conflicts of interest fairly, both between itself and its customers, and between customers and other clients.
9. **Customers: relationships of trust** – a firm must take reasonable care to ensure the suitability of its advice and discretionary decisions for any customer who is entitled to rely upon its judgment.
10. **Clients' assets** – a firm must arrange adequate protection for clients' assets when it is responsible for them.
11. **Relations with regulators** – a firm must deal with its regulators in an open and co-operative way and must disclose to the PRA/FCA appropriately anything relating to the firm of which the PRA/FCA would reasonably expect notice.

3.2 Fair Treatment

The concept of fair treatment is at the heart of the regulatory system. It is expressed in Principle 6 above, and also in an important conduct of business rule:

A firm must act honestly, fairly and professionally in accordance with the best interests of its client.

This rule is known as the **client's best interests rule**.

An important part of the FCA's supervision of firms involves assessing how they are able to demonstrate fair treatment of clients. The firm's management culture should be ethical and have the client's best interests at the heart of the firm. A firm also needs to ensure it gathers sufficient management information to help it monitor how well it is adhering to these obligations, and to help it identify where it might be failing.

As part of its **Treating Customers Fairly (TCF)** initiative, the FCA's predecessor, the FSA, defined six **consumer outcomes**. These are that:

1. Consumers can be confident that they are dealing with firms where the fair treatment of customers is central to the corporate culture.
2. Products and services marketed and sold in the retail market are designed to meet the needs of identified consumer groups and are targeted accordingly.
3. Consumers are provided with clear information and are kept appropriately informed before, during and after the point of sale.
4. Where consumers receive advice, the advice is suitable and takes account of their circumstances.
5. Consumers are provided with products that perform as firms have led them to expect, and the associated service is both of an acceptable standard and as they have been led to expect.
6. Consumers do not face unreasonable post-sale barriers imposed by firms to change product, switch provider, submit a claim or make a complaint.

The FCA is continuing with the work on TCF that the FSA started.

3.3   PRA Fundamental Rules

In June 2014 the PRA published its Fundamental Rules, which replaced the Principles for Businesses. The Rules are high-level and collectively set out the PRA's expectations of firms and act as an expression of the PRA's general objective of promoting the safety and soundness of regulated firms. They are a clearer expression of the PRA's expectations and more closely reflect the PRA's underlying detailed rules than the Principles.

The Rules apply proportionately to all PRA firms, taking into account the difference between sectors and between sizes of firms. They apply with respect of activities wherever they are carried on.

The Fundamental Rules are:

1. A firm must conduct its business with integrity.
2. A firm must conduct its business with due skill, care and diligence.
3. A firm must act in a prudent manner.
4. A firm must at all times maintain adequate financial resources.
5. A firm must have effective risk strategies and risk management systems.
6. A firm must organise and control its affairs responsibly and effectively.
7. A firm must deal with its regulators in an open and cooperative way and must disclose to the PRA appropriately anything relating to the firm of which the PRA would reasonably expect notice.
8. A firm must prepare for resolution so, if the need arises, it can be resolved in an orderly manner with a minimum disruption of critical services.

4. The Statements of Principle and Code of Practice for Approved Persons (APER)

Learning Objective

1.1.3 Know the Statements of Principle 1 to 4 and Code of Practice for approved persons for all approved persons functions [APER 1.1A, 1.2.3, 2.1A.2, 2.1A.3, 3.1.1A, 4.1, 4.2, 4.3.1 and 4.3.3, 4.4.1/3/4/9]

The FSMA recognises that certain roles within authorised firms are particularly important to the control or operation of the firm and to its capacity to meet its regulatory obligations. The roles are known as **controlled functions**, and a person has to apply to the PRA or the FCA for approval to carry out the role before they can start. Hence, individuals performing controlled functions are known as **approved persons**.

Controlled functions are grouped under two headings:

1. **Significant influence functions** – functions that are governing or managerial. They include the directors of the firm and other key personnel.
2. **Customer functions** – functions involving interaction with the customers of the firm, such as investment advice or management.

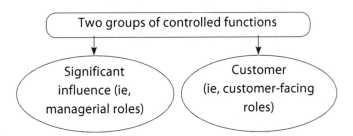

In a similar manner to the Principles for Businesses, the FCA Handbook details seven **Statements of Principle for Approved Persons** to observe as they carry out their duties.

4.1 Statements of Principle

There are seven Statements of Principle and the first four apply to all approved persons regardless of the controlled function that they perform. An approved person must:

1. act with **integrity** in carrying out his controlled function;
2. act with **due skill, care and diligence** in carrying out his controlled function;
3. observe **proper standards of market conduct** in carrying out his controlled function;
4. deal with the PRA/FCA and with other regulators **in an open and co-operative way** and must disclose appropriately any information of which the PRA/FCA would reasonably expect notice.

4.2 Code of Practice for Approved Persons – All Controlled Functions

Additionally, the rules include a Code of Practice for Approved Persons. Paradoxically, the Code of Practice describes behaviours which, in the opinion of the PRA/FCA, do not comply with the Statements of Principle and also factors that should be taken into account in determining whether or not an approved person's conduct complies with a Statement of Principle.

4.2.1 Code of Practice for Statement of Principle 1

In the opinion of the regulators, any of the following is a failure to comply with the requirement for an approved person to **act with integrity** in carrying out his controlled function:

1. Deliberately misleading (or attempting to mislead) a client, the firm (including the firm's auditors or appointed actuary) or the PRA/FCA by either act or omission. This includes deliberately:
   - falsifying documents;
   - misleading a client about the risks of an investment;
   - misleading a client about the charges or surrender penalties of investment products;
   - misleading a client about the likely performance of investment products by providing inappropriate projections of future investment returns;
   - misleading a client by informing him that products only require a single payment when that is not the case;
   - mismarking the value of investments or trading positions;
   - procuring the unjustified alteration of prices on illiquid or off-exchange contracts;
   - misleading others within the firm about the creditworthiness of a borrower;
   - providing false or inaccurate documentation or information, including details of training, qualifications, past employment record or experience;
   - providing false or inaccurate information to the firm (or to the firm's auditors or appointed actuary);
   - providing false or inaccurate information to the PRA/FCA;
   - destroying, or causing the destruction of, documents (including false documentation) or tapes or their contents, relevant to misleading (or attempting to mislead) a client, the firm or the PRA/FCA;
   - failing to disclose dealings where disclosure is required by the firm's personal account dealing rules; and
   - misleading others in the firm about the nature of risks being accepted.
2. Deliberately recommending an investment to a customer, or carrying out a discretionary transaction for a customer, if the approved person knows that he is unable to justify its suitability for that customer.
3. Deliberately failing to inform a customer, the firm (or its auditors or appointed actuary) or the PRA/FCA of the fact that their understanding of a material issue is incorrect. This includes deliberately failing to:
   - disclose the existence of falsified documents;
   - rectify mismarked positions immediately.
4. Deliberately preparing inaccurate or inappropriate records or returns in connection with a controlled function, such as:
   - performance reports for transmission to customers which are inaccurate or inappropriate (for example, by relying on past performance without giving appropriate warnings);

- ◦ inaccurate training records or details of qualifications, past employment record or experience;
- ◦ inaccurate trading confirmations, contract notes or other records of transactions or holdings of securities for a customer, whether or not the customer is aware of these inaccuracies or has requested such records.

5. Deliberately misusing the assets or confidential information of a client or the firm such as:
   - ◦ front running client orders ('front running' means handling the firm's own orders before those of its client, or before the firm's broker recommendations are released to clients, so as to benefit from price movements that may arise from client-dealing activity);
   - ◦ carrying out unjustified trading on client accounts to generate a benefit to the approved person (sometimes known as churning);
   - ◦ misappropriating a client's assets, including wrongly transferring cash or securities belonging to clients to personal accounts;
   - ◦ using a client's funds for purposes other than those for which they are provided;
   - ◦ retaining a client's funds wrongly;
   - ◦ pledging the assets of a client as security or margin in circumstances where the firm is not permitted to do so.

6. Deliberately designing transactions so as to disguise breaches of requirements and standards of the regulatory system.

7. Deliberately failing to disclose the existence of a conflict of interest in connection with dealings with a client.

8. Deliberately not paying due regard to the interests of a customer.

9. Deliberate acts, omissions or business practices that could be reasonably expected to cause consumer detriment.

4.2.2 Code of Practice for Statement of Principle 2

In the opinion of the PRA/FCA, any of the following is a failure to comply with the requirement for an approved person to **act with due skill, care and diligence** in carrying out his controlled function.

1. Failing to inform a customer or the firm (or the firm's auditors or appointed actuary) of material information in circumstances where he was aware, or ought to have been aware, of such information and the fact that he should provide it. Examples include:
   - ◦ failing to explain the risks of an investment to a customer;
   - ◦ failing to disclose details of the charges or surrender penalties of investment products;
   - ◦ mismarking trading positions;
   - ◦ providing inaccurate or inadequate information to the firm, its auditors or appointed actuary;
   - ◦ failing to disclose dealings where disclosure is required by the firm's personal account dealing rules.

2. Recommending an investment to a customer, or carrying out a discretionary transaction for a customer, where he does not have reasonable grounds to believe that it is suitable for that customer.

3. Undertaking, recommending or providing advice on transactions without reasonable understanding of the risk exposure of the transaction to the customer. For example, recommending transactions in investments to a customer without a reasonable understanding of the liability of that transaction.

4. Undertaking transactions without a reasonable understanding of the risk exposure of the transaction to the firm. For example, trading on the firm's own account, without a reasonable understanding of the liability of that transaction.

5. Failing without good reason to disclose the existence of a conflict of interest in connection with dealings with a client.

6. Failing to provide adequate control over a client's assets, such as failing to segregate a client's assets or failing to process a client's payments in a timely manner.
7. Continuing to perform a controlled function despite having failed to meet the standards of knowledge and skills as required by the PRA/FCA.
8. Failing to pay due regard to the interests of a customer, without good reason.

4.2.3 Code of Practice for Statement of Principle 3

Statement of Principle 3 requires an approved person to **observe proper standards of market conduct** in carrying out his controlled function. In terms of interpreting what might be regarded as proper standards of market conduct, the PRA/FCA states that compliance with its Code of Market Conduct will tend to show compliance with Statement of Principle 3.

4.2.4 Code of Practice for Statement of Principle 4

Statement of Principle 4 requires an approved person to **deal with the PRA/FCA and other regulators in an open and co-operative way** and to disclose appropriately any information of which the PRA/FCA would reasonably expect notice. In the opinion of the PRA/FCA, an approved person is not complying with Statement of Principle 4 in the following circumstances:

1. Failing to report promptly in accordance with his firm's internal procedures (or, if none exists, direct to the PRA/FCA) information which it would be reasonable to assume would be of material significance to the PRA/FCA, whether in response to questions or otherwise.
2. Failing without good reason to:
   i. inform a regulator of information of which the approved person was aware in response to questions from that regulator;
   ii. attend an interview or answer questions put by a regulator, despite a request or demand having been made;
   iii. supply a regulator with appropriate documents or information when requested or required to do so and within the time limits attaching to that request or requirement.

4.3 Code of Practice for Approved Persons – Significant Influence Functions (SIFs)

Learning Objective

1.1.5 Know the Statements of Principle 5 to 7 and Code of Practice for approved persons in respect of significant influence functions [APER 2.1A.3, 3.3.1, 4.5.1A/12/13/14 + 4.6.1A/2/3/5/6/8 & 4.7.1A/2/12/13]

Additionally, for significant influence functions (SIFs) there are three further principles:

An approved person must:

• take reasonable steps to ensure that the business of the firm for which he is responsible in his controlled function is organised so that it can be controlled effectively;

- exercise due skill, care and diligence in managing the business of the firm for which he is responsible in his controlled function; and
- take reasonable steps to ensure that the business of the firm for which he is responsible in his controlled function complies with the relevant requirements and standards of the regulatory system.

4.3.1 Code of Practice for Statement of Principle 5

Statement of Principle 5 requires an approved person performing a significant influence function to take reasonable steps to ensure that the business of the firm for which he is responsible in his controlled function is organised so that it can be controlled effectively.

The PRA/FCA expects this to include the following:

1. **Reporting lines** – the organisation of the business and the responsibilities of those within it should be clearly defined, with reporting lines clear to staff. If staff have dual reporting lines there is a greater need to ensure that the responsibility and accountability of each individual line manager is clearly set out and understood.
2. **Authorisation levels and job descriptions** – if members of staff have particular levels of authorisation, these should be clearly set out and communicated to staff. It may be appropriate for each member of staff to have a job description of which he is aware.
3. **Suitability of individuals** – if an individual's performance is unsatisfactory, then the appropriate approved person performing a significant influence function should review carefully whether that individual should be allowed to continue in that position. The approved person performing the significant influence function should not let the financial performance of the individual (or group) prevent an appropriate investigation into the compliance with the requirements and standards of the regulatory system.

Failure to comply with Principle 5 may include weaknesses and failings in any of these areas:

- failure to apportion responsibilities;
- poor systems and controls;
- failure to act upon relevant management information;
- failure to review the competence of individuals.

4.3.2 Code of Practice for Statement of Principle 6

Statement of Principle 6 requires an approved person performing a significant influence function to **exercise due skill, care and diligence** in managing the business of the firm for which he is responsible in his controlled function. In the opinion of the PRA/FCA, an approved person is not complying with Statement of Principle 6 when:

1. Failing to take reasonable steps adequately to inform himself about the affairs of the business for which he is responsible:
    - permitting transactions without understanding the risks;
    - permitting expansion of the business without assessing the risks;
    - inadequate monitoring of highly profitable or unusual transactions or practices;

◦   not testing the veracity of explanations from subordinates; not obtaining independent, expert opinion where necessary.

2. Delegating the authority for dealing with an issue or a part of the business to an individual or individuals (whether in-house or outside contractors) without reasonable grounds for believing that the delegate had the necessary capacity, competence, knowledge, seniority or skill to deal with the issue or to take authority for dealing with that part of the business.

3. Failing to take reasonable steps to maintain an appropriate level of understanding about an issue or part of the business that he has delegated to an individual or individuals (whether in-house or outside contractors):

    ◦   disregarding a delegated issue;

    ◦   not obtaining adequate reports;

    ◦   not testing the veracity of explanations from subordinates.

4. Failing to supervise and monitor adequately the individual or individuals (whether in-house or outside contractors) to whom responsibility for dealing with an issue or authority for dealing with a part of the business has been delegated:

    ◦   failing to take action where progress is unreasonably slow or unsatisfactory explanations given;

    ◦   failing to review the performance of an outside contractor.

4.3.3   Code of Practice for Statement of Principle 7

Statement of Principle 7 requires an approved person performing a significant influence function to take reasonable steps to ensure that the business of the firm for which he is responsible in his controlled function **complies with the relevant requirements and standards of the regulatory system**. This can be achieved, in part at least, by establishing a competent and properly staffed compliance department – though that may well not suffice in and of itself. The following does not comply with Statement of Principle 7:

- Failure to implement and oversee appropriate compliance systems and controls.
- Failure to monitor compliance against regulatory requirements.
- Failure to stay informed about, investigate and provide effective remedy for compliance breaches.
- For the Money Laundering Reporting Officer, failure to discharge these duties.

5.   Senior Management Arrangements

Learning Objective

1.1.6   Understand the rules and guidance regarding senior management arrangements, systems and controls for both MiFID and non-MiFID investment firms [SYSC 1.2.1, 3.1.1, 4.1.1/2]

The PRA/FCA places certain requirements on financial services firms' directors and senior managers in relation to the systems and controls in their businesses. These requirements are contained in the **Senior Management Arrangements, Systems and Controls (SYSC)** part of the Handbook. The overriding requirement is that a firm must take reasonable care to establish and maintain such systems and controls as are appropriate to its business.

The purpose of these requirements is to:

1. encourage firms' directors and senior managers to take responsibility for their firm's arrangements on matters likely to be of interest to the PRA/FCA (because they are relevant to the PRA/FCA's ability to discharge its regulatory obligations);
2. amplify Principle for Businesses 3, under which a firm must take reasonable care to organise and control its affairs responsibly and effectively, with adequate risk management systems;
3. encourage firms to vest responsibility for an effective and responsible organisation in specific directors and senior managers, so that everyone knows who is responsible for what activities and so that functions are not, therefore, in danger of falling between stools (each director/manager regarding another as being accountable for a given activity or function, so that no one person assumes responsibility for its oversight); and
4. create a common platform of organisational systems and controls for firms.

The systems and controls requirements apply to firms in two ways.

- For firms that are subject to the Capital Requirements Directive (CRD) and the Markets in Financial Instruments Directive (MiFID), the requirements are known as the **common platform** of organisational systems and controls; they have the status of **rule** and are legally binding on these firms and are expressed as **must** in the Handbook text.
- For firms that are not subject to the CRD and MiFID (and hence not 'common platform' firms) some of the requirements have the status of **rule** (for example, the provisions relating to financial crime) but other aspects apply as **guidance**; guidance is not legally binding on firms and so is expressed as **should** in the Handbook text and the FCA expects the firm to have regard to the guidance when designing and maintaining its arrangements.

The sections of SYSC that are relevant to investment firms are summarised below.

5.1   General Requirements (SYSC 4)

- **Sound governance:**
  - clear organisational structure and well-defined lines of responsibility;
  - adequate arrangements for business continuity to ensure that losses are minimised and essential data is preserved or recovered in a timely manner;
  - accounting policies and procedures to enable accurate and timely reporting to the FCA;
  - regular monitoring of the adequacy of systems and controls, and measures taken to address deficiencies that are identified;
  - an audit committee to be established (if relevant to the scale and complexity of the business).
- **Persons who direct the business** must be of good repute and sufficiently experienced as to ensure the sound and prudent management of the firm. There must be at least two independent minds formulating policy and controlling the business.
- **Senior personnel** must receive frequent written reports (not less than annually) on compliance and internal audit (where relevant) measures for protecting against financial crime and risk management.
- **Apportionment of responsibilities** must be done in such a way as to ensure that it is clear who has which responsibility and the firm's business and affairs can be adequately monitored and controlled by its senior personnel and governors. Controlled function 8 – Apportionment and oversight must be specifically allocated.

5.2   Employees, Agents and Other Relevant Persons (SYSC 5)

The requirements of SYSC apply to all persons appointed to a firm, whether on an employed basis, self-employed, acting as agent, appointed representatives and those appointed under outsourcing arrangements. In addition to these provisions, there are specific qualifications and competence requirements for certain roles.

- **Skills, knowledge and expertise** – firms must employ personnel with the skills, knowledge and expertise necessary for the discharge of their responsibilities. This is a very important requirement and is known as the **competent employees rule**.
- **Segregation of duties** – must be effective to ensure that persons performing several roles are able to perform each role soundly, honestly and professionally.
- **Awareness of procedures** – firms must ensure that persons are aware of the procedures that have to be followed for the performance of their duties.
- **Monitoring** – there must be regular evaluation of systems and controls specific to employee competence.

5.3   Compliance, Audit and Financial Crime (SYSC 6)

- **Compliance** – there must be adequate policies and procedures to ensure the firm's compliance with its obligations under the regulatory system, and to detect risk of failure. An effective compliance function must be maintained to monitor the firm's arrangements and to advise and assist personnel who conduct regulated activity. A compliance officer must be appointed. The compliance function must have the necessary authority, resources, expertise and access to relevant information and must be sufficiently independent. This means that, ideally, a person should not be involved in any activity that they monitor as part of the compliance function, but the rules allow flexibility in this requirement for small firms where this may not be possible.
- **Internal audit** – the requirement to maintain an independent internal audit function applies in a proportionate manner, that is, if the scale, nature and complexity of a firm's business is such that an internal audit function is appropriate.
- **Financial crime** – firms must establish systems and controls to enable them to identify, assess, monitor and manage money laundering risk, and regularly evaluate the adequacy of the arrangements. The firm must allocate overall responsibility for mitigating financial crime risk to a director or senior manager, and a Money Laundering Reporting Officer (MLRO) must be appointed (who may be the same person).

5.4   Risk Control (SYSC 7 and 12)

- **SYSC 7 Risk Control** – expands on the general requirement to manage risk, and requires firms to have arrangements for identifying and assessing the risks the firm may be exposed to, and to set a level of risk tolerance for the firm. Risk management policies must relate to the firm's level of risk tolerance. Senior personnel must review risk management strategies and ensure that the risks they relate to include the macroeconomic environment within which the firm operates.
- **SYSC 12 Group Risk Systems and Controls** – applies the risk control provisions to groups.

5.5   Outsourcing (SYSC 8)

Outsourcing is an arrangement between a firm and a provider concerning a function that the firm could otherwise have undertaken for itself, eg, where it has permission to safeguard client assets but chooses to outsource this to a third party custodian. This is a different situation from where a firm engages a provider for a service that the firm could not undertake for itself, eg, information technology (IT) support.

In either case, if a third party is engaged to provide operational support, the firm must ensure that it does not incur additional operational risk. If the arrangement counts as outsourcing, it must not compromise the quality of the firm's internal control nor the PRA/FCA's ability to monitor the firm.

The provisions in SYSC 8 differentiate between critical and non-critical operational functions. Critical functions are those where any defect would materially impair the continuance of sound regulated activity. Examples of non-critical functions on the other hand include:

- advisory services to the firm, eg, legal advice, training services, billing and security services;
- provision of market information/price feeds;
- telephone recording.

A firm that outsources a critical function or regulated activity remains fully responsible for the operation of that activity and its obligations under the regulatory system. Senior personnel may not delegate their responsibility, the firm's relationships with its clients must be unaltered and the conditions for the firm's authorised status must not be undermined or modified.

The due diligence conducted by the firm must ensure that the following conditions are satisfied:

- The service provider must be capable and have the necessary authority to perform the function.
- The firm must establish arrangements for monitoring effective performance of the function, ensuring that the service provider conducts internal supervision and risk management, and taking action if the service provider is not properly fulfilling the function.
- The firm must retain the necessary expertise to supervise and manage the risks of the outsourcing.
- The service provider must disclose any development that may impact on its continuing ability.
- The firm must be able to terminate the arrangement without detriment to its clients.
- The service provider must co-operate with the FCA, the firm and its auditors and allow access to its business premises and to relevant data.
- The service provider must protect confidential information concerning the firm and its clients.
- The firm and service provider must establish a contingency plan for disaster recovery and periodic testing of business continuity.
- Respective rights, obligations and authorities must be clearly allocated and subject to a written agreement.

The firm must notify the FCA when it intends to rely on a third party for the performance of critical operational functions.

5.6 Record-Keeping (SYSC 9)

This section requires firms to maintain orderly records of its business, internal organisation, services and transactions to enable the regulators to monitor the firm's compliance with regulatory requirements and its obligations towards its clients. Records for MiFID business must be retained for five years; the retention periods for other records vary and are specified in the rules relating to a particular record. Records must be retained in a durable medium that allows the following conditions to be met:

- The regulators must be able to access the record readily and be able to reconstitute each key state of processing a transaction.
- Corrections and amendments should be easily ascertained.
- It must not be possible for made records to be otherwise manipulated or altered.
- Generally, the records should be capable of being reproduced in English and on paper.

5.7 Conflicts of Interest (SYSC 10)

This section requires firms to maintain policies for identifying and managing conflicts of interest. This will be covered in detail in Chapter 4 when looking at Conduct of Business rules.

5.8 Remuneration (SYSC 19A)

All firms are required to establish remuneration policies that are consistent with and promote sound and effective risk management.

Additionally, some types of common platform firms are subject to the detailed requirements of the **Remuneration Code** in SYSC 19A.3.

The Code derives from the EU CRD and originally only applied to the largest banks, building societies and broker-dealers. However, from 1 January 2011, the requirements extended to many other types of firm including asset managers, hedge fund managers and investment firms, as well as some firms that engage in corporate finance, venture capital, the provision of financial advice and stockbrokers.

In summary, the Code covers:

- **12 principles** – the Code contains 12 principles with which firms must comply in a proportionate way, depending on the size, internal organisation nature, scope and the complexity of the firm's activities.
- **Code staff** – these are senior management and anyone whose professional activities could have a material impact on a firm's risk profile. The onus is on firms to identify their code staff in the first instance, but their lists will be subject to review and challenge by the PRA/FCA. Code staff earning above a specified threshold are subject to specific restraints concerning bonus payments and a restriction on variable remuneration.
- **Guarantees** – firms must not offer guaranteed bonuses of more than one year. Guarantees may only be given to new hires for the first year of service in exceptional circumstances.
- **Strengthening of capital base** – firms must ensure that their total variable remuneration does not limit the ability to strengthen their capital base. Total variable remuneration must be significantly reduced in circumstances where the firm produces a subdued or negative financial performance.

- **Voiding provisions** – a new rule will be introduced which defines instances where breaches of the code may render a contract void and/or require recovery of payments made.
- **Severance payments** – should reflect performance over time and failure must not be rewarded.
- **Pensions** – CRD3 states that enhanced discretionary pension benefits should be held for five years in the form of shares or share-like instruments.

5.9 Individual Accountability

Learning Objective

1.1.4 Know the requirements of the FCA & PRA individual accountability in banking [SMR C-CON 1.1.2, SYSC 5.2.1, Set of Conduct Rules C-CON 2.1/2 (FCA). SMF 2/3/4/5/6, 63E, 64 C, 137G (PRA)]

5.9.1 The Parliamentary Commission on Banking Standards (PCBS)

July and December 2014 saw the release of two joint Consultation Papers that are designed to remedy the perceived errant behaviour and culture within banks that played a major role in the 2008–09 financial crisis and in conduct scandals such as Payment Protection Insurance (PPI) mis-selling and the attempted manipulation of LIBOR, to mention but two examples.

Both FCA and PRA (the regulators) believe that holding individuals to account is a key component of effective regulation. The timing for implementation rests with the Treasury, although this will be later in 2015.

The proposals in the December CP, together with those set out in the July CP, reflect the recommendations of the final report of the Parliamentary Commission on Banking Standards (PCBS), *Changing Banking for Good and implement* changes required by amendments which the Financial Services (Banking Reform) Act 2013 made to the Financial Services and Markets Act 2000 (FSMA).

These changes are significant and include:

- A new **Senior Managers Regime (SMR)** for individuals who are subject to regulatory approval which will require firms to allocate a range of responsibilities to these individuals and to regularly vet their fitness and propriety. This will focus accountability on a narrower number of senior individuals in a firm than the current Approved Persons Regime (APR).
- A **Certification Regime** which will require relevant firms to assess the fitness and propriety of certain employees who could pose a risk of significant harm to the firm or any of its customers.
- A new set of **Conduct Rules**.

More generally, the following headlines have been proposed for implementation:

- Individual accountability will be enhanced through a range of measures, including identifying the senior individuals who run banks and clarifying their specific responsibilities, the introduction of a legislative presumption that they should be held accountable if they fail to act reasonably in discharging those responsibilities and expanding the population in relevant firms subject to rules of conduct. This should have a positive impact on individual behaviour and the general culture within firms which should, in turn, contribute to the advancement of both regulators' objectives.

- The PRA and FCA will work closely together when approving individuals and supervising firms' governance arrangements and it is important to consider the overall effect of their combined regimes. For that reason, the PRA and FCA have chosen to set out their respective proposals for consultation in a single document.

Now, the chairperson(s) and non-executive directors will be deemed as **senior management functions** and will be specifically accountable for boardroom decisions, and deemed potentially culpable for poor decisions as executive directors:

- Enhanced transparency through **prescribed responsibilities** will be introduced and will need to be allocated to the most senior of those performing 'senior management functions', recorded as part of their individual statements of responsibility describing the most senior executives' roles, demonstrable through day-to-day management.
- The concept of a **management responsibilities map** will be introduced, documenting a firm's governance and management arrangements. This includes how the statements of responsibility have been allocated, thus increasing reporting line information for those impacted.
- The introduction of a **presumption of responsibility** will reverse the burden of proof, and will require improved evidence of oversight to show that 'reasonable steps' have been taken to prevent, stop or remedy breaches.
- A new **Group Entity Senior Manager** will be introduced bringing individuals employed by a parent, holding or other group undertaking that exercises significant influence over activities in the UK into the scope of the regime, whether physically based in the UK or overseas.
- A **Certification Regime** will be created to cover material risk-takers, those performing significant harm functions, and anyone supervising a certified person.
- Senior managers must now provide annual attestations that the firm has complied with the new regime, specifying that those covered by the Certification Regime remain 'fit and proper' through arrangements designed and managed by the firm.
- The new framework of behavioural standards will be introduced against which individual conduct will be judged through Conduct Rules applicable to all individuals with a requirement to notify the regulator of any identified breaches and whether any formal disciplinary action was taken against this individual.

As noted above, these changes will become effective in 2015, with a specific time frame for implementation to be released shortly.

6. The Relationship Between the FCA and the PRA and Various Other Bodies

---

Learning Objective

Understand the wider structure of UK financial regulation including the responsibilities of the main regulating bodies and the relationship between them

1.2.1   Market regulators: The Financial Conduct Authority and the Prudential Regulation Authority

1.2.2   Other regulators: The UK Competition and Markets Authority, The Information Commissioner and The Pensions Regulator

1.2.3   The relationships and coordination between the following: The Financial Conduct Authority; The Prudential Regulation Authority; HMRC; Financial Ombudsman Scheme (FOS); Financial Services Compensation Scheme (FSCS); Financial Policy Committee; Upper Tribunal (Tax and Chancery); The Bank of England; HM Treasury

---

The FSMA required the establishment of two schemes to provide protection for consumers: the Financial Ombudsman Service (FOS) and the Financial Services Compensation Scheme (FSCS). We will look at these before considering the relationship between the PRA/FCA and various other relevant bodies.

6.1   The Financial Ombudsman Service (FOS)

Part XVI of FSMA provides for a single scheme for dealing with disputes between consumers and financial services firms. This single scheme replaced several ombudsman schemes that had existed previously. The FSMA required the establishment of a limited company (the Financial Ombudsman Service (FOS)) to administer the scheme and to make rules for its operation. The scheme is designed to provide quick resolution of disputes between **eligible complainants** and their product/service providers with a minimum of formality, by an independent person.

The FCA appoints the chairman and other directors of the FOS, but the terms of their appointment must be such as to secure their independence from the FCA. The FCA requires an annual report on the scheme. The FOS also has some rule-making power, and the FCA must approve any rules that the FOS makes.

The FCA's rules specify who is eligible to use the FOS (the eligible complainant) and also require financial services firms to set up and maintain complaints handling and resolution procedures themselves. The hope is that most disputes will be resolved between the firm and the customer, and that the customer will not need to resort to the FOS.

If an eligible complaint does reach the FOS, it is able to make judgments to compensate customers that are binding on the firm.

Consumers do not have to accept any decision the FOS makes and they can choose to go to court instead. But if they do accept the FOS decision, it is binding on them (and the firm). Further information on complaints-handling arrangements can be found in Chapter 5.

6.2   The Financial Services Compensation Scheme (FSCS)

Similarly, the FSMA required the establishment of a body, known as the Financial Services Compensation Scheme (FSCS), to provide a safety net for customers of financial services firms which become unable to repay them. This single scheme replaced several existing compensation schemes.

If an authorised financial services firm (eg, a bank) becomes insolvent, or appears likely to cease trading and fall insolvent, the customers of that firm (in our example, the people with money deposited at the bank) can make a claim under the FSCS for compensation for any loss – up to certain limits.

Details on the compensation limits are provided in Chapter 5.

As with the FOS, the FCA appoints the chairman and other board directors, with the terms of their appointment being designed to secure their independence from the FCA. The FSCS is required to make an annual report to the FCA.

6.3   Competition and Markets Authority (CMA)

The Competition and Markets Authority (CMA) took over the role and functions previously carried out by the Competition Commission and the Office of Fair Trading.

The CMA came into being on 1 April 2014. It works to promote competition for the benefit of consumers – both within and outside of the UK. Its main aim is to make markets work well for consumers, businesses and the economy. It is not solely looking into competition within the financial services industry.

The CMA has five strategic goals:

1. To deliver effective enforcement to deter wrongdoing, protect consumers and educate businesses.
2. To extend competition frontiers by using the markets regime to improve the way competition works, in particular within the regulated sectors.
3. To refocus consumer protection, working with its partners to promote compliance and understanding of the law, and empowering consumers to make informed choices.
4. To achieve professional excellence by managing every case efficiently, transparently and fairly, and to ensure all legal, economic and financial analysis is conducted to the highest international standards.
5. To develop integrated performance through ensuring that all staff are brought together from different professional backgrounds to form effective multi-disciplinary teams and to provide a trusted competition adviser across government.

The CMA is responsible for:

*   Investigating mergers which could restrict competition.
*   Conducting market studies and investigations in markets where there may be competition and consumer problems.
*   Investigating where there may be breaches of UK or EU prohibitions against anti-competitive agreements and abuses of dominant positions.
*   Bringing criminal proceedings against individuals who commit the cartel offence.

- Enforcing consumer protection legislation to tackle practices and market conditions that make it difficult for consumers to exercise choice.
- Co-operating with sector regulators and encouraging them to use their competition powers.
- Considering regulatory references and appeals.

6.4   The Information Commissioner's Office (ICO)

The Information Commissioner's Office (ICO) is an independent official body for upholding information rights. This entails both promoting access to official information in appropriate circumstances and protecting people's personal data. It is the ICO that is responsible for administering the provisions of the Data Protection Act (DPA) 1998 and the Freedom of Information Act 2000.

The Data Protection Act 1998 establishes a framework of rights and duties which are designed to safeguard personal data. This framework balances the legitimate needs of organisations to collect and use personal data for business and other purposes against the right of individuals to respect the privacy of their personal details.

The Freedom of Information Act 2000 provides public access to information held by public authorities. It obliges public authorities to publish certain information about their activities, and entitles members of the public to request information from public authorities.

6.5   The Pensions Regulator

The Pensions Regulator is the UK regulator of work-based pension schemes.

Under the Pensions Acts of 2004 and 2008 the Pensions Regulator has been given specific objectives:

- to protect the benefits of members of work-based pension schemes;
- to promote and to improve understanding of good administration of work-based pension schemes;
- to reduce the risk of situations arising which may lead to compensation being payable from the Pension Protection Fund (PPF);
- to maximise employer compliance with employer duties (including the requirement to enrol eligible employees automatically into a qualifying pension provision with a minimum contribution) and with certain employment safeguards.

The role of the Pensions Regulator is to ensure that people responsible for providing access to and managing work-based pensions fulfil their obligations. This includes trustees, employers, pension specialists and business advisers. The Pensions Regulator provides guidance and education to make clear what is expected.

6.6   The Financial Policy Committee (FPC) at the Bank of England

A stable financial system is a key ingredient for a healthy and successful economy. People need to have confidence that the system is safe and stable, and functions properly to provide critical services to the wider economy. It is important that problems in particular areas do not lead to disruption across the financial system.

Since 2009 the Bank of England has had a statutory objective to *'contribute to protecting and enhancing the stability of the financial systems of the UK'*. From April 2013 it took on further responsibilities that saw the creation of an independent FPC at the Bank and the PRA as a subsidiary of the Bank. The FPC is charged with identifying, monitoring and taking action to remove or reduce systemic risks with a view to protecting and enhancing the resilience of the UK financial system.

The FPC meets at least four times a year and publishes a record of its formal meetings. It is also responsible for the Bank's biannual Financial Stability Report (FSR), which covers the Committee's assessment of the outlook for the stability and resilience of the financial sector and the policy actions it advises to reduce and mitigate risks to stability.

6.7 The Upper Tribunal (Tax and Chancery)

The Upper Tribunal (Tax and Chancery Chamber) is an agency of the Ministry of Justice. It aims to assist those who wish to appeal against decisions made by:

* first-tier Tribunal in tax or charity cases;
* the financial services regulators (the FCA and the PRA);
* the Pensions Regulator.

6.7.1 Financial Services Cases

References can be made by the firm or the individual to whom the FCA/PRA or the Pensions Regulator notice is directed. The decision notices may cover a wide range of regulatory and disciplinary matters. Appeals can be made against the following types of decision notice:

Authorisation and Permission

For example, FCA/PRA decisions not to authorise a firm, or if the FCA/PRA have invoked their power to withdraw authorisation, or vary the scope of a firm's permission.

Penalties for Market Abuse

The FCA may impose penalties for market abuse. Its decisions on market abuse by people (whether authorised or unauthorised) can be referred to the Upper Tribunal.

Disciplinary Measures

The FCA/PRA may issue public statements about and/or impose penalties on authorised people who have failed to comply with requirements imposed by or under the Act. Such decisions can be referred to the Upper Tribunal.

Official Listing

Certain decisions by the FCA in its role as competent authority (UKLA) can be referred to the Upper Tribunal, for example, refusing to admit securities to the official list and suspending official listing of securities where necessary. The FCA is empowered to censure or impose penalties on issuers who breach listing rules.

Other Powers

The FCA will make decisions on the approval and discipline of employees and people who carry out certain functions on behalf of authorised people. They may prohibit certain people, including professionals, from carrying out particular functions.

7.   The FCA Handbook

Learning Objective

1.2.4   Know the six types of provisions used by the FCA and PRA in their Handbooks and the status of their approved industry guidance

7.1   The Handbooks and the Status of Provisions

The FSMA gives legal effect to the rules and guidance made by the regulators, which are set out in the Handbooks of the FCA and the PRA. The Handbooks contain a variety of provisions outlined below:

There are six different types of provisions, with each type being indicated by a single letter. The status of a provision is important because it determines the legal effect on a firm.

The six different types of provisions are:

R.   Rules – rules are binding on authorised persons (firms) and, if a firm contravenes a rule, it may be subject to discipline. The Principles for Businesses are given the status of rules.

E.   Evidential provisions – these are rules but they are not binding in their own right. They will always relate to another, binding rule. Evidential provisions give the required evidence which is expected to show that a person has complied with, or contravened, a rule. For example, the qualifications tables have the status of evidential provisions and they relate to the rule that requires firms to ensure certain employees attain appropriate qualifications.

G.   Guidance which may be used by the FCA or PRA to explain the implications of other provisions, to indicate possible means of compliance, or to recommend a particular course of action. Guidance is not binding, nor does it have **evidential** effect. As a result, a firm cannot be disciplined for a failure to follow guidance.

D.   Directions and requirements – these provisions dictate, eg, the form of content of applications for authorisation. They are binding on those to whom they are addressed.

P.   The Statements of Principle for Approved Persons, binding on approved persons.

C.   Conclusive behaviour that does not amount to market abuse. The letter 'C' is used because these types of behaviour are **conclusively not** market abuse (market abuse is covered in Chapter 3).

7.2 FCA and PRA Confirmation of Industry Guidance

Like the FSA before, the FCA and PRA encourage the financial industry to develop its own best practice and will give official recognition to guidance that has been developed by the industry for the benefit of practitioners.

FCA- or PRA-confirmed industry guidance does not create any new tier of regulation. It has the same status as the regulators' own guidance.

However, where a breach has been established, industry guidance is potentially relevant to enforcement deliberations. For example, to:

1. help assess whether it could reasonably have been understood or predicted at the time that the conduct in question fell below the standards required by the Principles;
2. explain the regulatory context;
3. inform a view of the overall seriousness of the breaches, eg, it could decide that the breach warrants a higher penalty in circumstances where the regulator had written to chief executives in that sector to reiterate the importance of ensuring a particular aspect of its business complied with relevant regulatory standards;
4. inform the consideration of a firm's defence that it was judging the firm on the basis of retrospective standards; and
5. be considered as part of expert or supervisory statements in relation to the relevant standards at the time.

8. The CISI Code of Conduct

Learning Objective

1.2.5   Know the Chartered Institute for Securities & Investment's Code of Conduct

Certain approved persons may, as well as having to comply with the FCA Statements of Principle, also be members of the **Chartered Institute for Securities & Investment (CISI)**. Membership of the CISI requires compliance with the CISI's own Code of Conduct – this includes an obligation to meet a set of standards set out within the **CISI Principles**. These Principles impose an obligation on members to act in a manner which goes beyond mere compliance, and which is consistent with the underlying values of the CISI.

A material breach of the Code of Conduct is incompatible with continuing membership of the CISI.

Members who find themselves in a position which might require them to act in a manner contrary to the Principles are encouraged to do the following:

1. discuss their concerns with their line manager;
2. seek advice from their internal compliance department;
3. approach their firm's non-executive directors or audit committee;

4. if unable to resolve their concerns and having exhausted all internal avenues, contact the CISI for advice.

8.1　CISI Principles

1. To act honestly and fairly at all times when dealing with clients, customers and counterparties and to be a good steward of their interests, taking into account the nature of the business relationship with each of them, the nature of the service to be provided to them and the individual mandates given by them.
2. To act with integrity in fulfilling the responsibilities of your appointment and to seek to avoid any acts, omissions or business practices which damage the reputation of your organisation or the financial services industry.
3. To observe applicable law, regulations and professional conduct standards when carrying out financial service activities, and to interpret and apply them to the best of your ability, according to principles rooted in trust, honesty and integrity.
4. To observe the standards of market integrity, good practice and conduct required or expected of participants in markets when engaging in any form of market dealing.
5. To be alert to and manage fairly and effectively and to the best of your ability any relevant conflict of interest.
6. To attain and actively manage a level of professional competence appropriate to your responsibilities, to commit to continuing learning to ensure the currency of your knowledge, skills and expertise and to promote the development of others.
7. To decline to act in any matter about which you are not competent unless you have access to such advice and assistance as will enable you to carry out the work in a professional manner.
8. To strive to uphold the highest personal and professional standards.

End of Chapter Questions

Think of an answer to each question and refer to the appropriate section for confirmation.

1. Who are the two regulators that together make up the twin peaks of UK financial services regulation and how do their responsibilities differ?
    Answer Reference: Section 1.1

2. To which government body is the FCA accountable?
    Answer Reference: Section 1.3

3. What are the statutory objectives of the FCA and the PRA?
    Answer Reference: Section 2.1

4. What are the four regulated firm categorisations?
    Answer Reference: Section 2.1.3

5. List the components of rules-based and forward-looking approaches.
    Answer Reference: Section 2.1.4

6. Give three examples of the regulators' powers additional to rule-making.
    Answer Reference: Section 2.2

7. List the 11 Principles for Businesses.
    Answer Reference: Section 3.1

8. What is the likely outcome for a firm that breaches a Principle?
    Answer Reference: Section 3.1

9. What Statements of Principle apply to approved persons performing significant influence functions?
    Answer Reference: Section 4.3

10. What is the purpose behind the FCA requirements for senior management?
    Answer Reference: Section 5

11. How do the requirements of SYSC apply to non-common platform firms?
    Answer Reference: Section 5

12. List five areas covered by SYSC.
    Answer Reference: Section 5.1–5.8

13. What is the relationship between the FCA and the FOS?
    Answer Reference: Section 6.1

14. What is the purpose of the FSCS?
    Answer Reference: Section 6.2

15. What is the role of each of the following: the CC, the ICO, the Pensions Regulator?
    Answer Reference: Sections 6.3–6.5

16. What is the FPC and what are its responsibilities?
    Answer Reference: Section 6.6

17. What is the purpose of the Upper Tribunal and who does it report to?
    Answer Reference: Section 6.7

18. What provision is indicated by the letters: G; D; P; E; R; C?
    Answer Reference: Section 7.1

19. What is the difference between a rule and an evidential provision in the Handbooks of the FCA or the PRA?
    Answer Reference: Section 7.1

20. What is the status of G provisions?
    Answer Reference: Section 7.1

21. What is the status of FCA- or PRA-confirmed industry guidance?
    Answer Reference: Section 7.2

22. What are members of the CISI expected to do should they be required to act in a manner contrary to the Principles?
    Answer Reference: Section 8

Chapter Two
The Financial Services Markets Act 2000 and Financial Services Act 2012

This syllabus area will provide approximately 10 of the 75 examination questions

1. Regulated and Prohibited Activities

Learning Objective

2.1.1 Know the regulated and prohibited activities (Part II/III of FSMA 2000, Regulated Activities Order 2001 and the under-noted guidance in the Perimeter Guidance Manual (PERG): authorised persons [PERG 2.2.3]; exempt persons [PERG 2.10] and FSMA Exemption Order 2001 [(SI 2001/1201)]; offences under the Act [PERG 2.2.1/2]; enforceability of agreements entered into with an unauthorised business [PERG 2.2.2]; defences available under the Act [PERG 2.2.1]

1.1 The General Prohibition

The FSMA is subdivided into 30 parts. Part II, **Regulated and Prohibited Activities**, includes the **general prohibition**, which simply states that no person can carry on a regulated activity in the UK, or purport to do so, unless he is either authorised or exempt. If a person contravenes the general prohibition it is a criminal offence; the maximum sanctions are up to two years' imprisonment and an unlimited fine.

A further effect of acting in contravention of the general prohibition is that any agreements made are unenforceable by the offending person against the other party. This is also the case for agreements made as a result of the activities of someone who was contravening the general prohibition, even if that person is not a party to the agreement.

The other party is entitled to recover any money or property transferred under the agreement, and to be compensated for any loss suffered.

It is a defence for a person to show that they took all reasonable precautions and exercised all due diligence to avoid committing the offence.

Example

Mrs X buys shares in ABC plc. The purchase is made following the recommendation of a firm of brokers, UNA Ltd. Mrs X subsequently discovers that UNA was not authorised under the FSMA.

Mrs X now has two choices: she can keep her shares in ABC and take no action against UNA, or she can sue UNA for the recovery of her money and damages (handing back her shares in ABC) because UNA has breached the general prohibition.

The relevant staff of UNA have also committed a criminal act, and will be liable to a potential punishment of up to two years in prison, plus an unlimited fine.

Chapter 1 gives examples of authorised and exempt persons. For a person to become authorised by the PRA and/or the FCA as appropriate, that person must first apply for permission to perform particular regulated activities; if that person satisfies the criteria, the regulator(s) will give permission.

You should remember from the previous chapter that the term 'person' here means the trading entity or firm, which could be incorporated as a company – or could be an unincorporated entity such as a sole trader or partnership.

There are various provisions in the FSMA whereby a person can be exempt from the general prohibition when carrying on regulated activity. The provisions are, in summary:

- **s.39 FSMA and the FSMA (Appointed Representatives) Regulations 2001** – for appointed representatives;
- **s.285 FSMA** – for recognised investment exchanges and clearing houses;
- **s.312A FSMA** – for operators of multilateral trading systems, exercising certain rights;
- **s.316 FSMA** – special provisions for members of the Society of Lloyd's;
- **FSMA Exemption Order 2001** – for central banks, supranational bodies, local authorities, charities, industrial and provident societies and certain organisations that are subject to some oversight by the government;
- **Part 20 FSMA** – the special regime for professional firms, subject to conditions.

Exempt persons are covered in more detail in Section 2 of this chapter.

1.1.1 Prohibition Orders

Learning Objective

2.1.2 Understand the regulator's actions in respect of prohibition orders and actions for damages and how private persons can sue for damages when a firm is declared in breach [(FSMA 2000, s.56, 59, 71) (FSA 2012 s.138D)]

Separately from the general prohibition, s.56 of FSMA gives the regulators (the FCA and the PRA) the power to make an order (prohibition order) prohibiting an individual from performing a specified function. Either regulator may do this if it considers the individual is not a fit and proper person to perform the function. The prohibition order may relate to a particular regulated activity or regulated activity generally. If the individual breaches the order, they are guilty of a criminal offence and liable to a fine. It is a defence for the person to show they took all reasonable care and exercised due diligence to avoid breaching the order.

An authorised person (the firm) must take reasonable care to ensure that individuals for whom they are responsible do not breach prohibition orders.

Prohibition orders may also be made against exempt persons, and also exempt professional firms who are acting in accordance with the

Part 20 regime of FSMA that enables professional firms (such as accountants, solicitors and actuaries) to undertake certain regulated activities under the supervision of their professional body rather than authorisation from the FCA or the PRA. These so-called designated professional bodies are covered in more detail in Section 2.3.2 of this chapter.

A person may apply to the FCA or the PRA to have a prohibition order varied or revoked.

Section 59 states that a person cannot carry out certain controlling functions in a firm without approval by the appropriate regulator.

Section 71 of FSMA provides for circumstances whereby a private person can sue a firm for damages if they suffer loss because the firm is found to be in breach of statutory duty in the following circumstances:

- an individual within a firm carries out a function in breach of a s.56 prohibition order;
- an individual carries out a controlled function but without prior approval (s.59).

Section 71 also provides for clients who are non-private persons (eg, businesses, trusts) to sue for damages as a consequence of negligence concerning prohibition orders, in prescribed circumstances.

Section 138D of the Financial Services Act 2012 sets out the circumstances in which a person who suffers losses, as a result of a breach of a rule, by an authorised person has the right to claim for damages for their resulting losses.

Breach of an FCA rule (unless otherwise stated) will, therefore, permit a person who has suffered a loss as a result of this breach a right to claim for damages; the person will only be required to show that the authorised person has breached a rule and that they have suffered a loss.

The only exemption is that they will not apply to listing rules, threshold conditions, short selling rules and the capital adequacy rules.

1.2 Regulated Activities

In order to understand whether someone is in breach of the general prohibition it is, of course, necessary to understand what the regulated activities themselves are. It is left to a separate statutory instrument, known as the **Regulated Activities Order (RAO) 2001**, to clarify precisely what these regulated activities are. FSMA provides that these will be defined by reference to two sets of criteria:

- a range of investments (including assets which we might typically think of as investments, such as shares and bonds, but also other assets such as deposits and contracts of insurance); and
- a range of activities which may be carried on in connection with those investments (such as dealing, managing or advising on investments, accepting deposits and effecting contracts of insurance).

Not all of the activities can be related to all the investments. Some are specific to just one type, eg, effecting a contract of insurance relates only to contracts of insurance.

If a person is performing one (or more) of these specified activities in relation to one (or more) of the specified investments, that person is performing a regulated activity and requires either authorisation or an exemption. It is the combination of carrying on a **specified activity**, in relation to a **specified investment**, which gives rise to **regulated activity**.

The investments and activities are detailed in secondary legislation issued under the FSMA – principally the RAO, as subsequently amended.

1.2.1 Specified Investments

Learning Objective

2.4.3 Know the investments specified in Part III of the Regulated Activities Order

The following are defined as specified investments within the RAO:

1. **Deposits** – money paid by one person to another, with or without interest being earned on it, and on terms that it will be repaid when a specified event occurs (eg, when a demand is made). The obvious example is deposits held with banks and building societies. For clarity, the RAO sets out certain exclusions – eg, electronic money (covered separately below), money paid in advance for the provision of goods or services and money paid as a security deposit.
2. **Electronic money** – monetary value (as represented by a claim on the e-money issuer) which is stored on an electronic device, issued on receipt of funds and accepted as a means of payment by third parties. In effect it is an electronic substitute for notes and coins.
3. **Rights under contracts of insurance** – includes both long-term insurance contracts (eg, life assurance or endowment policies) and general insurance (eg, motor or building insurance). The FCA gives guidance on identifying a contract of insurance (since this is not always as simple as you might think) in the Perimeter Guidance (PERG) Sourcebook.
4. **Shares** – defined widely as shares or stock in any company (wherever incorporated) or in any unincorporated body formed outside the UK. The RAO definition excludes shares in open-ended investment companies (OEICs), since an OEIC is a collective investment scheme (CIS) and is captured under a separate definition. It also excludes some building society shares, since these can behave like – and are, therefore, captured under – the definition of deposits.
5. **Instruments creating or acknowledging indebtedness** – including debentures, debenture stock, loan stock and, as a **mopping-up** clause, specifies also *'any other instrument creating or acknowledging debt'*. Again, the definition is wide, so the RAO provides for some exclusions – eg, trade bills, cheques and other bills of exchange, and (because they are separately captured) contracts of insurance and government and public securities.
6. **Government and public securities** – eg, gilts and US treasuries and local authority loan stocks. Again, certain instruments are excluded, such as trade bills issued by government bodies, and National Savings & Investments (NS&I) deposits and products.
7. **Alternative finance investment bonds/alternative debentures** – a form of Sharia'a-compliant bond or 'sukuk'.
8. **Instruments giving entitlements to investments** – essentially, warrants and similar instruments entitling the holder to subscribe for shares, debentures, government and public securities at a set price, and on or between set date(s) in the future.
9. **Certificates representing certain securities** – covers certificates which confer rights in (but are not themselves) other instruments such as shares, debentures, gilts and warrants. It includes, for example, American depositary receipts (ADRs), which typically give holders rights over a certain number of a UK company's shares. These ADRs are designed to offer the – typically US-based – investor a more convenient way to invest in UK shares, because they are dealt in, and pay dividends in, US dollars. Also covered here are other depositary receipts, such as global depositary receipts (GDRs).

10. **Units in a collective investment scheme** – covers holdings in any collective investment scheme, whether it is an authorised or an unregulated scheme. For example, it covers units in an authorised unit trust (AUT) or shares in an OEIC – which you may also see described as an investment company with variable capital (ICVC). This is why OEICs are specifically excluded from the heading of shares above. Unregulated schemes can also take other legal forms, such as limited partnerships, and so rights in such partnerships fall within the scope of units in a collective investment scheme.

11. **Rights under a stakeholder pension scheme** – stakeholder pensions are pension schemes set up under the Welfare Reform and Pensions Act 1999 which have to meet certain criteria and be run in a particular way.

12. **Rights under a personal pension scheme** – pensions designed for individuals who do not belong to a company scheme and/or who wish to take control of their own investment decisions for their pension provisions (for example, self-invested personal pensions (SIPPs). A wide range of investments may be held within a personal pension scheme.

13. **Options** – options (the right, but not the obligation, to buy or sell a fixed quantity of an underlying asset for a fixed price on or between fixed dates) are only covered if they relate to:
    - securities or contractually based investments (eg, stocks, shares, bonds, or futures on similar instruments);
    - currencies;
    - certain precious metals, including gold and silver;
    - options on futures contracts and other contracts for differences (see paragraph 15).

14. **Futures** – contracts for the sale/purchase of an asset where delivery and settlement will be made at a future date, at a price agreed when the contract is made. The RAO excludes futures agreed for commercial purposes as opposed to those made for investment/speculative purposes. Thus a contract to buy cocoa at an agreed price at some future date will not be caught if it is carried out by a chocolate maker to help him secure a certain price for the raw materials needed.

15. **Contracts for difference (CFDs)** – eg, spread bets, interest rate swaps. These are contracts where the investor's aim is to secure a profit (or avoid a loss) by making money by reference to fluctuations in the value of an index, or to the price of some other underlying property. The RAO excludes futures and options since these are separately caught.

16. **Lloyd's syndicate capacity and syndicate membership** – relates in the main to activities of Lloyd's members' agents and managing agents.

17. **Rights under a funeral plan contract** – ie, certain plans under which the customer pays for benefits which will pay for his (or someone else's) funeral upon their death.

18. **Rights under a regulated mortgage contract*** – ie, mortgage loans secured by first legal mortgages on property, at least 40% of which is to be used for the borrower's, or some related party's, dwelling. This specified investment also includes lifetime mortgages, a type of equity release transaction.

19. **Rights under a home reversion plan*** – another type of equity release transaction, whereby the customer sells part or all of his home to the plan provider in return for a lump sum or series of payments; he retains the right to stay in his home until he dies or moves into residential care.

20. **Rights under a home purchase plan*** – alternatives to mortgages, which allow people to buy their homes while complying with Islamic principles (financing via an interest-bearing mortgage is not permitted under a strict interpretation of these principles).

21. **Rights under a regulated sale and rent back agreement*** – whereby a person sells all or part of qualifying interest in land/property but remains in occupation of at least 40% of the land/property.

22. **Emissions auction products**.

23. **Credit agreement** with respect to the regulated activities of entering a regulated credit agreement as lender and exercising (or having the right to exercise) the lender's rights and duties under a regulated credit agreement. This is sub-divided into four different types.
24. **Consumer hire agreement.**
25. **Rights to or interests in other specified investments** – rights in anything that is a specified investment listed, excluding rights in home finance transactions, are themselves a specified investment.

The investments marked * are collectively known as **home finance transactions**.

1.2.2 Regulated Activities

Learning Objective

2.4.1 Know the activities specified in Part II of the Regulated Activities Order

An activity is a regulated activity for the purposes of the FSMA if it is an activity specified as such under an order made by the Treasury. Some of the activities are only specified if they are carried out in relation to investments. Others can be carried out in relation to property of any kind.

As we have already noted, the RAO defines regulated activities by reference:

• first to the range of specified investments; and
• then to the activities a firm might carry on in relation to those investments.

The specified activities themselves are as follows:

1. **Accepting deposits** – mainly the preserve of banks and building societies, but other firms may find themselves caught under this activity.
2. **Issuing e-money** – ie, acting as the issuer of e-money, as it is described in Section 1.2.1.
3. **Effecting or carrying out contracts of insurance as principal** – this essentially applies to insurers.
4. **Dealing in investments as principal or agent** – this applies only to certain of the specified investments. Dealing is buying, selling, subscribing for or underwriting the investments concerned. When the firm deals as principal (ie, on its own account), it applies only to those investments that are:
   • securities – shares, debentures and warrants, or
   • contractually based investments, such as options, futures, CFDs, and life policies.
   When the firm deals as agent (ie, on behalf of someone else), it applies to securities (as for dealing as principal) and relevant investments. Relevant investments include contractually based investments (as for dealing as principal) and additionally rights under pure protection and general insurance contracts.
5. **Arranging deals in investments** – covers:
   • bringing about deals in investments – that is, the involvement of the person is essential to bringing about/concluding the contract, and also

- making arrangements with a view to transact in investments (which may be quite widely interpreted as any arrangement pursuant to transactions in investments, such as making introductions).

The arranging activities relate only to specified investments which are:

- securities (eg, shares, debentures or warrants);
- relevant investments, eg, options, futures, CFDs and rights under insurance contracts;
- underwriting capacity of a Lloyd's syndicate or membership of a Lloyd's syndicate; and
- rights to or interests in any of the above.

A typical example is a broker making arrangements for its client to enter into a specific insurance contract.

6. **Arranging home finance transactions** – the arranging and making of arrangements in relation to mortgages, home reversion or home purchase plans, and regulated sale and rent-back agreements are captured in the same way as arranging deals in investments.

7. **Operating a multilateral trading facility (MTF)** – an MTF is any system that brings together multiple third-party buying and selling transactions in financial instruments (eg, shares, units in collective investment schemes, derivatives). Retail investors and other investment firms can all trade together via the MTF. MTFs purport to be faster and more cost effective than the traditional exchanges and they have had some impact on trading practices. One example of an MTF that has had a significant impact is BATS Chi-X Europe. An important distinction between stock exchanges and MTFs is that the latter do not have the power to list a security to enable the security to be traded on a regulated market.

8. **Managing investments** – this applies in respect of investments belonging to someone other than the manager, and when the manager exercises discretion over the management of the portfolio. The portfolio must include, or be able to include, securities or contractually based investments. A typical example is a portfolio manager. Non-discretionary management (when the firm does not make the final decision) is not covered under this heading: it is be captured under the separately defined regulated activities of dealing in investments and advising on investments.

9. **Assisting in the administration and performance of a contract of insurance** – this is activity carried on by an intermediary after conclusion of a contract of insurance, eg, loss assessors.

10. **Safeguarding and administering investments** – again, this applies in the context of securities (eg, shares, debentures) and contractually based investments (eg, options, futures, CFDs, qualifying insurance contracts). The firm must be holding the assets for someone else, and it must be both safeguarding and administering the assets to be caught under this heading. A typical example is a custodian bank, which might hold title documents to investments, hold dematerialised investments in its name, and administer the collection of interest/dividends or the application of corporate actions.

11. **Sending dematerialised instructions** – covers firms which operate systems that allow for the electronic transfer of title in certain investments (again, securities and contractually based investments), and those which cause instructions to be sent on those systems. An example of such a system is CREST.

12. **Establishing, operating and winding up a collective investment scheme** – this activity captures persons who set up, operate/administer and wind up any type of CIS, whether an authorised scheme or an unregulated scheme. Acting as a trustee of an AUT, or as the depository or sole director of an OEIC, are also separate regulated activities.

13. **Establishing, operating and winding up a pension scheme** – captures those who set up, operate/administer and wind up stakeholder pension schemes and self-invested personal pensions (SIPPs). These activities may be carried out by the scheme trustees and/or the scheme administrators.

14. **Providing basic advice on stakeholder products** – this is a special regulated activity, for those who advise only on stakeholder products. Stakeholder products conform to certain criteria for cost and accessibility.

15. **Advising on investments** – this covers giving advice on securities and relevant investments. It does not extend to giving advice about deposits, nor to occupational pensions schemes, nor to generic advice (eg, '*invest in the US, not in Europe*'). Neither does it extend to giving information – facts, which are not tailored to constitute a recommendation – instead of advice.

16. **Advising on home finance transactions** – advising on the merits of entering into, or varying the terms of, a regulated mortgage, a home reversion plan, a home purchase plan or a regulated sale and rent-back agreement is a regulated activity.

17. **Lloyd's market activities** – in addition to those mentioned above under arranging investments, there are three further Lloyd's-related regulated activities:
    - advising on syndicate participation;
    - managing underwriting capacity as a managing agent;
    - arranging deals in contracts of insurance at Lloyd's.

18. **Entering into a funeral plan contract** – a firm that enters into funeral plan contracts as provider (ie, being the person to whom the pre-payments are made) is conducting a regulated activity.

19. **Entering into and administering home finance transactions** – captures the activity of regulated mortgage lenders, home reversion providers, home purchase providers and regulated sale and rent-back agreement providers.

20. **Dormant account funds** – meeting repayment claims and managing dormant account funds are specified activities.

21. **Agreeing to carry on a specified activity** – is itself a regulated activity (and so a firm should not agree to carry on a regulated activity until it is properly authorised, notwithstanding that it may not intend to actually carry out that activity until it has its authorisation).

22. **Certain activities relating to entering forms of consumer credit as lender** – rights under any contract under which one person provides another with credit and contracts for hire of goods – rights under a contract for the bailment or hiring of goods to a person other than a body corporate.

23. **Providing credit reference services** – furnishing persons with information that is relevant to the financial standing of persons other than bodies corporate and is provided to that person for that purpose.

24. **Providing credit information services** – taking steps on behalf of a person other than a body corporate in connection with information relevant to that person's financial standing that is or may be held by a regulated person.

25. **Certain other activities relating to consumer credit** are regulated including credit broking, debt adjusting, debt counselling, debt collecting and debt administration.

26. **The setting of benchmarks** – providing information, administration and the determining or publishing of a benchmark or publishing connected information.

Advising, dealing and arranging activities when carried on in connection with a contract of insurance, and the activity of assisting in the administration and performance of a contract of insurance, are collectively known as **insurance mediation activity** and subject to the provisions of the Insurance Mediation Directive.

The above is a high level summary of the main provisions. The complete unabridged list can be located using this weblink https://fshandbook.info/FS/glossary-html/handbook/Glossary/R?definition=G974

1.3 Exclusions

Learning Objective

2.4.2 Know the main exclusions from the need for authorisation under the FSMA 2000 [Regulated Activities Order]: dealing as principal [PERG 2.8.4]; advice in newspapers [PERG 2.8.12 & 7.1.2]; trustees, nominees and personal representatives [PERG 2.9.3]; employee share schemes [PERG 2.9.13]; overseas persons [PERG 2.9.15]

There are a significant number of exclusions provided in the FSMA; those carrying on regulated activities falling entirely within the scope of an exclusion can conduct the activity without having to apply to the PRA/FCA for authorisation for the activity in question. Some key examples follow.

1.3.1 Exclusions from Dealing as Principal

Absence of Holding Out

Dealing in investments as principal is a regulated activity. This means that persons dealing for themselves in the hope of making profits are required to be authorised or exempt. However, this regulated activity is restricted to those persons who are holding themselves out as and acting as **market makers**, and who regularly solicit the public with the purpose of inducing them to deal. The result is that a wide range of activity is excluded from the regulated activity of dealing as principal.

This means that:

- firms which are professional dealers, such as market makers, and which hold themselves out as such, are carrying on a regulated activity; but
- individuals or companies which are not in the business of dealing in investments, and which invest only for themselves in the hope of making a profit, are excluded.

This exclusion relates to securities (shares and bonds) and assigning rights under a life policy, as long as they are entered into by an unauthorised person.

Furthermore, there is an exclusion relating to contractually based investments (futures, options and CFDs) if the transaction is entered into by an unauthorised person and it takes place in either of the following circumstances:

- First, where the person with whom the unauthorised person deals is either an authorised person or an exempt person who is acting in the course of a business comprising a regulated activity in relation to which he is exempt.
- Secondly, where the unauthorised person enters into a transaction through a non-UK office (which could be his own) and he deals with or through a person who is based outside the United Kingdom. This non-UK person must be someone who, as his ordinary business, carries on any of the activities relating to securities or contractually based investments that are generally treated as regulated activities.

Other Exclusions

There are other exclusions where dealing as principal is not classified as a regulated activity:

1. a bank providing finance to another person and accepting an instrument acknowledging the debt;
2. a company or other organisation issuing its own shares, warrants or debentures, or purchasing its own shares in accordance with certain provisions of the Companies Act 1985 (Treasury shares);
3. using options, futures and CFDs for risk management purposes, as long as the company's business is mainly unregulated activities and the sole or main purpose of the deals is to limit identifiable risks;
4. entering into transactions as principal for, or in connection with, the following:
   - while acting as bare trustee (or as nominee in Scotland);
   - the sale of goods or supply of services;
   - between members of a group or joint enterprise;
   - the sale of a body corporate;
   - an employee share scheme;
   - an overseas person;
   - an incoming electronic commerce provider.

1.3.2   Exclusions for Advice in Newspapers

There is a particular exclusion from the regulated activity of advising on investments and on home finance transactions, in relation to newspapers and other media. If a newspaper includes investment advice, and that advice is not the principal purpose of the newspaper, it is excluded from the regulated activity of advising on investments. The existence of money and city pages or subsections within a newspaper does not make the principal purpose of the paper anything other than the provision of news, so there is no need for authorisation.

If the principal purpose of a publication is the provision of investment advice, with a view to encouraging investors or prospective investors to undertake investment activity, authorisation is required. This is the case for periodicals that tip certain investments and are often sold on a subscription basis. They are often referred to as 'tipsheets' and include publications like Warrants Alert (which highlights those warrants that offer good value to the investor).

1.3.3   Trustees, Nominees and Personal Representatives

There is an exclusion from the need for authorisation if the person carrying on the regulated activity is:

- acting as the representative of another party;
- not generally holding himself out as carrying on regulated activities; and
- not receiving additional remuneration for providing these investment services.

This exclusion can apply to the following types of regulated activity:

- dealing in investments as principal;
- arranging deals in investments and making arrangements with a view to transactions in investments;
- arranging a home finance transaction;
- managing investments;

- safeguarding and administering investments;
- sending dematerialised instructions;
- advising on investments or advising on a home finance transaction;
- assisting in the administration and performance of a contract of insurance;
- entering into, or administering a home finance transaction.

It is important to note that this exclusion is not available if the person is carrying on, dealing, arranging or advising activity in connection with a contract of insurance.

1.3.4   Employee Share Schemes

In order to encourage companies to set up schemes enabling their employees to hold shares in the company they work for, there are exclusions from the need to be authorised to operate such schemes. The exclusion covers four types of activity:

- dealing in investments as principal;
- dealing in investments as agent;
- arranging deals in investments and making arrangements with a view to transactions in investments; and
- safeguarding and administering investments.

1.3.5   Overseas Persons

There are a number of exclusions for overseas persons carrying on regulated activities, providing that they do not do so from a permanent place of business in the UK. These exclusions apply only if the business is done through an authorised, or exempt, UK person, or if they are the result of a **legitimate approach**, such as a UK client approaching an overseas person in an unsolicited manner.

The exclusions mainly cover the following types of activity:

- dealing in investments as principal;
- dealing in investments as agent;
- arranging deals in investments and making arrangements with a view to transactions in investments;
- arranging a home finance transaction;
- advising on investments;
- agreeing to carry on the regulated activities of managing investments, making arrangements with a view to transactions in investments, assisting in the performance and administration of a contract of insurance, arranging deals in investments, safeguarding and administering investments or sending dematerialised instructions;
- operating a MTF; and
- entering into, or administering a home finance transaction.

2. Exemptions

Learning Objective

2.1.1   Know the regulated and prohibited activities [Parts II/III of FSMA 2000, Regulated Activities Order 2001 and the under-noted guidance in the Perimeter Guidance Manual (PERG)]: authorised persons [PERG 2.2.3]; exempt persons [PERG 2.10] and FSMA Exemption Order 2001 [(SI 2001/1201)]; offences under the Act [PERG 2.2.1/2]; enforceability of agreements entered into with an unauthorised business [PERG 2.2.2]; defences available under the Act [PERG 2.2.1]

As mentioned previously, the FSMA provides for certain persons to be exempt from the general prohibition in the conduct of regulated activity. These exempt persons are summarised below.

2.1   Appointed Representatives

An appointed representative can be any type of person (ie, a natural person or any other legal person) who has entered into a contract with an authorised person (**the principal**) for the purpose of conducting regulated activity. The authorised person becomes the principal and accepts legal responsibility for the regulated activity conducted by the appointed representative. In this way, the appointed representative becomes an exempt person under FSMA for the conduct of permitted regulated activity.

The FCA and the PRA rules do not apply to appointed representatives because they are not authorised persons. However, any business conducted by the appointed representative for which the principal has accepted responsibility will be treated as having been conducted by the principal. The principal itself must have the permissions for the activity that is to be carried out by the appointed representative.

Additionally, some persons within the appointed representative firm must be approved for controlled functions, namely, the governors (directors, partners) and individuals who will be performing customer functions (CF30, see Section 5.3).

The regulators expect principals to conduct thorough reviews of the suitability and conduct of their appointed representatives. The exempt status that appointed representatives enjoy (s.39 FSMA and the FSMA (Appointed Representatives) Regulations 2001) comes at the price of ongoing supervision and monitoring by the principal.

The appointed representatives regulations only allow certain regulated activities to be conducted by appointed representatives on an exempt basis. These activities are:

- dealing in investments as agent (pure protection or general insurance contracts only);
- arranging deals in investments and making arrangements with a view to transactions in investments;
- arranging deals in home finance transactions and making arrangements with a view to home finance transactions;
- assisting in the administration and performance of a contract of insurance;
- arranging the safeguarding and administration of assets;
- advising on investments;
- giving basic advice on stakeholder products;

- advising on home finance transactions;
- agreeing to carry on a regulated activity.

In particular, appointed representatives are not permitted to deal in investments as principal or manage investments.

2.2 Recognised Investment Exchanges (RIEs) and Recognised Clearing Houses (RCHs)

Substantial amounts of trading in, and issuance of, securities is conducted through formal exchanges such as the LSE. There are often separate clearing systems connected to these formal exchanges that facilitate the settlement of the trades that take place. The firms operating these systems are referred to as **clearing houses**.

The FSMA gives the FCA the responsibility of recognising, regulating and supervising exchanges and clearing houses.

In order to be recognised by the FCA, these exchanges and clearing houses need to be fit and proper for their purpose. Once recognised, the exchanges are referred to as **recognised investment exchanges** (RIEs) and the clearing houses are referred to as **recognised clearing houses** (RCHs). RIEs and RCHs are exempt persons in that they do not need to seek authorisation from the FCA to do regulated activities – they are, instead, **recognised**.

2.3 FSMA Exemption Order 2001

The Treasury has established certain exemptions from the need to be authorised for particular persons. Some of these exemptions are restricted in that they only apply in certain circumstances.

For example supranational bodies of which the UK or another European Economic Area (EEA) member state is a member and central banks of the UK or another EEA member state are exempted from the need to be authorised to carry on any regulated activity, apart from effecting or carrying out contracts of insurance. Obvious examples are the Bank of England, the European Investment Bank (EIB) and the International Monetary Fund (IMF).

In contrast, certain bodies are exempted from the need to be authorised for the sole regulated activity of accepting deposits; these include municipal banks, local authorities and charities.

Certain persons are able to perform limited regulated activities without the need to be authorised or exempt. In effect, the general prohibition of FSMA does not apply to them. Such persons include the members of Lloyd's insurance market and members of certain designated professional bodies (DPBs).

2.3.1 Members of Lloyd's

Several activities carried on in connection with business at Lloyd's are regulated activities. These include:

- advising on syndicate participation;
- acting as a managing agent for one or more syndicates; and

• arranging deals in insurance contracts.

However, FSMA disapplies the general prohibition for members of Lloyd's in relation to contracts of insurance written at Lloyd's. This is further extended to those members that ceased to be an underwriting member at any time on or after 24 December 1996; these former members can carry out insurance contracts underwritten at Lloyd's without the need for authorisation.

The reason why the general prohibition does not apply is because the activities at Lloyd's are expected to be suitably supervised and executed by the Society of Lloyd's, and so additional FCA authorisation of members is unnecessary. The regulators do, however, have certain powers to impose rules on the members (or former members) of Lloyd's if it is felt necessary.

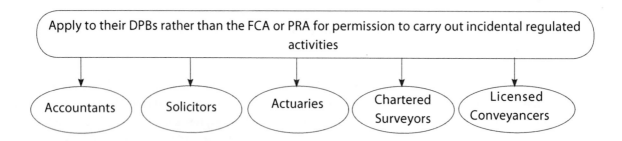

2.3.2 Members of the Professions

Part 20 of the FSMA provides for five professions where individual firms are permitted to carry on particular regulated activities without the need to apply to the regulators for authorisation. Firms are required to apply to their relevant professional body for permission to conduct these activities. The individual professions are accountants, solicitors, actuaries, chartered surveyors and licensed conveyancers.

The professional bodies that are able to grant permissions are known as designated professional bodies (DPBs). They include the Institute of Chartered Accountants in England and Wales (ICAEW), the Law Society, the Institute of Actuaries and the Royal Institution of Chartered Surveyors.

The DPB must operate a set of rules with which its members must comply and the regulated activity must be incidental to the provision of professional services. For example, a firm of accountants providing tax advice might give a client advice as to which investments might best be sold to avoid the accrual of a tax liability.

In order to be able to rely on the Part 20 regime, the activities carried out by member firms of DPBs are restricted. For example, such firms are allowed to receive pecuniary reward only from the client (ie, they must return to the client any commissions received from the providers of products held); and certain regulated activities may not be carried out by the members, namely:

1. accepting deposits;
2. dealing in investments as principal (ie, acting as market maker);
3. lending or administering home finance transactions (unless the firm is acting as trustee or personal representative);

4.   establishing, operating or winding up a CIS;
5.   establishing, operating or winding up a stakeholder pension scheme or a personal pension scheme;
6.   acting as stakeholder pension scheme manager;
7.   managing the underwriting capacity of a Lloyd's syndicate or advising on syndicate participation;
8.   effecting or carrying out contracts of insurance (including Lloyd's business);
9.   providing funeral plan contracts.

With regard to the regulated activity of managing investments, the firm may exercise discretion to sell investments but may only purchase investments where the decision is taken, or an authorised person gives advice.

Advising on investments can only be done in specified circumstances in order for it to be exempt.

3.   Authorisation

Learning Objective

2.4.4   Know the authorisation procedures for firms: the need for authorisation [FSMA s.19, PERG 2.3, Annex 1 & 2, 2.10.9–16]; the threshold conditions for authorisation [FSMA sch.6, COND 2]

Persons wishing to carry on regulated activities in the UK, by way of business, need to be authorised or exempt, unless their activity falls wholly within the scope of one or more exclusions. **By way of business** broadly means holding oneself out as carrying on the activity on a commercial basis.

Although regulated activities must be carried out 'by way of business', what this includes or excludes partly depends upon the nature of the activities undertaken. For example:

*   Accepting deposits is not considered to be carried out by way of business by a person if he does not hold himself out as accepting deposits on a day-to-day basis and if the deposits he accepts are accepted only on particular occasions. In determining whether deposits are accepted only on particular occasions, the frequency of the occasions and any distinguishing characteristics are taken into account.
*   A person who carries on an insurance mediation activity will not be regarded as doing so by way of business unless he takes up or pursues that activity for remuneration.

Whether or not an activity is carried on by way of business is ultimately a question of judgement that takes account of several factors (none of which is likely to be conclusive). These include the degree of continuity, the existence of a commercial element, the scale of the activity and the proportion the activity bears to other activities carried on by the same person but which are not regulated. The nature of the particular regulated activity that is carried on will also be relevant to the factual analysis.

More generally, the following questions summarise what a person concerned that his proposed activities may require authorisation should consider:

1.   Will I be carrying on my activities by way of business?

2. Will I be managing the assets of an occupational pension scheme?
3. If the answer is 'Yes' to (1) or (2), will my activities involve specified investments in any way?
4. If so, will my activities be, or include, regulated activities?
5. If so, will I be carrying them on in the United Kingdom?
6. If so, will my activities be excluded?
7. If not, will I be exempt?
8. If not, am I allowed to carry on regulated activities without authorisation?
9. If not, do I benefit from the few provisions of the Act that authorise me without permission?
10. If not, what is the scope of the permission that I need to seek from the regulator?

3.1 The Permissions Regime

The term **authorised person** includes those who have been authorised by the FCA or the PRA and also other persons such as overseas firms and the Society of Lloyd's. This section looks at those who are authorised by the FCA or the PRA.

Authorisation provided in this way is through the regulators' powers under Part 4A of FSMA (as amended) so is referred to as a **Part 4A permission**. The FCA or PRA gives Part 4A permission as appropriate and, once granted, the firm becomes an authorised person. As an authorised person, the firm can carry on regulated activities without breaching the general prohibition.

We have seen that there is a very wide range of specified investments and activities. The Part 4A permission specifies precisely which activities the firm can carry on, the investments those activities may relate to, and any further requirements or special conditions attaching to the permission. For example, the holding or controlling of client money is not, in itself, a regulated activity. However, if a firm does not wish to hold client money the FCA will impose a requirement on the firm's scope of permission that the firm may not hold or control client money.

The activities which a firm is given permission to conduct can be limited. For example, it may be permitted to deal as principal, but only for a particular type of client.

3.2 The Authorisation Process

Depending on the type of firm, it would apply to either the PRA and/or the FCA (for FCA-only regulated firms).

If a firm is dual-regulated the PRA will not authorise the firm unless it engages with the FCA – and they authorise.

The applicant completes an application pack, available from the regulators. The packs are tailored depending on the type of activity that is to be applied for. The pack requires information on:

- **core details** – the applicant's legal form, summary details of ownership, accounting year end, organisational structure and IT systems;
- **controllers** – detailed information about the firm's owners and controllers;
- **business supplement** – a detailed form covering the business plan, type of activity, anticipated business levels, financial forecasts showing how the applicant will meet capital adequacy tests, details of professional indemnity insurance and compliance procedures;

- **disclosure of significant events** – if the firm has traded before (perhaps as an appointed representative), this questionnaire must be completed to disclose any trading issues;
- **approved persons forms** – each person who is to be carrying out a controlled function must send an individual form;
- **checklist and declaration** – including the application fee – this is £1,500 for straightforward cases (eg, advising and arranging) and £5,000 for moderately complex cases (eg, managing investments); this fee is not refundable in any circumstances.

A case officer is appointed to review the case and obtain further information from the applicant. The case officer prepares a report and a committee then signs this off and the applicant is notified that they are an authorised person with effect from a specified date. The regulators have statutory deadlines for determining cases: six months for complete cases and up to 12 months for incomplete cases.

If an authorised firm that was previously unincorporated (eg, sole trader, partnership) decides to incorporate (limited company or limited liability partnership (LLP)), the new entity will require authorisation. In these circumstances, and so long as there are no material changes and the activities are to be the same, the regulator allows a simplified pack to be submitted (change of legal status) with a reduced application fee.

3.3   The Threshold Conditions (TCs)

The Threshold Conditions (TCs) were effectively the minimum standards for being, and remaining, authorised. The Financial Services and Markets Act 2000 (Threshold Conditions) Order 2013 has changed and re-distributed responsibility for TCs between the FCA and the PRA. Some FCA TCs will apply to all firms, including dual-regulated firms.

The revised TCs became effective from 1 April 2013. The FCA conditions have been widened in scope, allowing the regulator to exercise a greater degree of subjective judgment. In particular it currently sees rigorous business model analysis as the key to an effective supervisory regime that avoids the alleged deficiencies of past approaches.

The FCA assess applicants only for conduct if they are dual-regulated firms, with the PRA assessing prudential issues. For single-regulated firms, the FCA will assess the applicant for both conduct and prudential issues.

Although the process is the same the FCA will work to a set of principles, which are:

- Align the assessments of new applications to the risk they pose to the FCA's statutory objectives; firms will not be authorised whose products and services pose a risk to customers.
- Be open with all potential applicants as they go through the authorisations process, making sure that communication occurs early on so that the firm understands what is required of it. Then the FCA will look closely at the proposed business model and the viability of the firm over a medium-term horizon.
- Processes will be structured to support the operational objectives.
- Refuse applications at an earlier stage if do not think the proposed offering of products or services is in the interests of consumers or, more broadly, if it poses a significant risk to the FCA's objectives.
- Share any risks and underlying themes that are identified with supervision colleagues, so they can monitor and assess them on an ongoing basis once a firm or individual is authorised.

3.3.1   Business Model Threshold Condition

A new business model threshold condition will demonstrate the importance that the FCA places on a firm's ability to put forward an appropriate, viable and sustainable business model, given the nature and scale of business that it intends to carry out. Then the FCA expects firms to demonstrate adequate contingency planning in their business model. Firms will need to make clear how their business model meets the needs of clients and customers, not placing them at undue risk, or placing at risk the integrity of the wider financial services system, for example, from financial crime. The FCA will also expect firms to provide clear information, with evidence of how they will meet this threshold condition.

The FCA has stated that it will recommend refusal at an early stage where it is not satisfied that a firm meets, or will continue to meet, this minimum expected standard.

3.3.2   PRA Additional Conditions

Firms will need to meet both the PRA-specific and FCA-specific threshold conditions. The PRA-specific threshold conditions will apply for banks, building societies, credit unions and designated investment firms that are regulated by the PRA for prudential purposes.

No significant amendments were made to the legal status and location of offices conditions.

In granting Part 4A permission, the regulators are required to ensure that the applicant satisfies the minimum standards for being an authorised person. These are the **threshold conditions**, namely:

1. **Legal status** – the regulators broadly accept individuals, companies, branches of companies, partnerships and unincorporated associations as authorised persons. However, there are some restrictions on the legal form that is acceptable for a firm wishing to undertake certain activities; for example, an individual or partnership does not meet the criteria for banking deposits or insurance business.
2. **Location of offices** – the regulators require companies established under UK law to have their head and registered offices in the UK if they are to be authorised. For firms other than companies, the FSMA stipulates that a *'non-body corporate with its head office in the UK must carry on business in the UK'*.
3. **Business to be conducted in a prudent manner** – the new condition incorporates some of the considerations in the former adequate resources condition and requires firms to have appropriate (rather than 'adequate') financial and non-financial resources. To have appropriate financial resources, the firm must have appropriate capital, liquidity and must be willing and able to value its assets and liabilities appropriately. To have appropriate non-financial resources, the firm must have appropriate resources to monitor, manage and take action to remove or reduce risks to the firm's safety and soundness, and to the firm's valuation of its assets and liabilities. The firm's business must be managed effectively and the firm's non-financial resources must be sufficient for the firm to comply with the PRA's requirements.
4. **Effective supervision (including the existing close links condition)** – this is a new condition from the 2013 Order. The effective supervision condition includes the former close links TC, (eg, the effect of group structures on supervision) and, in addition, firms will need to ensure that there is no impediment to their effective supervision by virtue of:
    *   the nature and complexity of regulated activities undertaken;
    *   products offered; and
    *   the business organisation.

5. **Appropriate resources** – the need to have 'appropriate' resources will replace the former 'adequate' resources test, reflecting the importance of considering the quality as well as quantity of resources available. The revised threshold condition lists two extra matters as relevant: the nature and scale of the firm's business; and the risks to the continuity of the services provided by the firm. Additional new material specifically addresses a firm's 'non-financial resources' – these include any *systems, controls, plans or policies... any information that the firm holds and the human resources that the firm has available'.* In assessing appropriateness of non-financial resources, the FCA will consider the skills and experience of those who manage the firm's affairs.

6. **Suitability** – the firm is required to prove itself fit and proper to be granted Part 4A permission. The fit and proper requirement is considered in the context of all of the firm's circumstances; this includes the range and nature of its proposed regulated activities, the need to be satisfied that its affairs are conducted soundly and prudently, and its connections with other persons. The regulators will assess an applicant's fit and proper status in the light of the specific activities it wishes to carry on. Just because an applicant is suitable to carry on one regulated activity, it does not mean that it is suitable to carry on all regulated activities. In addition, for FCA-regulated firms, the current condition of suitability has been amended and contains additional references to the firm's affairs being conducted in an appropriate manner with regard to the interests of consumers and the integrity of the UK financial system and the need to minimise the extent to which the business carried on by a firm can be used for a purpose connected with financial crime. Firms must also be generally co-operative in the provision of information to the FCA, and the firm's management must act with probity, in addition to having adequate skills and experience. For PRA-regulated firms, the amended condition of suitability contains requirements for firms to comply on a pro-active basis with the PRA's requests relating to the provision of information, and that the firm's management act with probity, in addition to having adequate skills and experience.

7. **Business model –** this is a new condition and it states that the firm's strategy for doing business must be suitable for its regulated activities, having regard to whether the business model is compatible with the firm's affairs being conducted in a sound and prudent manner, the interests of consumers and the integrity of the UK financial system.

8. **Appointment of claims representatives** – the 2013 Order did not change this TC and is only relevant to motor insurers who must have a claims representative in each EEA state for dealing with claims and as such isn't reflected in the table below.

The table below summarises the applicability of the threshold conditions:

Condition	FCA firm	Dual-regulated firm	
		FCA	PRA
Legal status	N/A	No	Yes
Location of offices	Yes	No	Yes
Prudent conduct	N/A	No	Yes
Effective supervision	Yes	Yes	Yes
Appropriate resources	Yes	Yes	No
Suitability	Yes	Yes	Yes
Business model	Yes	Yes	No

4.   Supervision

Learning Objective

2.4.5   Know the supervisory process: purpose of supervision arrangements [SUP 1A.2/3]; focus on a firm's senior management [SUP 1A.1.4, SYSC 1.2.1(1)/4.2.1/4.3.1]; tools for supervision [SUP 1.4.1/2/4/51A.4.1/2/4/5]; transaction reporting regime [SUP 17.1.4]

Under FSMA, the relevant regulator (the FCA and/or the PRA) is required to maintain arrangements to supervise compliance with the requirements imposed on authorised persons.

The supervisory approach has to work to ensure the statutory objectives are met. However, there is also the need to ensure that supervision does not impose an unnecessary restriction or burden on firms. In this respect, the regulators also emphasise the role of senior management to organise and control the business for which they are responsible. This includes implementing sound internal risk management systems and making sure that individuals are suitable and competent for the roles they are appointed to carry out. We looked at the main systems and controls requirements in Chapter 1. You may wish to review these in the context of regulatory supervision.

The purpose of the regulators' supervision arrangements is to mitigate and manage risks to the statutory objectives. The FCA's supervision efforts focus on the conduct of both FCA-authorised and PRA-authorised firms, plus prudential regulation for those authorised firms that are not authorised by the PRA. The PRA supervises the prudential aspects of those firms that it authorises.

A structured approach is adopted which is designed to:

- **identify the main risks to objectives as they arise** – the regulators   use intelligence from a wide range of sources such as firm visits, enforcement actions, regulatory reporting, transaction monitoring, sector and environmental analysis; and consultation with market participants, consumer and practitioner panels, and the FOS for information on complaints trends;
- **measure the importance of the risk** – score the risk according to the impact on the regulator's objectives (were the risk to crystallise) and the probability of this happening;
- **mitigate the risk** – assess how to respond, having regard to costs and benefits, and the best use of supervisory resources;
- **monitor the progress of the risk** – reports are produced to assess that risks are being managed and that internal controls are adequate.

The approach adopted by the FCA starts by categorising firms according to their potential impact on the FCA's objectives. This results in more supervisory effort being allocated to firms with the greatest potential to cause risks to consumers or market integrity. For FCA-only regulated firms the supervisory efforts will also include the impact the firm's failure might have.

The FCA's supervision model is based on three pillars:

1. **The Firm Systematic Framework (FSF)** – preventative work through structured conduct assessments of firms. This involves looking at the business model and strategy of the firm along with an assessment of how the firm embeds fair treatment of customers and ensures market integrity in the way it conducts its business. The result is that the FCA can decide on what actions are required by the firm. These required actions are communicated to the firm, and subsequently followed up.
2. **Event-driven work** – problems that are emerging or have happened are dealt with faster, securing customer redress or other remedial work where necessary. Events that may give rise to such issues might include a whistleblower alleging misconduct, or a sudden increase in reported complaints at a firm.
3. **Issues and products** – fast intensive campaigns on sectors of the market or products that are putting or may put consumers at risk. An example might be where market intelligence suggests that a product is being sold to customers who do not need it, or do not fully understand it.

The supervisory approach adopted by the PRA uses its Proactive Intervention Framework (PIF). The PIF captures the PRA's assessment of the proximity of each of its authorised firms to failure. This assessment is drawn from a variety of elements including business risk, management and governance, risk management and controls, capital and liquidity. The PRA continually reviews its judgement of the risks to the firm's safety and soundness, and requires action from the firm where necessary. Significantly, if a firm's viability is assessed as deteriorating, the PRA supervisors will review their supervisory actions accordingly.

In contrast to the PRA, the general approach to prudential supervision adopted by the FCA is based on managing failure when it happens rather than focusing on reducing its probability. This is because isolated failures of FCA-only firms will not present a risk to the integrity of the financial system since the PRA authorises all deposit takers, insurers and significant investment firms. The focus of the FCA is on ensuring that client assets are protected and that a firm can be run down without adversely affecting consumers.

4.1   Tools of Supervision

The regulators have a range of supervisory tools available to them that can be classified under four headings:

1. **Diagnostic tools** – designed to identify, assess and measure risk such as those described above.
2. **Monitoring tools** – to track the development of identified risk, wherever this arises.
3. **Preventative tools** – to limit or reduce identified risks and so prevent them crystallising or increasing.
4. **Remedial tools** – to respond to risks when they have crystallised.

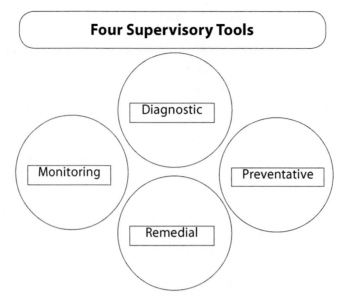

Some tools involve the regulators in a direct client relationship with firms, such as **supervisory visits** by the regulator's staff. Others do not involve firms directly; for example, the FCA may make **public statements** to consumers about the risks of particular types of products.

The regulators also have statutory powers under FSMA whereby either regulator can impose certain requirements on firms. For example, they can change the scope of a firm's Part 4A permission to prevent the conduct of activity that poses risks to the regulator's objectives.

The regulators also use a variety of methods for checking whether individual firms remain compliant. These include:

- desk-based reviews;
- liaison with other agencies and regulators;
- meetings with a firm's management;
- on-site inspections;
- analysis of periodic returns and notifications;
- reviews of past business;
- transaction monitoring;
- auditor's reports;
- skilled persons reports – under s.166 of FSMA, the regulator can require a firm to appoint an independent skilled person to conduct a report on an aspect of the firm's business. The regulator defines the scope of the review, but the contract is between the firm and the skilled person.

4.2   Transaction Reporting

Firms that execute transactions in financial instruments or certain over-the-counter (OTC) derivatives are required to report details of the transaction to the FCA through an Approved Reporting Mechanism (ARM). This helps in the surveillance of market operations. The report must include information about the:

- **reporting firm** – unique identification code and the capacity in which the firm dealt (principal or agent);
- **trade** – date, time, buy or sell;
- **instrument(s) as relevant** – identification code, type of instrument, maturity date, derivative details, put or call status;
- **price** – unit price, strike price of an option, price multiplier, price notation (currency);
- **quantity** – number and value of instruments;
- **counterparty**;
- **venue** – where the transaction was executed;
- **customer identification**;
- **other** – as required by the system.

Discretionary portfolio managers that send orders to other firms for execution do not have to make transaction reports themselves so long as they know the firm carrying out the order has to make such reports.

The transaction reporting regime is undergoing changes designed to harmonise transaction reporting across the EU.

5. The Process for Approved Persons

Learning Objective

2.4.6 Know the approval processes for Approved Persons: the application process [SUP 10A.13.1/2/3]; the criteria for approval as an Approved Person [FIT 1.3, 2.1, 2.2, 2.3]

Section 59 of FSMA requires persons fulfilling controlled functions to first be approved by the regulator as fit and proper. This is the approved persons regime which we first encountered in Chapter 1. As we saw, approved persons – having been assessed as fit and proper – are also then expected to comply with the Statement of Principles and Code of Practice for Approved Persons.

5.1 The Approval Process

An individual may be permitted to perform a controlled function only after they have been granted approved person status by the regulator. The candidate completes a form and this is notified to the regulator by the firm. The form includes a comprehensive list of questions to establish a person's employment history and give the regulator the information it needs to conduct the assessment of fitness and propriety.

In certain circumstances an abbreviated form may be completed, for example if the person is already an approved person executing similar controlled functions.

The amount of time the regulator takes to determine an application varies depending on any additional checks that have to be made.

If adverse information about the candidate comes to light during the determination process, the firm must notify the regulator.

If a person does not wish to proceed with an application, the regulator must be formally notified using a separate form notification.

5.2 The Fit and Proper Test

The regulator may grant an application for approved person status only if it is satisfied that the candidate is a fit and proper person to perform the controlled function stated in the application form. Responsibility lies with the firm making the application to satisfy the regulator that the candidate is fit and proper to perform the controlled function applied for.

During the application process, the regulator may discuss the assessment of the candidate's fitness and propriety with the firm, and may retain notes of such discussions. In making its assessment, the regulator will consider the controlled function to be fulfilled, the activities of the firm and the permission which has been granted to the firm. If any information comes to light that suggests that the individual might not be fit and proper, the regulator will take into account how relevant and important it is.

In assessing the fitness and propriety of a person within the approved persons' regime, the regulator will look at a number of factors against a set of criteria, of which the most important will be the person's:

- honesty, integrity and reputation;
- competence and capability; and
- financial soundness.

The following criteria are among those which will be considered when assessing an individual's fitness and propriety. These are examples of the type of information that the regulator will want; it does not, however, constitute a definitive list of the matters which might be relevant.

5.2.1 Honesty, Integrity and Reputation

The regulator will have regard to whether a person has been:

- convicted of a criminal offence; particular consideration will be given to offences of fraud, dishonesty and financial crime;
- the subject of an adverse finding or settlement in a civil case, again with particular consideration given to cases involving financial businesses and fraud;
- the subject of previous investigation or disciplinary proceedings by the FSA, FCA or PRA or another regulatory authority;
- the subject of a justified complaint in relation to regulated activities;
- refused a licence to trade, or had a licence or registration revoked;
- involved in an insolvent business; or
- disqualified as a director, or dismissed from a position of trust.

The person must be able to demonstrate a readiness and willingness to comply with the requirements and standards of the regulatory system.

Each application will be treated on its merits, considering the seriousness and circumstances of any matters arising, as well as (in some cases) the length of time which has elapsed since the matter arose.

5.2.2 Competence and Capability

In assessing an applicant's competence and capability, the regulator will have particular regard to whether the person:

- satisfies the relevant requirements laid down in the Training and Competence Sourcebook (TC is covered in Section 6 of this chapter);
- has demonstrated the experience and training needed for them to fulfil the controlled function applied for; and
- has adequate time to perform the controlled function and meet the responsibilities associated with that function.

The regulator will consider previous convictions or dismissals/suspensions from employment for drug or alcohol abuse or other abusive acts only if they relate to the continuing ability of the person to perform the controlled function for which they are to be employed.

5.2.3 Financial Soundness

In assessing an applicant's financial soundness, the regulator will have particular regard to whether the person:

- has been subject to any judgement to repay a debt or pay another award that remains outstanding or was not satisfied within a reasonable period;
- has filed for bankruptcy, been adjudged bankrupt, had his assets sequestrated or made arrangements with his creditors.

The regulator will not normally require a statement of a person's assets and liabilities. The fact that a person may be of limited financial means will not of itself affect his suitability to perform a controlled function.

5.3 Controlled Functions

Learning Objective

2.4.7 Understand the FCA's and PRA's controlled functions: the five functional areas, the required functions, the four areas of significant influence functions, the requirement for FCA or PRA approval prior to performing the function [SUP 10A.4/5/6/7/8/9/10/13 and the types of functions listed under Table 10.4.5. FSMA s.59]

Prior to the introduction of the PRA and its transition to the FCA, the FSA had identified five types of controlled functions:

1. **Governing functions** – these are the persons responsible for directing the affairs of the business. If the business is a company, they will be the directors of that company. If the business is a partnership, they will be the partners. It is important to remember, however, that the deciding factor is not just whether the person has the title of director – someone who acts as a director, even if they are not formally registered as such (eg, a shadow director) will also require FCA/PRA approval because of the influence they exert over the firm.
2. **Required functions** – these are specific functions which the FSA considered to be fundamental to effective control within an authorised firm, as appropriate to the nature of the business. For example, every firm should have appointed someone to fulfil the compliance oversight function and the money laundering reporting functions.
3. **Systems and control functions** – these functions are held by persons responsible for reporting to a firm's governors on its financial affairs, risk exposure and adherence to internal systems and controls.
4. **Significant management function** – this function occurs only in larger firms where there is a layer of management below the governing body which has responsibility for a significant business unit, for example, the head of equities, the head of fixed income and the head of settlements. The function also applies to a firm that conducts proprietary trading.

The above four groups of functions are collectively termed significant influence functions as the persons fulfilling these roles exercise a significant influence over the conduct of a firm's affairs.

5. **Customer function** – this function involves giving advice, dealing, arranging deals and managing investments. The individuals have contact with customers in fulfilling their role. Examples of customer functions are investment adviser and investment manager. The function only extends to activities carried on from a UK establishment.

Customer functions are not significant influence functions.

The Financial Services Act of 2012 amended the FSMA definition of controlled functions to embrace both the FCA and the PRA. It specifies that the FCA may specify a description of a controlled function if it is satisfied that the function is a customer-dealing function or a significant influence function. The PRA is only able to specify the description in relation to significant influence functions in PRA-authorised firms.

The table below sets out Part 1 of the FCA-controlled functions (FCA-authorised persons and appointed representatives).

Type	CF	Description of controlled function
FCA-governing functions*	1	Director function
	2	Non-executive director function
	3	Chief executive function
	4	Partner function
	5	Director of unincorporated association function
	6	Small friendly society function
FCA-required functions*	8	Apportionment and oversight function
	10	Compliance oversight function
	10A	CASS operational oversight function
	11	Money laundering reporting function
	40	Benchmark submission function
	50	Benchmark administration function
Systems and control function*	28	Systems and controls function
Significant management function*	29	Significant management function
Customer-dealing function	30	Customer function
	31	Mortgage customer function
* FCA-significant influence functions		

The table below sets out Part 2 of the FCA-controlled functions (PRA-authorised persons).

Type	CF	Description of controlled function
FCA-required functions*	8	Apportionment and oversight function
	10	Compliance oversight function
	10A	CASS operational oversight function
	11	Money laundering reporting function
FCA-required functions	40	Benchmark submission function
	50	Benchmark administration function
Significant management function*	29	Significant management function
Customer function	30	Customer function
* FCA-significant influence functions		

The table below sets out the PRA-controlled functions for a PRA-authorised firm.

Type	CF	Description of controlled function
PRA-governing functions*	1	Director
	2	Non-executive director function (PRA)
	3	Chief executive function
	4	Partner
	5	Director of unincorporated association
	6	Small friendly society
PRA-required functions*	12	Actuarial function
	12A	With-profits actuary function
	12B	Lloyd's actuary function
Significant management function*	28	Systems and controls function
* PRA-significant influence functions		

5.3.1   Governing Functions

Every authorised firm will have one or more persons responsible for directing its affairs. These persons are performing FCA-governing functions, unless the firm is a PRA-authorised firm, when some of those persons will be performing PRA-governing functions and required to be PRA-approved persons instead. If the PRA receives and considers applications relating to the most senior functions, such as chief executive and other senior directors, the FCA must also give or refuse consent. Unsurprisingly, the FCA view will be based on whether the applicants have the conduct-related skills and experience.

5.3.2   The CASS Oversight Function

The Client Assets Sourcebook (CASS) oversight controlled function applies to firms that hold client money and/or assets (CASS firms). The role includes general oversight of the firm's compliance with CASS, reporting to the firm's governing body in respect of that oversight and completing and submitting the monthly client money and assets return (CMAR).

6. Training and Competence

Learning Objective

2.4.8   Know the Training and Competence regime: the application of the systems and control responsibilities in relation to the competence of employees [SYSC 3.2.13/14/5.1.1 (FCA/PRA)]; the application of T&C for retail activities [TC 1.1.1/3]; assessing and maintaining competence [TC 2.1.1(1), 2.1.2]; the examination requirements before starting activities [TC 2.1.6/7(1)]; firms must assess at the outset and at regular intervals the training needs of its employees [TC 2.1.11]; maintaining competence [TC 2.1.12/13] and the need for a Statement of Professional Standing; activities to which the T&C rules apply [TC Appendix 1]

6.1   Overview

The Principles for Businesses require that firms take reasonable care to 'organise and control their affairs responsibly and effectively'. To comply with this requirement, they must, clearly, ensure that any employee involved with a regulated activity achieves and maintains the competence needed for this role.

The Principles are built on further in the section of the Handbook dealing with senior management arrangements, systems and controls (SYSC). This stipulates a high-level competence requirement which applies to all UK authorised firms, whereby firms must employ personnel with the skills, knowledge and expertise necessary for the discharge of the responsibilities allocated to them.

Additionally, it is incumbent upon individuals who carry out significant influence functions to make sure that there are policies and procedures in place for reviewing the competence of personnel.

This high-level approach is then supplemented – for firms carrying on activities with or for retail clients – by the Training and Competence (TC) Sourcebook. This Sourcebook emphasises the outcomes achieved by firms through their internal training and competence arrangements, as opposed to prescribing how the arrangements should work.

The following activities fall within the scope of the TC Sourcebook, when they are conducted with or for retail clients:

- providing basic advice on stakeholder products;
- advising on/dealing in the following investments – securities*, derivatives*, packaged products, friendly society life policies, friendly society tax-exempt policies, long-term care insurance contracts, corporate finance advice, and advising on Lloyd's syndicate participation*;
- acting as broker fund adviser*;
- acting as pension transfer specialist*; managing investments;
- overseeing CISs, safeguarding assets or client money, administrative functions relating to managing investments, administrative functions concerning contracts of insurance, and the operation of stakeholder pension schemes;
- advising on and overseeing various activities concerning regulated mortgages and equity release transactions;

- advising on non-investment contracts of insurance;
- advising on and overseeing regulated sale and rent-back agreements.

Note that, although all the activities involve dealing with retail clients, only those involving advising and dealing in investments require the person to be approved for a customer function.

6.2   Assessing Competence

The TC Sourcebook requires that firms do not assess an employee as competent to carry on one of the specified activities until that employee has demonstrated the necessary competence to do so and has (if required) attained an appropriate qualification. The list of appropriate qualifications is an Appendix to the TC Sourcebook and has the status of evidential provision.

For those activities marked with an asterisk in Section 6.1, the individual must have attained the full qualification before commencing the activity, even under supervision.

For the other activities requiring a qualification, as long as the person has attained the regulatory module of a qualification, they may commence the activity under supervision. The exception to this is the overseers' roles, as they may commence the activity under supervision without having attained any aspect of their qualifications.

But the overriding rule is that no one conducting a specified activity is eligible for assessment as competent until they have attained the full qualification requirement. There is a time limit of 30 months for attaining a qualification – apart from the overseer roles, where this is a suggested time limit but is not mandatory.

If a person doesn't attain a qualification within 30 months they have to cease the activity to which the qualification relates and they may not recommence the activity until they attain the qualification.

It is ultimately up to the firm to define precisely job roles and standards of competence and to conduct a proper assessment of competence. This may mean that a person has passed the required qualification but is still not deemed competent by the firm.

There is an exemption from the qualification requirements in certain circumstances, to help people who have been based overseas. These conditions are that the firm must be satisfied that the employee:

- has at least three years' up-to-date relevant experience in the activity, which he gained while employed outside the UK;
- has not previously been required to comply fully with the relevant examination requirements; and
- has passed the relevant module of an appropriate examination.

This exemption is not available for those roles (asterisked in Section 6.1) where the person must always attain the full qualification before commencing the activity. It may also not be available to a person who is benefiting from the **30-day rule**. This is a special dispensation for individuals who are largely based overseas and who spend no more than 30 days in the UK under appropriate supervision. In these circumstances, such a person does not have to apply to be approved for a customer function.

Since 1 January 2013 certain provisions also apply to those advising on retail investment products as a result of the implementation of the Retail Distribution Review. This is covered in more detail in Chapter 4 of this workbook.

Firms are required to notify the FCA if any of the following events occur:

- an adviser who was previously assessed as competent is no longer considered competent;
- an adviser has failed to attain an appropriate qualification within the prescribed time limits;
- an adviser has failed to comply with a Statement of Principle in carrying out his controlled function;
- an adviser has performed one of the specified activities before being assessed as competent, and without appropriate supervision.

6.3   Supervision

Further, firms must not allow an employee to carry on any of those specified activities without appropriate supervision. They are required to ensure that employees are appropriately supervised at all times. The level and intensity of that supervision will be significantly greater in the period before a firm has assessed its employee as competent than after. Firms should thus have clear criteria and procedures relating to the specific point at which their employees are assessed by them as being competent so as to be able to demonstrate when and why a reduced level of supervision was considered appropriate.

At all stages, firms are required to consider the level of relevant experience that an employee has in determining the level of supervision required.

Firms must ensure that supervisors have the necessary coaching and assessment skills, as well as the technical knowledge associated with the activity, so as to act as competent supervisors and assessors. In particular, firms should consider whether it is appropriate to require the supervisor to have attained an appropriate qualification. This is a mandatory requirement for supervisors of those who advise on retail investment products, who have not yet been assessed as competent.

6.4   Maintaining Competence

Firms are also required to review regularly their employees' competence – and to take appropriate action, where needed, to ensure that they remain competent for their role. In doing so, they should take account of:

- the individual's technical knowledge and its application;
- their skills and expertise; and
- changes in the market and to products, legislation and regulation.

Firms must assess their employees' training needs at the outset, and again at regular intervals (including if their role changes). They should also review the quality and effectiveness of their training.

7.   Whistleblowing

Learning Objective

2.4.9   Know the legal and regulatory basis for whistleblowing [SYSC 18.1.2, 18.2.3]

The Public Interest Disclosure Act (PIDA) 1998, which came into force on 2 July 1999, introduced legislation to protect persons from retaliation, if they inform regulatory authorities of concerns that might come to their attention at their place of work; this is generally referred to as **whistleblowing**. The FCA provides guidance to authorised firms as to how they might want to adopt internal procedures to facilitate whistleblowing as part of an effective risk management system.

PIDA makes any clause or term in an agreement between a worker and his employer void if it precludes the worker from making a **protected disclosure** (sometimes known as 'blowing the whistle'). A protected disclosure is one, made in good faith, where information is revealed by a worker that shows that one of the following has been, is being, or is likely to be, committed:

- a criminal offence;
- a failure to comply with any legal obligation;
- a miscarriage of justice;
- the putting of the health and safety of an individual in danger;
- damage to the environment;
- deliberate concealment of any of the above.

It is irrelevant whether any of the above occurred in the UK or elsewhere, or whether the law is the law of the UK or any other country.

Firms are encouraged to consider adopting (and encouraged to invite their appointed representatives or, where applicable, their tied agents to consider adopting) appropriate internal procedures which will encourage workers with concerns to blow the whistle internally about matters which are relevant to the functions of the financial services regulators (the FCA and the PRA).

Smaller firms may choose not to have as extensive procedures in place as larger firms. For example, smaller firms may not need written procedures. The following is a list of things that larger and smaller firms may want to do.

Appropriate internal procedures for larger firms include:

- a clear statement that the firm takes failures seriously;
- an indication of what is regarded as a failure;
- respect for the confidentiality of workers who raise concerns, if they wish this;
- an assurance that, if a protected disclosure has been made, the firm will take all reasonable steps to ensure that no person under its control engages in victimisation;
- the opportunity to raise concerns outside the line management structure, such as with the compliance director, internal auditor or company secretary;
- penalties for making false and malicious allegations;
- an indication of the proper way in which concerns may be raised outside the firm, if necessary;

- providing access to an external body such as an independent charity for advice;
- making whistleblowing procedures accessible to staff of key contractors.

Appropriate internal procedures for smaller firms include:

- telling workers that the firm takes failures seriously and explaining how wrongdoing affects the organisation;
- telling workers what conduct is regarded as failure;
- telling workers who raise concerns that their confidentiality will be respected, if they wish this;
- making it clear that concerned workers will be supported and protected from reprisals;
- nominating a senior officer as an alternative route to line management and telling workers how they can contact that individual in confidence;
- making it clear that false and malicious allegations will be penalised by the firm;
- telling workers how they can properly blow the whistle outside the firm if necessary;
- providing access to an external body such as an independent charity for advice; and
- encouraging managers to be open to concerns.

Firms should also consider telling workers (through the firm's internal procedures, or by means of an information sheet available from the regulator, or by some other means) that they can blow the whistle to the FCA, as the regulator prescribed in respect of financial services and markets matters under PIDA.

8. The Regulators' Enforcement and Decision-Making Process

Learning Objective

2.2.1 Know the role of the FCA and PRA enforcement divisions, the power of the FCA and PRA to make decisions by executive procedures and the role, scope and consequences of the Regulatory Decisions Committee's responsibility for decision making [DEPP 3.1–3.4, 4.1]

The criteria and procedures for making decisions concerning disciplinary matters are set out in a Handbook module called Decisions, Procedures and Penalties Manual (DEPP). This covers:

- the various statutory notices that the FCA or PRA may issue;
- the Regulatory Decisions Committee (RDC);
- settlements, penalties and the power to impose suspension or restrictions;
- the FCA's and PRA's policy on assisting overseas regulators.

In addition, the Enforcement Guide (EG), which is in the same block, sets out the regulators' approach to how they exercise the main enforcement powers, both under the FSMA and under the Unfair Contract Terms Regulations, and how the appropriate regulator operates through the activities of their Enforcement Divisions.

The regulators' approach to the enforcement of financial penalties supports their ongoing commitment to the principle of credible deterrence and the improvement of standards within firms in relation to market misconduct and their dealings with customers. The previous regulator, the FSA, created a structured framework, based on the following steps:

- removing profits made from the misconduct;
- setting a figure to reflect the seriousness of the breach;
- considering any aggravating and mitigating factors;
- achieving the appropriate deterrent effect;
- applying any settlement discount.

The settlement discount is designed to provide for earlier redress, protection to consumers and cost savings for both the regulator and the firm involved by allowing the firm to agree the amount of financial penalty and other conditions imposed by the regulator in return for a discount of up to 30%.

The FCA received new powers from the Financial Services Act 2012. It will be allowed to announce publicly that it has begun disciplinary action against a firm or individual. The FCA will be able to publish details of a warranty notice proposing disciplinary action, to signal the start of formal enforcement proceedings. It will have to consult the recipient concerned before publishing.

8.1   The Regulatory Decisions Committee (RDC)

In the interests of fairness, the FSMA requires that, when it makes decisions about the issue of warning and decision notices, the regulator follows procedures that are *'designed to secure, among other things, that the decision which gives rise to the obligation to give any such notice is taken by a person not directly involved in establishing the evidence on which that decision is based'*.

Thus, rather than allowing the enforcement team to make the decisions which are implemented in the statutory notices outlined above, these decisions are made by a relatively independent committee: the RDC.

The RDC is a committee of the FCA's board, and is accountable to that board; however, it is independent to the extent that it is outside the FCA's management structure. Only the chairman is an FCA employee; the rest of the members represent the public interest and are either current or retired practitioners with financial services knowledge and experience, or non-practitioners.

The RDC meets either in its entirety, or as a panel – depending on the issue under review. In either case, the chairman or deputy must be present. The RDC also has its own legal function, so it is not advised on cases by the same legal team that advises the regulator's enforcement team who will have originally brought the case to the RDC.

The RDC has responsibility for statutory decisions, such as to:

- specify a narrower description of a regulated activity than that applied for in a Part 4A permission, or to limit Part 4A permission in a way which would make a fundamental change;
- refuse an application for Part 4A permission, or to cancel an existing Part 4A permission;
- refuse an application for approved person status, or withdraw an existing approval;
- make a prohibition order in relation to a person that will prohibit them from gaining approved person status, or to refuse to vary such an order;
- exercise the regulator's powers to impose a financial penalty, make a public statement on the misconduct of an approved person, issue a public censure against an authorised person, or make a restitution order against a person.

If a statutory notice decision is not made by the RDC, it will be made under the **executive procedures** of the FCA. These executive procedures enable the FCA to use statutory powers when individual guidance or voluntary agreement is felt to be inappropriate. A typical example of when these executive procedures might be used is if the FCA had particular concerns and, therefore, required a firm to submit reports, such as those on trading results, customer complaints, or detailing the firm's management accounts.

8.2   Statutory Notices

Learning Objective

2.2.2   Know the outcomes of the FCA's and PRA's statutory notices [DEPP 1.2], the regulatory enforcement processes: warning, decision, supervisory and final notices [DEPP 2.2 + 2.3] and the firm's right to refer to the tribunal [DEPP 2.3.2/3]

FSMA gives the FCA the power to issue a variety of notices to authorised firms and/or approved persons, collectively referred to as **statutory notices**. These are:

- **Warning notices** give the recipient details about the action the FCA proposes to take and why it proposes to do so. They also give the recipient the right to make representations as to why the FCA should not take this action. New powers provided in the Financial Services Act 2012 permit the FCA to announce publicly that it has begun disciplinary action against a firm or individual. It can be able to publish details of a **warning notice** proposing disciplinary action, to signal the start of formal enforcement proceedings. However, the FCA will have to consult with the recipient of the warning notice before publishing the details.
- **Decision notices** give details of the action that the FCA has decided to take, leaving room for appeal by the recipient.
- **Supervisory notices** give the recipient details regarding the action the FCA has taken, or proposes to take. A typical supervisory notice might limit a firm's Part 4A permission with immediate effect (and hence it would seem reasonable for the FCA to alert the public to the fact that the firm is no longer permitted to carry on certain activities).

In addition, the FCA can issue the following notices, but they are not referred to as 'statutory notices'. These are:

- **Further decision notices** may follow the issue of a decision notice, when the FCA has agreed with the recipient to take a different action from that proposed in the original decision notice. The FCA can issue a further decision notice only with the consent of the recipient.
- **Notices of discontinuance** let the recipient know that if the FCA has previously sent it a warning notice and/or a decision notice, it has decided not to proceed with the relevant action.
- **Final notices** set out the terms of the final action which the FCA has decided to take and the date that it is effective from. They are also – unlike warning and decision notices – published by the FCA, on its website. The FCA would need to get approval from the recipient if it wished to publish a warning notice.

8.3   The Regulatory Enforcement Processes

Learning Objective

2.2.2   Know the outcomes of the FCA's and PRA's statutory notices ([DEPP 1.2]), the regulatory enforcement processes: warning, decision, supervisory and final notices ([DEPP 2.2 + 2.3]) and the firm's right to refer to the tribunal [DEPP 2.3.2/3]

Regulatory enforcement measures are one of the ways the regulators can address instances of non-compliance with their requirements. There are three possible forms of formal disciplinary sanction:

1.   public statements of misconduct (relating to approved persons, ie, individuals);
2.   public censures (relating to authorised persons, ie, firms); and
3.   financial penalties (fines).

The imposition of regulatory enforcement measures (such as fines and public statements/censures) assists the regulators in meeting their statutory objectives.

In addition to these formal measures, you should remember that the FCA can take a lower-key approach if it feels this would be more appropriate. It could, for example:

- issue a private warning, or
- take supervisory action, such as:
  - varying or cancelling the firm's Part 4A permissions, or removing its authorisation;
  - withdrawing an individual's approved person status;
  - prohibiting an individual from performing a particular role in relation to a regulated activity.

These might be used if the regulator considers it necessary to take protective or remedial action (rather than disciplinary action), or if a firm's ability to continue to meet its threshold conditions (see Section 3.3), or an individual approved person's fitness and propriety, is called into question.

When the regulator is considering formal discipline against an authorised firm and/or an approved person, it is required by the FSMA to issue one or more notices. These are the statutory notices we looked at in Section 8.2. As we saw, these notices fall into two categories: warnings and decisions.

Warnings are not in themselves disciplinary events, since for an action to be regarded as disciplinary action a decision must have been made – and a warning is just that, no more and no less. Indeed, the decision notices themselves may not be absolutely final – they may be:

- discontinued by the issue of a notice of discontinuance;
- varied with agreement in a further decision notice; or
- simply confirmed in a final decision notice.

8.3.1   Criteria for Disciplinary Action

In determining whether to take regulatory enforcement measures, the regulator will consider the full circumstances which may be relevant to the case. This would include, but not be limited to:

- The nature and seriousness of the suspected breach.
    - Was it deliberate or reckless?
    - Does it reveal serious or systemic weakness of the management systems or internal controls of the firm?
    - How much loss, or risk of loss, was there to consumers and other market users?
- The conduct of the firm after the breach.
    - How quickly, effectively and completely was the breach brought to the attention of the regulator?
    - Has the firm taken remedial steps since the breach was identified? For example, by identifying and compensating consumers who suffered loss, taking disciplinary action against the staff involved, addressing systemic failures and taking action to avoid recurrence of the breach in the future?
- The previous regulatory record of the firm or approved person.
    - Has the regulator (or a previous regulator) taken any previous disciplinary action?

8.3.2   The Measures

1. **Private warnings** – these are issued by the regulator when it has concerns regarding the behaviour of the firm or approved person, but decide it is not appropriate to bring formal disciplinary action. It might include cases of potential (but unproven) market abuse, or where the FCA considered making a prohibition order but decided not to do so.

   In such circumstances, the regulator believes it is helpful to let the recipient know that they came close to disciplinary action and the private warning serves this purpose. The circumstances giving rise to a private warning might include a minor matter (in nature or degree), or where the firm or approved person has taken full and immediate remedial action. The benefit of a private warning is that it avoids the reputational damage that would follow from more public sanctions, such as a fine or public censure.

   The private warning will state that the regulator has had cause for concern but, at present, does not intend to take formal disciplinary action. It will also state that the private warning will form part of the firm's compliance history and will require the recipient to acknowledge receipt and invite a response.

That said, where an individual accepts a private warning concerning 'fitness', serious consideration needs to be given as a future approved persons application may encounter problems given the earlier warning 'acceptance'. This is increasingly being used as a less resource-intensive regulatory approach by the FCA. Be warned!

2. **Variation of permission** – the Part 4A permission granted to the firm can be varied on the relevant regulator's own initiative. The relevant regulator's powers to vary and cancel a person's Part IV permissions are exercisable in the same circumstances. However, the statutory procedure for the exercise of each power is different and this may determine how the regulator acts in a given case. When it considers how it should deal with a concern about a firm, the regulator will have regard to its regulatory objectives and the range of regulatory tools that are available to it. It will also have regard to:

    1. the responsibilities of a firm's management to deal with concerns about the firm or about the way its business is being or has been run; and
    2. the principle that a restriction imposed on a firm should be proportionate to the objectives the regulator is seeking to achieve.

    Examples of circumstances in which the relevant regulator will consider varying a firm's Part 4A permission because it has serious concerns about a firm, or about the way its business is being or has been conducted, include where:

    1. in relation to the grounds for exercising the power under section 45(1)(a) of the Act, the firm appears to be failing, or appears likely to fail, to satisfy the threshold conditions relating to one or more, or all, of its regulated activities, because for instance:
        a. the firm's material and financial resources appear inadequate for the scale or type of regulated activity it is carrying on, for example, where it has failed to maintain professional indemnity insurance or where it is unable to meet its liabilities as they have fallen due; or
        b. the firm appears not to be a fit and proper person to carry on a regulated activity because:
            *   it has not conducted its business in compliance with high standards which may include putting itself at risk of being used for the purposes of financial crime or being otherwise involved in such crime;
            *   it has not been managed competently and prudently and has not exercised due skill, care, and diligence in carrying on one or more, or all, of its regulated activities;
            *   it has breached requirements imposed on it by or under the Act (including the Principles and the rules), eg, in respect of its disclosure or notification requirements, and the breaches are material in number or in individual seriousness;
    2. in relation to the grounds for exercising the power under section 45(1)(c), it appears that the interests of consumers are at risk because the firm appears to have breached any of Principles 6 to 10 of the Principles (see PRIN 2.1.1R) to such an extent that it is desirable that limitations, restrictions, or prohibitions are placed on the firm's regulated activity.

3. **Withdrawal of a firm's authorisation** – the regulator will consider cancelling a firm's Part 4A permission in two major circumstances:

    *   if it has very serious concerns about a firm, or the way its business is conducted; or
    *   if a firm's regulated activities have come to an end, but it has not applied for cancellation of its Part 4A permission.

The grounds on which the regulator may exercise its power to cancel an authorised person's permission under section 45 of the Act are the same as the grounds for variation. They are set out in section 45(1) and described in EG 8.1. Examples of the types of circumstances in which the FCA may cancel a firm's Part 4A permission include:

1. non-compliance with a FOS award against the firm;
2. material non-disclosure in an application for authorisation or approval or material non-notification after authorisation or approval has been granted. The information which is the subject of the non-disclosure or non-notification may also be grounds for cancellation;
3. failure to have or maintain adequate financial resources, or a failure to comply with regulatory capital requirements;
4. non-submission of, or provision of false information in, regulatory returns, or repeated failure to submit such returns in a timely fashion;
5. non-payment of the relevant regulator's fees or repeated failure to pay those fees, except under threat of enforcement action;
6. failure to provide the regulator with valid contact details or failure to maintain the details provided, so that the regulator is unable to communicate with the firm;
7. repeated failures to comply with rules or requirements;
8. a failure to co-operate with the regulator which is of sufficient seriousness that the regulator ceases to be satisfied that the firm is fit and proper, eg, failing without reasonable excuse to:
   a. comply with the material terms of a formal agreement made with the regulator to conclude or avoid disciplinary or other enforcement action; or
   b. provide material information or take remedial action reasonably required by the regulator.

Section 45(2A) of the Act sets out further grounds on which the regulator may cancel the permission of authorised persons which are investment firms.

Depending on the circumstances, the regulator may need to consider whether it should first use its own-initiative powers to vary a firm's Part 4A permission before going on to cancel it. Among other circumstances, the regulator may use this power if it considers it needs to take immediate action against a firm because of the urgency and seriousness of the situation.

4. **Withdrawal of approval** – as well as having the power to withdraw authorisation for the firm, the regulator has the power to withdraw the approval of particular individuals which allows them to fulfil controlled functions. The regulator is required first to issue a warning notice to the approved person and the firm, followed by a decision notice. The regulator's decision can be referred to the Tax and Chancery Chamber of the Upper Tribunal.

The regulator recognises that withdrawing approval will often have a substantial impact on those concerned. When considering withdrawing approval it will take into account the cumulative effect of all relevant matters, including the following:

- The competence and capability of the individual (embracing qualifications and training). Does he have the necessary skills to carry out the controlled function he is performing?
- The honesty, integrity and reputation of the individual. Is he open and honest in dealings with consumers, market participants and regulators? Is he complying with his legal and professional obligations?
- The financial soundness of the individual. Has he been subject to judgment debts or awards that have not been satisfied within a reasonable period?

- Whether he failed to comply with the Statements of Principle, or was knowingly involved in a contravention of the requirements placed on the firm.
- The relevance, materiality and length of time since the occurrence of any matters indicating the approved person is not fit and proper.
- The degree of risk the approved person poses to consumers and the confidence consumers have in the financial system.
- The previous disciplinary record and compliance history of the approved person.
- The particular controlled function and nature of the activities undertaken by the approved person.

The regulator will publicise the final decision notice in relation to the withdrawal of approval, unless this would prejudice the interests of consumers.

5. **Prohibition of individuals** – under Section 56 of FSMA, the regulator has the right to make a prohibition order against an individual. This order can prohibit the individual from carrying out particular functions, or from being employed by any authorised firm if the relevant regulator considers it necessary for the achievement of their four statutory objectives. The prohibition order may relate just to a single specified regulated activity, or to all regulated activities. It may also relate to the individual's ability to work for a particular class of firms, or to all firms.

   Prohibition orders will generally be used by the regulator in cases which it sees as more serious than those that merit mere withdrawal of approval, ie, there may be a greater lack of fitness and propriety. The regulator will consider all the factors listed above which could otherwise have resulted in a withdrawal of approval. It will also consider factors such as whether the individual has been convicted of, or dismissed or suspended from employment for, the abuse of drugs or other substances, or has convictions for serious assault. The regulator might feel it appropriate to issue a prohibition order against someone who continues to fulfil a controlled function after approval has been withdrawn.

   As with withdrawal of approval, the regulator is required first to issue a warning notice to the approved person and the firm, followed by a decision notice. The regulator's decision can be referred to the Tax and Chancery Chamber of the Upper Tribunal. Generally it will publicise the final decision notice in relation to the prohibition of an individual.

6. **Public censure and statement of misconduct** – the relevant regulator is empowered under the FSMA to issue a public censure on firms it considers to have contravened a requirement imposed on them by, or under, the Act. For approved persons, FSMA may issue a public statement of misconduct where a person has failed to comply with the Statement of Principles, or has been knowingly involved in a firm's contravention of a requirement imposed on it by, or under, the Act. As with other disciplinary actions, the steps required of the regulators are to:
   - issue a warning notice (including the terms of the statement or censure the regulator is proposing to issue);
   - follow this by a decision notice;
   - subsequently provide the right to go to Upper Tribunal.

7. **Financial penalties** – as an alternative to public censures/statements of misconduct, the regulator is able to impose financial penalties on firms contravening requirements imposed on them by, or under, the FSMA, and on approved persons failing to comply with the Statements of Principle, or having been knowingly involved in a firm's contravention of requirements.

The regulator provides guidance as to the criteria used to determine whether to issue public censures/statements (and no fine), rather than impose a financial penalty. It includes the following factors:

- If the firm or person avoided a loss or made a profit from their breach, a financial penalty is more appropriate to prevent the guilty party from benefiting from its/his actions.
- If the breach or misconduct is more serious in nature or degree, a financial penalty is likely to be imposed.
- Admission of guilt, full and immediate co-operation and taking steps to ensure that consumers are fully compensated may lessen the likelihood of financial penalty.
- A poor disciplinary record or compliance history may increase the likelihood of a financial penalty, as a deterrent for the future.
- Whether the firm has followed the regulator's guidance.

As is usual for disciplinary matters, there will be a warning notice, decision notice and final decision notice and ordinarily the final decision will be made public by the regulator issuing a press release. However, in circumstances where it would be unfair on the person, or prejudicial to the interests of consumers, the regulator may choose not to issue a press release.

When the regulator publishes a notice of financial penalty on its website it will also publish the rationale for the decision and the specific rules that were breached. Holders of significant influence functions should regularly review the notices to keep themselves informed of the regulator's approach and to help them mitigate against similar failings in their own firm.

8.4 The Upper Tribunal (Tax and Chancery)

Learning Objective

2.2.2 Know the outcomes of the FCA's and PRA's statutory notices [DEPP 1.2], the regulatory enforcement processes: warning, decision, supervisory and final notices [DEPP 2.2, 2.3] and the firm's right to refer to the tribunal [DEPP 2.3.2/3]

As has been noted previously, any person who receives a decision notice (including a supervisory notice) has the right to refer the regulator's decision to the Upper Tribunal. The individual or firm has 28 days in which to do so, and during this period the regulator cannot take the action it has proposed; it must give the person or firm the full 28 days to decide whether to refer the decision.

The Upper Tribunal is independent of the regulator and is appointed by the Government's Ministry of Justice (formerly the Department of Constitutional Affairs).

The Upper Tribunal will involve a full rehearing of the case and will determine on the basis of all available evidence whether the regulator's decision was appropriate. The rehearing may include evidence that was not available to at the time.

The Upper Tribunal's decision is binding on the regulator. While the Upper Tribunal has generally not overturned many of the regulator's decisions to date (indeed, it would be worrying if it had!), it has been known to do so – an important factor in demonstrating that it is independent in its decision-making and prepared to challenge the regulator where it sees fit.

It is possible for a firm or individual to appeal a decision of the Upper Tribunal itself (but only on a point of law: for this, permission is needed either from the Upper Tribunal itself or from the Court of Appeal).

8.5   New Enforcement Powers

Learning Objective

2.2.3   Know the FCA's powers of intervention (products and financial promotions)

The Financial Services Act 2012 provided the FCA with additional enforcement powers, which are:

- short-selling disclosure rule-making power and the power to impose financial penalties on those who breach short-selling rules;
- power to suspend firms and individuals;
- power to impose financial penalties on individuals who have carried out controlled functions without approval;
- financial stability information-gathering power.

The intention is to use the suspension power only if the imposition of a suspension will be a more effective and persuasive deterrent than the imposition of a financial penalty alone.

The Financial Services Act 2012 gave the FCA the power to make rules to ban products that pose unacceptable risks to consumers. This power is normally subject to a consultation process before it can be implemented, but in cases where there is a need for prompt intervention, products can be banned (for no more than 12 months) without consultation. This is referred to as the **temporary product intervention rules**, and will be applied with a focus on consumer protection.

Additionally, the FCA is able to ban financial promotions where they are deemed to be misleading. This power can be applied to remove promotions from the market immediately, without the need to go through the normal enforcement process. The intention of the FCA is to give a direction to an authorised firm to remove its own financial promotion or the financial promotion it has approved on behalf of an unauthorised firm. The direction will set out the reasons for banning the promotion. The firm is then given the opportunity to make representations, after which the FCA will decide whether to confirm, amend or revoke the direction. Confirmed directions will be published along with a copy of the promotion and the reasons behind the decision. Firms can appeal against the decision to the Upper Tribunal.

The power to ban financial promotions helps the FCA to raise standards in particular areas, such as new products or the use of new channels like social media. The FCA's intention is to use the power not only in cases which may harm consumers in terms of actual or potential financial loss, but also where promotions adversely affect consumers' ability to make informed choices and secure the best deal for themselves.

9. Information Required by the Regulators

Learning Objective

2.3.1 Know the regulators' power to require information and to appoint persons to carry out investigations [FSMA 2000 s.165/7/8]

Under Section 165 of FSMA, the financial services regulators (the FCA and the PRA) are given wide-ranging powers to require information. These powers extend to authorised persons, persons connected with authorised persons, RIEs and RCHs.

Essentially, either regulator is able to give written notice to an authorised person requiring information and/or documents to be provided within a reasonable period. Indeed, the regulator's staff (such as supervisors) are able to require documents and/or information without delay. This requirement applies only to information and documents reasonably required in connection with the exercise by the regulator of functions conferred on it by or under this Act.

Section 167 of the FSMA gives the regulators further information-gathering powers:

- It requires authorised firms (and certain persons connected with such firms) to appoint one or more competent persons to provide a report on any matter about which the regulator has required or could require the provision of information under Section 167. The nature of that/ those competent person/persons will depend on the issue being investigated – they are often solicitors or accountants. The purpose of the appointment by the regulator of a competent person/ persons to carry out general investigations is to identify the nature, conduct or state of business of an authorised person or an appointed representative; a particular aspect of that business or the ownership or control of an authorised person (firm).

Section 168 of the FSMA permits either regulator to appoint competent persons (one or more) to carry out investigations on its behalf in particular cases, such as:

- if a person may be guilty of an offence under Sections 177/191 (offences) or 398(1) (misleading the regulator);
- if an offence has been committed under Section 24(1) (false claim to be authorised or exempt); or misleading statements and practices;
- if there may have been a breach of the general prohibition of regulated activities, market abuse may have taken place and there may have been a contravention of Sections 21 or 238 of the Act (Restrictions on Financial Promotions).

In addition, the regulator may undertake the appointment of a person to carry out investigations in particular cases where it appears to them that someone:

- may be carrying out authorised activities when they are not authorised to do so (s.20 of the FSMA);
- may be guilty of an offence under prescribed regulations relating to money laundering;
- may have contravened a rule made by the regulator;
- may not be a fit and proper person to perform functions in relation to a regulated activity carried on by an authorised or exempt person;
- may have performed or agreed to perform a function in breach of a prohibition order;

or if:

- an authorised or exempt person may have failed to comply with a prohibition order (s.56(6));
- a person for whom the regulator has given approval under s.59 (approval for particular arrangements) may not be a fit and proper person to perform the function to which that approval relates or a person may be guilty of misconduct for the purposes of s.66 (disciplinary powers).

10. Misleading Statements and Practices

Learning Objective

2.5.1 Know the purpose, provisions, offences and defences of FSA 2012 s.89–s.92 – misleading statements and practices

10.1 The Offences

Part 7, Section 95 of the FSA 2012 Act repealed Section 397 of FSMA and replaced the criminal offence relating to misleading statements and practices with three new criminal offences.

The offences are:

- making false or misleading statements (Section 89);
- creating false or misleading impressions (Section 90); and
- making false or misleading statements or creating false or misleading impressions in relation to specified benchmarks (Section 91).

The first two offences together largely replicate the now-repealed FSMA Section 397 offence. The misleading impressions offence, however, is now wider in scope and covers recklessly created misleading impressions as well as those created intentionally.

The new Section 91 offence has been introduced as a result of the recommendations made in the final report of the Wheatley Review of the London Interbank Offered Rate (LIBOR). (The only benchmark to which this new offence currently applies is LIBOR.)

For an offence to occur the offending behaviour must take place within the UK, or have an effect within the UK.

The sanctions are serious – under Section 92, a person found guilty of a s.89–s.91 offence is liable to:

- six months' imprisonment and/or a maximum fine of £5,000 if the matter is tried in a magistrate's court (summary conviction);
- seven years' imprisonment and/or an unlimited fine if the matter is so serious that it is tried in a crown court.

Example

A stockbroker might tell a potential investor that the shares in XYZ plc (a property developer) are very cheap because XYZ has just won a major contract to build a shopping centre in central London. If the information about the award of the contract to XYZ was false, the FCA could bring a criminal prosecution on the stockbroker under s.89 for making a false and misleading statement to persuade their client to purchase shares.

Example

A firm of fund managers might let the market know that it is very keen to buy substantial quantities of shares in ABC plc, when actually it holds a smaller quantity of shares in ABC that it plans to sell. The fund manager's expressions of interest in buying ABC shares might mislead participants in the market to pay more money for the shares in ABC that the fund manager anonymously sells. The fund manager is guilty under s.90.

10.2 Defences

The potential defences to a charge under s.89–s.92 are:

- The person reasonably believed that his conduct would not create an impression that was false or misleading.
- The person was acting in conformity with the **price stabilisation rules** of the FCA. These allow market participants, such as investment banks, to support the price of a new issue of securities for their clients, with the aim of preventing the market from being excessively volatile. The rules themselves require certain disclosures to investors considering investing in the stabilised securities and restrict the support operation to a particular period.
- The person was acting in conformity with the **control of information** rules of the FCA. These rules relate to statements, actions or forecasts being made on the basis of limited information. The remainder of the information may be known to the firm, but it rests behind so-called Chinese walls, and is not known to the relevant individual.
- The person was acting in conformity with certain **EU provisions** with regards to stabilising financial instruments.

End of Chapter Questions

Think of an answer to each question and refer to the appropriate section for confirmation.

1.   Is a bank deposit a specified investment as defined in the Regulated Activities Order?
     Answer Reference: Section 1.2.1

2.   Does a firm that accepts deposits from customers need to be regulated and authorised to carry
     out this activity?
     Answer Reference: Section 1.2.2

3.   Is a market maker required to be regulated and authorised when carrying on such activity for a
     firm?
     Answer Reference: Section 1.3.1

4.   State three exclusions relating to regulated activity.
     Answer Reference: Sections 1.3.1–1.3.5

5.   How are appointed representatives exempt from the requirement to be regulated and authorised?
     Answer Reference: Section 2.1

6.   Name two types of exempt person under the FSMA Exemption Order 2001.
     Answer Reference: Section 2.3

7.   What are the threshold conditions for being granted Part 4A permission?
     Answer Reference: Section 3.3

8.   What is the purpose of the regulators' supervision arrangements?
     Answer Reference: Section 4

9.   What factors are taken into account when assessing an individual as fit and proper for approval?
     Answer Reference: Section 5.2

10. State the five types of controlled function.
     Answer Reference: Section 5.3

11. Which type of firm must comply with the Training and Competence Sourcebook?
     Answer Reference: Section 6.1

12. True or false; a person who advises on derivatives may do so under supervision so long as they
     have passed a regulatory module?
     Answer Reference: Sections 6.1 and 6.2

13. What is the status of the list of appropriate qualifications in the TC Sourcebook?
     Answer Reference: Section 6.2

14. What are the qualification requirements for supervisors?
     Answer Reference: Section 6.3

15. Which act provides the legal basis for the protection of whistleblowers?
    Answer Reference: Section 7

16. What are the responsibilities of the RDC?
    Answer Reference: Section 8.1

17. What are the different types of statutory notices that the regulator can issue and what are their outcomes?
    Answer Reference: Section 8.2

18. What is the aim of a private warning made by the regulators to a firm?
    Answer Reference: Section 8.3.2

19. What does Section 165 of the FSMA permit the regulators to do?
    Answer Reference: Section 9

20. What are the offences under the FSA 2012 Sections 89–92 and what are the potential defences available?
    Answer Reference: Sections 10.1 and10.2

Chapter Three

Associated Legislation and Regulation

This syllabus area will provide approximately 18 of the 75 examination questions

1. Insider Dealing

1.1 Introduction

When a director of, or someone otherwise linked to, a listed company buys or sells shares in that company there is a possibility that they are committing a criminal act – insider dealing.

This would be the case, for example, if that director or other linked person bought in the knowledge that the company's last six months of trade were better than the market expected (and that information is price-sensitive and had not yet been made publicly available).

The person buying the shares has the benefit of this information because he is an **insider** in the company. Under the Criminal Justice Act 1993 (CJA) this is a criminal act, punishable by a fine and/or a jail term.

1.2 Inside Information and the Insider

Learning Objective

3.1.1   Understand the meaning of inside information and insider; the offences and the instruments covered by the legislation [CJA 1993 s.52/56/57/58 + Schedule 2]

To be found guilty of insider dealing, a person must commit one of three specific offences; to do this, he must be an insider in possession of inside information.

The CJA defines both of these terms, as well as the offences that may be carried out.

Inside information is information which:

- relates to particular securities or to one or more particular issuers (ie, it is not so wide as to apply to securities or issuers of securities generally). It could, however, include information about the particular market or sector the issuer is active in;
- is specific or precise;
- has not been made public; and
- is price-sensitive (ie, if it were made public, it would be likely to have a significant effect on the price of any securities).

Some of these criteria may seem quite subjective; for example, what is specific or precise? In practice the meaning will be determined by the courts when cases come before them.

The CJA does give some assistance in interpretation, however; for example, it includes a (non-exhaustive) list of what **made public** means (from which we can work out when information has not been made public). For example, information becomes public when it is:

- published in accordance with the rules of a regulated market to inform investors, eg, a UK-listed company publishing price-sensitive news through the LSE's Regulatory News Service (RNS); or

- contained within records open to the public (eg, a new shareholding that is reflected in the company's register of shareholders); or
- it can be readily acquired by those likely to deal in securities to which the information relates, or securities of an issuer to which it relates.

This tells us that it need not be actually published – it just needs to be available to someone who **exercises diligence or expertise** in finding it (ie, you might have to look quite hard for it). It may also be regarded as made public even if it has to be paid for (ie, by subscription).

Inside information is often referred to as **unpublished price-sensitive information**, and the securities which may be affected by it are referred to as **price-affected securities**.

A person in possession of price-sensitive information is an insider if he knows that it is inside information and that it has been knowingly acquired from an **inside source**. He has obtained it from an inside source if he has got it:

- **because he is an inside source** himself (by being a director, employee or shareholder of an issuer of securities; and this need not necessarily be the company whose securities are the subject of the insider dealing); or
- **because he has access to the information by virtue of his employment, office or profession** (and, again, this need not necessarily be in relation to the company to which the information relates). An example might be the auditor, legal adviser or corporate finance adviser to a company; or
- **directly or indirectly from a person who obtained it in one of these two ways.** For example, a director's husband or wife will have information from an inside source if s/he sees confidential information at home about a takeover bid and then buys shares in the listed company which is the takeover target.

1.3   The Offences

Learning Objective

3.1.1   Understand the meaning of inside information and insider; the offences and the instruments covered by the legislation [CJA 1993 s.52/56/57/58 + Schedule 2]

Someone commits the offence of insider dealing if they:

- deal in price-affected securities when in possession of inside information;
- encourage someone else to deal in price-affected securities when in possession of inside information; or
- disclose inside information, otherwise than in the proper performance of their employment, office or profession.

For a deal (ie, an acquisition or a disposal of price-affected securities) to be caught under the insider dealing legislation, it must take place on a regulated market, or through a professional intermediary – otherwise the legislation does not apply to it.

These offences can be committed only by an individual (and, of course, only then by someone holding inside information as an insider); a company cannot commit the offence. However, by arranging for a company to deal, an individual could commit the offence of encouraging it to do so.

The offence of encouraging someone to deal need not result in an actual deal for the offence to have been committed (though it may be unlikely that the offence will come to light if no deal results).

1.4 The Instruments

Learning Objective

3.1.1 Understand the meaning of inside information and insider; the offences and the instruments covered by the legislation [CJA 1993 s.52/56/ 57/58 + Schedule 2]

Only certain investment instruments are caught under the insider dealing legislation; they are, for the purposes of the CJA, those described as securities (note, you may find the term 'securities' defined differently in different legislation).

For the purpose of the CJA and insider dealing, securities are:

- shares;
- debt securities (issued by a company or a public sector body);
- warrants;
- depositary receipts;
- options (to acquire or dispose of securities);
- futures (to acquire or dispose of securities); and
- CFDs based on securities, interest rates or share indices.

You will see that this definition of securities does not embrace:

- commodities, and derivatives on commodities such as options and futures on agricultural products, metals or energy products;
- foreign exchange, and derivatives on foreign exchange, such as forward foreign exchange contracts. This is because these will not be price-sensitive or be affected in the same way as individual securities.
- units or shares in open-ended collective investment schemes (CISs). The reason is that the price of the fund is determined by the prices of the underlying investments held and owing to the fund's investment and borrowing restrictions, a single stock in the fund will not have a material effect on the fund's price.

1.5   General Defences

Learning Objective

3.1.2   Know the general defences available with regard to insider dealing [CJA 1993 s.53]

The defences available to the defendant in an insider dealing case are as follows:

For the offence of **insider dealing**, or of **encouraging another to deal**, the defences are:

- the defendant did not expect the dealing to result in a profit (or avoid a loss) due to the information; or
- he believed, on reasonable grounds, that the information had been sufficiently widely disclosed to ensure none of those taking part in the dealing would be prejudiced by not having the information; or
- he would have acted in the same way regardless of being in possession of the information.

For the offence of **disclosing only**, the defences are:

- he did not expect any person to deal; or
- although he may have expected a person to deal, he did not expect the dealing to result in a profit (or avoid a loss) due to the information.

1.6   Special Defences

Learning Objective

3.1.3   Know the special defences: market makers acting in good faith, market information and price stabilisation [CJA 1993 s.53 and Schedule 1 paras 1–5]

There are further defences available to defendants in particular circumstances (special defences). These are for market makers, in relation to market information and to price stabilisation activities.

1.6.1   Market Makers

As long as a market maker can show that he acted in good faith in the course of his business as a market maker, he will not be deemed guilty of insider dealing or encouraging another to deal. So, a market maker (or his employee) could have unpublished price-sensitive information as an insider and continue to make a market in that security.

A further defence is available if the market maker shows he was acting in connection with an acquisition or disposal where the price was under negotiation, and he acted in order to facilitate the deal. He would have to show that the information was market information arising directly out of the negotiations.

1.6.2 Market Information

Market information includes information such as the fact that the sale of a block of securities is under consideration, or the price at which such a transaction is likely to be done.

An insider is not guilty of dealing or encouraging others to deal if he can prove that the information he held was market information, and it was reasonable for him to act as he did despite having the information as an insider at the time. Whether or not the action was reasonable depends on:

- the content of the information;
- the circumstances in which he first had the information and in what capacity;
- the capacity in which he now acts.

A further defence is where a person can show that his dealing or encouragement of another person was in connection with an acquisition or disposal that was the subject of negotiation, and with a view to facilitating the acquisition or disposal; and that the market information in his possession arose directly out of the acquisition or disposal.

Example

A client had been discussing the possibility of purchasing a block of 10,000 shares in XYZ plc with their broker. The client instructs the broker to buy. Clearly, the broker has the unpublished information that the buy order exists before he deals. However, this is market information and is a specific defence against a charge of insider dealing.

The defence would apply equally if it was market information relating to a client's planned disposal of securities.

What needs to be considered is the size of the order, and whether the order size is significant enough to move the underlying share price.

1.6.3 Price Stabilisation

The FCA has a set of rules that allow the stabilisation of a security's price after a new issue in order to prevent too much volatility. These are known as the **price stabilisation rules** and they provide a safe harbour for a number of activities, including insider dealing. As long as a person can show that they are acting in conformity with these rules, they are not deemed to have undertaken insider dealing. The rules can be found in Chapter 2 of the FCA's Market Conduct (MAR) Sourcebook.

1.7 FCA Prosecution Powers

Learning Objective

3.1.4 Know the FCA's powers to prosecute insider dealing [FSMA s.402, EG 12.7–10]

The FCA has been given the powers by FSMA to prosecute certain criminal offences. In particular, it is able to institute proceedings for an offence, under Part V of the CJA, of insider dealing.

In deciding whether to bring a criminal prosecution under the CJA, the FCA uses the same principles as the Code for Crown Prosecutors. If the following aspects are present, the FCA may consider that a criminal prosecution is appropriate:

- the conduct is so serious that it would lead to a significant sentence;
- there are victims who have suffered significant and substantial loss;
- the misconduct has severely damaged markets or confidence;
- substantial profits have been achieved (or substantial loss avoided);
- there are grounds for believing the misconduct may be repeated;
- the person has a relevant history, whether criminal, civil or regulatory;
- there is the likelihood that prosecution may result in an effective remedy for the victims;
- there is a lack of co-operation with the FCA in taking corrective measures;
- dishonesty or abuse of authority or trust is present;
- the person took a leading role in group activity (if relevant).

However, the importance of any of these factors will vary from case to case and the FCA will also have regard to the individual's circumstances. The FCA also has wide powers under the Market Abuse regime (see Section 2) and will not start a prosecution if it intends to bring disciplinary proceedings for the same misconduct.

2. Market Abuse

2.1 The Statutory Offence

Learning Objective

3.2.1 Understand the statutory offence of market abuse [FSMA 2000 s.118(1–8)]

Market abuse is a statutory offence that covers stock market manipulation and insider dealing. It is a serious offence that damages investor confidence and the integrity of financial markets.

The **Market Abuse Directive (MAD)** was introduced to create a regime to tackle market manipulation in the EU and legislate for the proper disclosure of information to the market. It also aimed to update the then EU insider dealing legislation. MAD defines and prohibits market abuse and provides for a number of preventive measures such as prompt disclosure of inside information and management transactions or safeguards of impartiality of investment research.

The UK's own market abuse (an offence under the FSMA) regime came into force on 30 November 2001. However, the new regulations introduced by the Directive came into effect on 1 July 2005. This required the previous regulator, the FSA, to make amendments to relevant rules such as the market conduct, UK listing rules and the price stabilisation rules.

Market abuse relates to **behaviour** by a person, or a group of persons working together, which occurs in relation to **qualifying investments** on a **prescribed market** that satisfies one or more of the following three conditions. The behaviour as it is currently defined is:

1. based on information that is not generally available to those using the market and, if it were available, it would have an impact on the price;
2. likely to give a false or misleading impression of the supply, demand or value of the investments concerned; and
3. likely to distort the market in the investments.

In certain cases, the behaviour is judged on the basis of what a **regular user** of the market would view as a failure to observe the standards of behaviour normally expected in the market.

The Treasury has determined the **qualifying investments** and **prescribed markets** – broadly, they are the investments traded on any of the UK's RIEs, investments where application has been made for trading on such markets, and related investments such as derivatives.

The behaviour will amount to market abuse as long as it relates to these investments, regardless of where it takes place. There is some overlap with the insider dealing legislation under the CJA, but:

- the CJA provides for a criminal regime, whereas the FSMA market abuse regime provides for civil penalties and, consequently, a lower required standard of proof; and
- the CJA insider dealing regime applies to a more restricted range of investments, whereas the FSMA market abuse regime extends its insider dealing provision to other markets, such as commodity and energy.

2.2   The FCA Code of Market Conduct

Learning Objective

3.2.2   Know the status of the FCA's Code of Market Conduct [FSMA 2000 s.119(1)–(3)]; the territorial scope of the legislation and regulation [FSMA s.118]

3.2.3   Know the offences outlined in the Code of Market Conduct [MAR 1.2.2/7, 1.3.1, 1.4.1, 1.5.1, 1.6.1, 1.7.1, 1.8.1, 1.9.1, 1.2.22]

The FCA is tasked under FSMA s.118 to prepare and issue a code containing such provisions as they consider will give appropriate guidance to those determining whether or not behaviour amounts to market abuse. This is called the **Code of Market Conduct** and forms part of the Handbook. The FCA must have regard to European directives when formulating such guidance.

The Code provides guidance on what does and does not amount to market abuse and the factors that are taken into account in the determination of whether market abuse has occurred.

The territorial scope of FSMA s.118 is such that it only extends to the behaviour of market abuse undertaken in the UK or in relation to qualifying investments traded on any of the UK's RIEs which are either situated in the UK or which are accessible electronically in the UK.

The Code includes aspects of insider dealing as well as expanding on behaviours that constitute market abuse.

2.2.1   Code of Market Conduct Offences

The FCA's Code of Market Conduct Sourcebook explains the types of behaviour caught by the market abuse regime. They extend to seven circumstances:

1. **Insider dealing** – where an insider deals in, or attempts to deal in, a qualifying investment or a related investment on the basis of inside information. For market abuse purposes, an insider has inside information:
    a. as a result of his membership of the administrative, management or supervisory bodies of the issuer of the investment;
    b. as a result of his holding in the capital of the issuer of the investment;
    c. as a result of having access to the information through his employment, profession or duties;
    d. as a result of criminal activities; or
    e. which he has obtained by other means and which he knows, or could reasonably be expected to know, is inside information.
2. **Improper disclosure** – where an insider discloses inside information to another person otherwise than in the proper course of the exercise of his employment, profession or duties.
3. **Misuse of information** – where behaviour is not covered by 1 above (insider dealing) or 2 above (improper disclosure) but is based on information that is not generally available to those using the market and which a regular user would regard as relevant and a failure to observe the standard of behaviour reasonably expected.
4. **Manipulating transactions** – where the behaviour consists of effecting transactions or orders to trade that are not for legitimate reasons and in conformity with accepted practices on the relevant market, and which:

    a.   give, or are likely to give, a false or misleading impression as to the supply or demand for, or the price of, the qualifying investment; or

    b.   secure the price of such investments at an abnormal or artificial level.

5. **Manipulating devices** – behaviour that consists of effecting transactions or orders to trade which employ fictitious devices or any other form of deception or contrivance.

6. **Dissemination** – where the behaviour consists of the dissemination of information by any means which gives, or is likely to give, a false or misleading impression as to a qualifying investment by a person who knew, or could reasonably be expected to have known, that the information was false or misleading.

7. **Misleading behaviour and distortion** – where behaviour which is not covered by 4 above (manipulating transactions), 5 above (manipulating devices) or 6 above (dissemination):

    a.   is likely to give a regular user a false or misleading impression as to the supply of, demand for, or price or value of, a qualifying investment: or

    b.   would be regarded by a regular user as behaviour likely to distort the market in such investments.

In both circumstances, the regular user must view the behaviour as a failure to observe the standard of behaviour reasonably expected of a person in his position in relation to the market.

The practical examples given below for each of the seven circumstances are drawn from the factsheet *'Why market abuse could cost you money'* published by the previous regulator (the FSA) in June 2008.

Examples of Market Conduct

Offences

Circumstances 1 and 2 – Insider Dealing and Improper Disclosure

An employee finds out that his company is about to become the target of a takeover bid. Before the information is made public, he buys shares in his company because he knows a takeover bid may be imminent. He then discloses the information to a friend. This behaviour creates an unfair marketplace because the person who sold the shares to the employee might not have done so if he had known of the potential takeover. The employee's friend also has this information and could profit unfairly from it.

Circumstance 3 – Misuse of Information

An employee learns that his company may lose a significant contract with its main customer. The employee then sells his shares, based on his assessment that it is reasonably certain the contract will be lost. This behaviour creates an unfair marketplace, as the person buying the shares from the employee might not have done so had he been aware of the information about the potential loss of the contract.

Circumstance 4 – Manipulating Transactions

A person buys a large number of a particular share near the end of the day, aiming to drive the stock price higher to improve the performance of their investment. The market price is pushed to an artificial level and investors get a false impression of the price of those shares and the value of any portfolio or fund that holds the stock. This could lead to people making the wrong investment decisions.

Circumstance 5 – Manipulating Devices

A person buys shares and then spreads misleading information with a view to increasing the price. This could give investors a false impression of the price of a share and lead them to make the wrong investment decisions.

Circumstance 6 – Dissemination

A person uses an internet bulletin board or chat room to post information about the takeover of a company. The person knows the information to be false or misleading. This could artificially raise or reduce the price of a share and lead to people making the wrong investment decisions.

Circumstance 7 – Distortion and Misleading Behaviour

An empty cargo ship that is used to transport a particular commodity is moved. This could create a false impression of changes in the supply of, or demand for, that commodity or the related futures contract. It could also artificially change the price of that commodity or the futures contract, and lead to people making the wrong investment decisions.

2.3 The Regular User

Learning Objective

3.2.4 Know the concept of effect rather than intention [MAR 1.2.3]; the concept of a reasonable regular user [MAR 1.2.20/21] and accepted market practices [MAR 1 Annex 2]

The Regular User test is used to assess behaviour for the offences of Market Abuse (Misuse of Information) and Market Abuse (Misleading Behaviour and Distortion). Whether or not behaviour amounts to market abuse does not require there to be an element of intention. Rather, it depends on how a hypothetical reasonable person (the regular user), familiar with the market in question, would view the behaviour. If a regular user would feel that the behaviour falls below the standards expected on the market in question, it will be market abuse.

In assessing whether the behaviour falls below the standards expected, the following will be considered:

- The characteristics of the market, the investments traded there and the users of that market.
- The rules and regulations of the market in question and any applicable laws (eg, if the behaviour occurred overseas, compliance with the law overseas will be a consideration).
- The prevailing market mechanisms, practices and codes of conduct applicable to the market in question.
- The standards reasonably expected of the person in the light of their level of skill and knowledge (eg, the standards expected of a retail investor may differ from those expected of an institutional investor).
- The need for market users to conduct their affairs in a manner that does not compromise the fair and efficient operation of the market as a whole, or damage the interests of investors.

It is not essential for the person responsible for the behaviour in question to have intended to commit market abuse, although the regular user test may determine that market abuse has not occurred unless the intention of the person was to engage in market abuse.

2.3.1 Accepted Market Practices

An Accepted Market Practice is relevant to the market abuse regime in the following ways:

a. it is an element in deciding what is inside information in the commodity markets; and
b. it provides a defence for Market Abuse (Manipulating Transactions).

The FCA will take the following non-exhaustive factors into account when assessing whether to accept a particular market practice:

- The level of transparency of the relevant market practice to the whole market.
- The need to safeguard the operation of market forces and the proper interplay of the forces of supply and demand (taking into account the impact of the relevant market practice against the main market parameters, such as the specific market conditions before carrying out the relevant market practice, the weighted average price of a single session or the daily closing price).
- The degree to which the relevant market practice has an impact on market liquidity and efficiency.

- The degree to which the relevant practice takes into account the trading mechanism of the relevant market and enables market participants to react properly and in a timely manner to the new market situation created by that practice.
- The risk inherent in the relevant practice for the integrity of, directly or indirectly, related markets, whether regulated or not, in the relevant financial instrument within the whole EEA.
- The outcome of any investigation of the relevant market practice by any competent authority or other authority mentioned in Article 12(1) of MAD; in particular, whether the relevant market practice breached rules or regulations designed to prevent market abuse, or codes of conduct, be it on the market in question or on directly or indirectly related markets within the EEA.
- The structural characteristics of the relevant market, including whether it is regulated or not, the types of financial instruments traded and the type of market participants, including the extent of retail investors' participation in the relevant market.

2.4 Penalties

Learning Objective

3.2.5 Understand the enforcement regime for market abuse [MAR 1.1.3] and a firm's duty to report suspicious transactions [SUP 15.10.2]

FSMA gives the FCA the power to impose a penalty, or to make a statement that a person has engaged in market abuse. These powers can be exercised if the FCA is satisfied that a person has engaged in market abuse, or if the person has taken (or refrained from taking) any action which required or encouraged another party to engage in behaviour that would amount to market abuse.

The penalties available to the FCA are essentially those outlined in Chapter 2 (ie, they are the sanctions that FSMA empowers the FCA to use). They include:

- withdrawal of approval or authorisation;
- imposing an unlimited civil fine;
- making a public statement that a person has engaged in market abuse;
- applying to the court for an injunction to restrain threatened or continued market abuse, an injunction requiring a person to take steps to remedy market abuse or a freezing order;
- applying to the court for a restitution order; and
- requiring the payment of compensation to victims of the abuse.

However, if there are reasonable grounds for the person to believe that the behaviour in question did not amount to market abuse, or the person had taken all reasonable precautions and exercised all due diligence to avoid engaging in market abuse, the FCA cannot impose a penalty.

2.5   Reporting of Suspicions

Learning Objectives

3.2.5   Understand the enforcement regime for market abuse [MAR 1.1.4/5/6] and a firm's duty to report suspicious transactions [SUP 15.10.2]

The Supervision (SUP) Manual states that authorised investment firms and credit institutions, which arrange or execute a transaction with or for a client in a qualifying investment, and which have **reasonable grounds** to suspect that the transaction might constitute market abuse, must notify the FCA without delay. Qualifying investments are those admitted to trading on a prescribed market (SUP 15.10.2R).

Strictly, this obligation extends only to executed transactions and not to unexecuted orders – but a firm may voluntarily bring a suspicious order to trade to the FCA's attention. The provisions require that firms decide on a case-by-case basis whether there are reasonable grounds for suspecting that a transaction involves market abuse, taking into account the circumstances. Further, Principle 11 of the Principles for Businesses requires that a firm discloses to the FCA everything of which the FCA would reasonably expect notice, and many firms (or rather their employees) would interpret this as giving them grounds to report unexpected transactions as well.

2.6   Safe Harbours

Learning Objective

3.2.6   Know the statutory exceptions (safe harbours) to market abuse [MAR 1.10.1–4 (excl. table 1.10.5)]

There are certain safe harbours against a charge of market abuse. Safe harbours outline situations where the behaviour in question is categorically not deemed to be market abuse.

1. **FCA rules** – some FCA rules make specific reference to the fact that behaviour conforming to the rules does not amount to market abuse. Therefore, people acting in accordance with these rules will not be deemed to be engaging in market abuse. They are:
    *   the rules relating to Chinese walls (covered in more detail in the SYSC Sourcebook); and
    *   the disclosure rules relating to the timing, dissemination or availability, content and standard of care applicable to the announcement, communication and release of information for listed companies.
2. **Takeover Code** – during the course of a takeover, both the predator company and its target have to comply with certain rules laid down in the Takeover Code. There are no rules in the Takeover Code that permit or require a person to behave in a way that amounts to market abuse. Specifically, as long as any announcements or the release of information conforms with the timing, dissemination and availability required by the rules of the Takeover Code, is expressly permitted or required by such rules and conforms with the Takeover Code's relevant general principle, it will not amount to market abuse.

3. **Price stabilisation and buy-backs** – price-support activities carried out in accordance with the price stabilisation rules will not amount to market abuse (you should remember that this was also the case with insider dealing; see Section 1.6.3).

2.7   Relationship with Other Legislation

Learning Objective

3.2.7   Understand the distinction between offences under market abuse, insider dealing [CJA] and under FSA 2012 s.89-92 misleading statements

The first two behaviour types that are potentially market abuse, namely insider dealing and improper disclosure, and behaviour which is likely to give a false or misleading impression of the supply, demand or value of the investments concerned, are, to an extent, already covered by the legislation relating to insider dealing (CJA, see Section 1) and the legislation relating to misleading statements and practices in Section 89–92 of FSA 2012 (see Chapter 2, Section 10).

As we have already noted, the FSMA market abuse regime is designed to complement the criminal regime for insider dealing and misleading statements and practices. There will be cases where a possible breach of both the criminal law, as well as the market abuse regime, occurs and the FCA is required to assess whether it has sufficient evidence, and whether it is in the public interest, to commence criminal proceedings rather than impose sanctions for market abuse. The regulator has stated that it is its policy not to impose a sanction for market abuse if a person is being prosecuted for insider dealing or misleading statements and practices. Similarly, it will not commence criminal proceedings if it has brought, or is seeking to bring, disciplinary proceedings for market abuse.

2.7.1 Regulatory Developments

The following notes are for information only and will not be examined.

In October 2011 the European Commission (EC) published proposals for new criminal sanctions for insider dealing and market abuse. The new regulations will replace MAD, and will have a direct impact on member states, which means that there will be no need for national implementing legislation. The new regime is expected to apply from July 2016.

The Commission published proposals for a Regulation (MAR) and a Directive (MAD). At the time of writing, the Level 1 text for MAR has been published. The Level 1 text for MAD has been agreed, but is yet to be published. It is aligned with MiFID II/Markets in Financial Instruments Regulation (MiFIR).

In summary, the proposals:

- extend the scope of the existing directive to include MTFs, organised trading facilities (OTFs), financial instruments traded OTC, spot commodity markets and emission allowances;
- amend the definition of inside information to include reference to specified instruments such as emission allowances and spot commodity contracts, and to introduce information that a reasonable investor would regard as relevant;
- include behaviours such as cancelling and amending orders, where the information used is inside information; attempted market abuse; and attempted insider dealing;
- prohibit certain manipulative trading strategies (such as spoofing and quote stuffing);
- require controls for the prevention and detection of market abuse, including protection for whistleblowers;
- revise and extend disclosure requirements;
- require co-operation and co-ordination between the competent authorities in member states;
- specify heavy administrative sanctions, such as fines of up to 10% of annual turnover on firms, and up to €5,000,000 on individuals; and criminal sanctions, where insider dealing or market manipulation is intentional.

3. Money Laundering

Learning Objective

3.3.1 Understand the terms money laundering, criminal conduct and criminal property and the application of money laundering to all crimes [Proceeds of Crime Act 2002 s.340] and the power of the Secretary of State to determine what is relevant criminal conduct

3.3.2 Understand that the UK legislation on money laundering is found in the Proceeds of Crime Act 2002 (POCA), as amended by the Serious Organised Crime and Police Act 2005 (SOCPA), the Money Laundering Regulations 2007, the Senior Management Arrangements, Systems and Controls Sourcebook [SYSC] and that guidance to these provisions is found in the Joint Money Laundering Steering Group guidance and Financial Crime Guide and understand the interaction between them

---

3.1 Introduction

Money laundering (ML) is the process of turning **dirty** money (money derived from criminal activities) into money that appears to be from legitimate origins. Dirty money is difficult to invest or spend, and carries the risk of being used as evidence of the initial crime. Laundered money can more easily be invested and spent without risk of incrimination.

Increasingly, anti-money laundering provisions are being seen as the frontline against drug dealing, organised crime and the financing of terrorism. Much police activity is directed towards making the disposal of criminal assets more difficult and monitoring the movement of money.

The current rules and regulations in relation to money laundering cover a variety of sources:

- **The Proceeds of Crime Act (POCA) 2002** – POCA 2002 is widely drafted. It specifies that ML relates to criminal property – that is, any benefit (money or otherwise) that has arisen from criminal conduct. Property is criminal property only if the alleged offender knows or suspects it is criminal property. The broad requirement is for firms to report suspicions of ML to the authorities.
- **The Serious Organised Crime and Police Act (SOCPA) 2005** – this Act amended certain sections of POCA. In particular, one feature of POCA was that criminal conduct was deemed to include anything which would have been an offence had it been done in the UK, regardless of where it had actually happened. This resulted in the often-cited Spanish bullfighter problem. Bullfighting is illegal in the UK, but not in Spain, meaning that, arguably, a financial institution should regard deposits made by a Spanish bullfighter as the proceeds of crime, even if they represented his legitimate earnings in Spain. SOCPA addresses this difficulty – in part at least – in that there is a defence for alleged offenders if they can show that they know, or believe on reasonable grounds, that the conduct was not criminal in the country where it happened. However, the Secretary of State has reserved the right to prescribe certain offences as relevant criminal conduct that might be legal where they occurred but would be illegal in the UK and still need to be reported. For example, the government may specify serious tax evasion or drug cultivation as types of criminal conduct which do need to be reported, despite occurring overseas.

- **The Money Laundering Regulations (ML Regs)** – these are relatively detailed regulations, implemented as the result of EU directives, which deal predominantly with the administrative provisions that firms need to have to combat ML. For example, they deal with firms' requirements for systems and training to prevent ML and their obligations to check the identity of new customers. The most recent version was issued in 2007.
- **The Senior Management Arrangements, Systems and Controls (SYSC) Sourcebook** – this provides high-level rules and guidance for authorised firms in formulating their anti-money laundering policies and controls. However, the regulator does not provide rules for procedures but rather refers firms to the Joint Money Laundering Steering Group (JMLSG) guidance.
- The **Joint Money Laundering Steering Group (JMLSG) guidance** – this is provided by a combination of UK trade associations including the British Bankers' Association (BBA), the Council of Mortgage Lenders (CML) and the Association of British Insurers (ABI). Guidance is provided to firms on how they should interpret and implement anti-money laundering provisions. They are not mandatory but do highlight industry best practice and provide procedural guidance for firms to follow. They are also approved by the Treasury, which means that if a firm can show that it adhered to them, the courts will take this into account as evidence of compliance with the legislation.

3.1.1 Financial Crime Guide

In April 2013 the FCA published two documents on financial crime as a guide for firms – Part 1 is titled *A Firm's Guide to Preventing Financial Crime* and Part 2 is called *Financial Crime Thematic Reviews*.

This guide consolidates FCA guidance on financial crime. It does not contain rules and its contents are not binding. It provides guidance to firms on steps they can take to reduce their financial crime risk and aims to enhance understanding of FCA expectations and help firms to assess the adequacy of their financial crime systems and controls and remedy deficiencies.

An aim of the guide is to help firms adopt a more effective, risk-based and outcomes-focused approach to mitigating financial crime risk.

The guide provides practical examples, but not the only way, in which firms might comply with applicable rules and requirements.

The Part 1 is divided into the following sections:

- financial crime systems and controls;
- money laundering and terrorist financing;
- fraud;
- data security;
- bribery and corruption;
- sanctions and asset freezes.

Part 2 is divided into 14 sections, listing all of the thematic work that the UK regulator (including the FSA and the FCA) have undertaken since 2006. In each section the FCA provides examples of good and poor practice – by way of guidance to firms.

3.2   The Stages of Money Laundering

Learning Objective

3.3.4   Understand the three stages of money laundering

There are three stages to a successful ML operation.

1. **Placement** – introduction of the money into the financial system; typically, this involves placing the criminally derived cash into a bank or building society account, a bureau de change or any other type of enterprise which can accept cash, such as, for example, a casino.
2. **Layering** – involves moving the money around in order to make it difficult for the authorities to link the placed funds with the ultimate beneficiary of the money. This might involve buying and selling foreign currencies, shares or bonds in rapid succession, investing in CISs, insurance-based investment products or moving the money from one country to another.
3. **Integration** – at this final stage, the layering has been successful and the ultimate beneficiary appears to be holding legitimate funds (clean money rather than dirty money). The money is regarded as integrated into the legitimate financial system.

Broadly, the anti-money laundering provisions are aimed at identifying customers and reporting suspicions at the placement and layering stages, and keeping adequate records that should prevent the integration stage being reached.

3.3   The Offences

3.3.1   Money Laundering Regulations 2007

Learning Objective

3.3.3   Understand the main offence set out in the Money Laundering Regulations (internal controls), which includes obligations on firms for adequate training of individuals on money laundering

The ML Regulations 2007 impose obligations on a wide range of businesses – from financial services firms to casinos – to apply customer due diligence when establishing a business relationship or carry-out transactions. If there is any suspicion of ML or terrorist finance or doubt about the veracity of the customer's identity, the firm has to take action.

The obligations can be summarised as:

1. **Administrative** – carry out certain identification procedures, implement certain internal reporting procedures for suspicions and keep records in relation to anti-money laundering and terrorist financing activities.
2. **Training** – adequately train staff in the law relating to ML and terrorist financing, and how to recognise and deal with suspicious transactions.

3. **Preventative** – ensure the establishment of internal controls appropriate to identify and prevent ML and terrorist financing. This is a catch-all requirement.

It is an offence, liable to a maximum jail term of two years and an unlimited fine, for firms to fail to comply with the ML Regulations. It is a defence for a person to show that he took all reasonable steps and exercised due diligence to avoid committing the offence. This means that the court may consider whether the firm followed the relevant guidance at the time.

3.3.2   Proceeds of Crime Act (POCA) 2002

Learning Objective

3.3.5   Understand the main offences set out in POCA Part 7 Sections 327, 328, 329, 330, 333A, 342 (Assistance, ie, concealing, arrangements, acquisition, use and possession; failure to disclose; tipping off in the regulated sector) and the implications of Part 7 regarding the objective test in relation to reporting suspicious transactions; that appropriate disclosure [internal for staff and to the National Crime Agency for the firm] is a defence

The Proceeds of Crime Act (POCA) 2002 establishes five offences:

1. **Concealing (s.327)** – it is an offence for a person to conceal or disguise criminal property.
2. **Arrangements (s.328)** – that is, being concerned in an arrangement which the person knows, or suspects, facilitates the acquisition, retention, use or control of criminal property for another person. Being concerned in an arrangement may be widely interpreted – it could include a person working within a financial organisation giving advice on a transaction, for example.
3. **Acquisition, use and possession (s.329)** – acquiring, using or having possession of criminal property. The person must know or suspect that the property arose out of criminal conduct.

These offences are punishable by a fine and a jail term of up to 14 years.

4. **Failure to disclose (s.330)** – there is a duty on employees in the regulated sector to make reports if they know or suspect that another person is engaged in ML or terrorist financing activity. It is an offence for employees to fail to disclose such information. Three conditions need to be satisfied for this offence:
   a. the person knows or suspects (or has reasonable grounds to know or suspect) that another person is committing an offence;
   b. the information giving rise to the knowledge or suspicion came to them during the course of business in a regulated sector (such as the financial services sector); and
   c. the person does not make the required disclosure to a nominated officer (NO), such as the firm's money laundering reporting officer (MLRO), as soon as is practicable.

These offences are punishable by a fine and a jail term of up to five years.

5. **Tipping off (s.333A)** – this is a particular offence applying only to persons in working in the regulated sector, and it involves disclosing a suspicious activity report or investigation. It is committed if a person knows or suspects that by disclosing the information this is likely to prejudice the investigation, and the information came to them in the course of business in the regulated sector. It is possible to commit this offence even if you do not know that a report has actually been made.

These offences are punishable by a fine and a jail term of up to two years.

As further detailed below, a person has a defence against the first three offences (concealing, arrangements, and acquisition, use and possession) if they make the required disclosure to the MLRO or, if the person was the MLRO, to the National Crime Agency (NCA).

The offence of failure to disclose suspicions of ML may be committed, not only when the person knows or suspects ML, but also when there are reasonable grounds to know or suspect ML (even if the person did not know or suspect it). The test as to whether there are reasonable grounds is called the **objective test**; whether a **reasonable person** would have known or been suspicious, even though the offender protests their innocence.

Part 7 of POCA concerns investigations, and s.342 describes the offence of prejudicing investigations, which applies generally, that is not only to those working in the regulated sector. A person commits this offence if they:

- make a disclosure that is likely to prejudice an investigation; or
- falsify, conceal, destroy or otherwise dispose of documents relevant to an investigation, or permit such falsification.

The offence is not committed if:

- the person did not know or suspect that the disclosure would prejudice an investigation;
- the disclosure was made in the performance of a duty under POCA or other similar enactment;
- the person is a legal adviser acting in his professional capacity in advising his client or in contemplation of legal proceedings (apart from where the disclosure is made with the purpose of furthering a criminal purpose);
- the person did not know or suspect that documents were relevant to the investigation;
- the person did not intend to conceal from an investigator any facts disclosed by the documents.

These offences are punishable by a fine and a jail term of up to five years.

3.4   Systems and Controls in Relation to Money Laundering

3.4.1   The FCA's Requirements

Learning Objective

3.3.6   Understand the approach adopted covered by the Senior Management Arrangements, Systems and Controls Sourcebook [SYSC], in particular, the systems and controls that the FCA and PRA expect firms to have adopted, the role of the Money Laundering Reporting Officer, Nominated Officer and the Compliance function [SYSC 3.2.6, 3.2.6 (A)–(J) (FCA), 3.2.7 (FCA/PRA), 3.2.8, SYSC 6.3 (FCA)]

The FCA's expectations for investment firms concerning financial crime systems and controls are set out in SYSC 6.3. In summary, the requirements are that firms establish and maintain effective systems and controls for compliance with the various requirements and standards under the regulatory system and for countering the risk that the firm might be used to further financial crime. The provisions are principles-based as opposed to prescribing detail as to how firms must do this, and it is up to firms to implement arrangements that are proportionate to the nature, scale and complexity of the business.

Firms are required to ensure that their systems and controls enable them to identify, assess, monitor and manage **ML risk**. They must carry out regular assessments of the adequacy of these systems and controls.

ML risk is the risk that a firm may be used to launder dirty money. Failure by a firm to manage this risk effectively will increase the risk to society of crime and terrorism. When considering whether a breach of its rules on systems and controls against ML has occurred, the FCA will look to see if the firm has followed relevant provisions in the guidance for the UK financial sector provided by the JMLSG.

In identifying its ML risk, and in establishing its systems and controls, a firm should consider a range of factors, including:

- its customer, product and activity profiles;
- its distribution channels;
- the complexity and volume of its transactions;
- its processes and systems; and
- its operating environment.

A firm should ensure that the systems and controls include appropriate:

- training for its employees in relation to ML;
- provision of information to its governing body and senior management, including a report at least annually by the firm's MLRO (see below) on the operation and effectiveness of those systems and controls;
- documentation of its risk management policies and risk profile in relation to ML;

- measures to ensure that ML risk is taken into account in its day-to-day operation and also with the development of new products, the taking on of new customers, and changes in its business profile; and
- measures to ensure that new client identification procedures do not unreasonably deny access to persons who may not be able to produced detailed evidence of identity.

Each authorised firm must give a director or senior manager (who may also be the MLRO) overall responsibility for the establishment and maintenance of effective anti-money laundering systems and controls.

A firm must also appoint an MLRO, who is responsible for receiving and assessing internal suspicion reports, and determining – after a proper investigation – whether to report them to the NCA. The MLRO is a controlled function, so the individual holding this role is subject to the approved persons' regime. The firm must ensure that its MLRO has an appropriate level of authority and independence within the firm and access to resources and information sufficient to enable them to carry out their responsibilities. The MLRO acts as a central point for all activity within the firm relating to anti-money laundering and should be based in the UK.

Depending on the nature, scale and complexity of its business, it may be appropriate for a firm to have a separate compliance function. This function may be heavily involved in monitoring the firm's compliance with its anti-money laundering procedures. The organisation and responsibilities of a compliance function should be documented. A compliance function should be staffed by an appropriate number of competent staff who are sufficiently independent to perform their duties. It should be adequately resourced and should have unrestricted access to the firm's relevant records.

3.4.2 The Joint Money Laundering Steering Group (JMLSG) Requirements

Learning Objective

3.3.7 Understand the standards expected by the JMLSG Guidance particularly in relation to: risk-based approach; requirements for directors and senior managers to be responsible for money laundering precautions; need for risk assessment; need for enhanced due diligence in relation to politically exposed persons (JMLSG 5.5.1–5.5.29); need for high level policy statement; detailed procedures implementing the firm's risk–based approach [JMLSG 1.20, 1.27, 1.40–1.43, 4.17–4.18]; financial sanctions regime [JMLSG Part III 4.1–4.10]

As mentioned in Section 3.1, the primary source of procedural guidance for firms is the JMLSG Guidance. The JMLSG is in three parts:

- **Part I** is general guidance applicable to all types of firms in the financial sector. This part also explains the international context and the UK legislative framework.
- **Part II** is sectoral guidance where each chapter is specific to a particular type of firm, such as retail banking, wealth management, execution-only stockbrokers, wholesale markets, and so on.
- **Part III** is specialist guidance, for example relating to electronic payments (wire transfers); this section also contains the UK financial sanctions regime.

The JMLSG approach is essentially risk-based that is, firms must identify the risks that their own business faces in conducting financial transactions, and then implement arrangements and controls to mitigate against the risk that the firm will be used for financial crime.

In 2009, the JMLSG issued revised guidance notes setting out how authorised firms should manage their risk in terms of ML and terrorist financing. The revised notes reflected the changes introduced under the ML Regulations 2007, which were, in summary:

- some new or revised definitions, including to beneficial owners of businesses and trusts, and politically exposed persons (PEPs);
- expansion of the guidance on customer due diligence measures to be applied in various circumstances, and how to operate a risk-based approach;
- an explanation of the extent to which reliance may be placed on the customer due diligence work of other regulated firms;
- the setting out of situations where simplified customer due diligence measures may be applied;
- guidance for when enhanced due diligence must be applied in higher-risk situations, eg, with individuals who are PEPs, on the basis that these people may be more vulnerable or susceptible to corruption; in non-face-to-face situations, and in connection with correspondent banking.

Politically Exposed Persons (PEPs)

A politically exposed person is defined in the JMLSG guidance as *'an individual who is or has, at any time in the preceding year, been entrusted with prominent public functions and an immediate family member, or a known close associate, of such a person'*.

This is only if the person holds such office outside the UK, or in an EC institution or other international body. For example:

- heads of state, heads of government, ministers and deputy or assistant ministers;
- members of parliaments;
- members of supreme courts, constitutional courts or other high-level judicial bodies whose decisions are not normally subject to further appeal;
- members of courts of auditors or on the boards of central banks;
- ambassadors, *chargés d'affaires* and high-ranking officers in the armed forces;
- members of administrative, management or supervisor boards of state-owned enterprises.

However, it does not normally include middle-ranking or junior officials, although firms must apply a risk-based approach and take enhanced measures if the person's political exposure places them on a basis similar to national level.

Immediate family members are spouses, partners, children and their spouses or partners, and parents. Close associates include someone who is known to have joint beneficial ownership of a legal entity or other arrangement, or any other close business relationship with a PEP, and extends to a person who has sole beneficial ownership of a legal entity or arrangement known to have been set up for the benefit of a PEP. Enhanced due diligence is required because a PEP or connected person may be vulnerable to corruption, and so this makes them a higher ML risk than the norm. PEP enhanced due diligence involves procedures for:

- determining whether or not a person is a PEP or is connected to a PEP – note that firms only need to have regard to information that is in their possession or publicly known to establish the connection;
- obtaining senior management approval for establishing a business relationship with the person;
- establishing the source of wealth and source of funds; and
- conducting enhanced monitoring of the business relationship.

These procedures are not prescribed; it is up to firms to make their own arrangements, having regard to the scale and complexity of the firm's activity. The JMLSG guidance suggests that firms use internet search engines, published reports and databases such as the Transparency International Corruption Perceptions Index, which ranks around 150 countries in order of perceived corruption.

Although technically a person ceases to be a PEP after one year, firms are encouraged to continue enhanced due diligence and monitoring and to take a risk-based approach in deciding whether the higher risks associated with the person's position have abated to allow normal procedures to be applied. Different types of due diligence are covered in Section 3.4.3.

Senior Management Responsibilities and Policy Statement

Senior management of regulated firms must appoint an appropriately qualified senior member of staff who will have overall responsibility for the maintenance of the firm's anti-money laundering systems and controls.

Firms must also have an anti-money laundering policy statement in place. This provides a framework to the firm and its staff and must identify named individuals and functions responsible for implementing particular aspects of the policy. The policy must also set out how senior management undertakes its assessment of the ML and terrorist financing risks the firm faces and how these risks are to be managed.

The firm's policy statement might include such matters as:

- **Guiding principles:**
  1. Customers' identities need to be satisfactorily verified before the firm accepts them.
  2. A commitment to the firm knowing its customers appropriately – both at acceptance and throughout the business relationship – through taking appropriate steps to verify a customer's identity and business.
  3. Staff will need adequate training and need to be made aware of the law and their obligations.
  4. Recognition of the importance of staff promptly reporting their suspicions internally.

- **Risk mitigation approach:**
  1. A summary of the firm's approach to assessing and managing its ML and terrorist financing risk.
  2. Allocation of responsibilities to specific persons and functions.
  3. A summary of the firm's procedures for carrying out appropriate identification and monitoring checks on the basis of their risk-based approach.
  4. A summary of the appropriate monitoring arrangements in place to ensure that the firm's policies and procedures are being carried out.

The Sanctions Regime

An important aspect of the JMLSG guidance concerns the UK **financial sanctions** regime. Sanctions can take the form of any restrictive or coercive measure on another state, business or individual, including trade embargoes. When an embargo is in place this means that the firm must not do business with the state, entity or business in question. The sanctions regime requires absolute compliance – which means that firms need to keep fully updated with the latest sanctions lists and have robust arrangements in place to prevent business being conducted in breach of the sanctions regime. Anyone guilty of an offence in breach of the sanctions regime may be imprisoned and/or fined.

The responsibility for the UK sanctions regime lies with:

- HM Treasury;
- the Foreign and Commonwealth Office; and
- the UK Department for Business Innovation and Skills.

HM Treasury regularly publishes consolidated lists: www.hm-treasury.gov.uk/fin_sanctions_index.htm.

3.4.3   JMLSG Guidance on Know Your Customer (KYC)

Learning Objective

3.3.8   Understand the money laundering aspects of know your customer (Joint Money Laundering Steering Group's Guidance for the Financial Sector [Para 5.1.1–5.1.14])

Chapter 5 of the JMLSG guidance explains that the requirement to conduct **customer due diligence (CDD)** derives from the Money Laundering Regulations 2007. The requirements are there for two broad reasons:

- to help the firm be satisfied that the customers know who they say they are and that there are no legal reasons preventing the relationship;
- to assist law enforcement.

The CDD requirements should be applied by firms having regard to the risks associated with different types of business relationship. There are three aspects to CDD at the outset of a new business relationship:

- identify the customer – obtain their name, address and date of birth; for non-personal customers the beneficial owners must be identified;
- obtain verification of the customer's identity – conduct additional checks to verify the information;
- obtain information about the intended nature of the business relationship.

This is **standard due diligence**, and Chapter 5 of the JMLSG notes gives practical guidance of the due diligence required for different types of customer. For personal customers, standard verification requirements may be satisfied by the production of a valid passport or photocard driving licence. For non-personal customers, such as companies, partnerships and clubs, it will be necessary to conduct checks on public registers such as Companies House.

Enhanced due diligence is where the firm conducts more checks than for standard cases. This is obligatory in three circumstances:

- if the client is a PEP – see Section 3.4.2;
- if the client is not physically present (non-face-to-face cases); and
- in respect of a correspondent banking relationship.

But the firm may choose to conduct enhanced due diligence for any case where this is deemed necessary.

Simplified due diligence means not having to conduct due diligence at all, and is permissible if the customer falls into one of the following types:

- certain regulated financial services firms;
- listed companies;
- beneficial owners of pooled accounts held by notaries or legal professionals;
- UK public authorities;
- community institutions;
- certain products/arrangements where the risk of their being used for ML is inherently low: life assurance, e-money products, pension funds, child trust funds and other low risk products.

If simplified due diligence does not apply, then satisfactory identification evidence for the customer should be obtained, and verified, as soon as is reasonably practicable after first contact between the firm and the customer. If there is a delay between the forming of the business relationship and the verification of the customer's identity (eg, in the case of non-face-to-face business), firms' risk management procedures should limit the extent of the relationship. They could do this, eg, by placing restrictions on the transactions the customer can enter into, or on the transfer of funds, until verification is complete.

If a firm cannot satisfactorily verify a customer's identity, it should not proceed with the business relationship, and should consider whether this should cause it to make a report to the NCA. If it is simply the case that the customer cannot produce the correct documents or information, the firm may consider whether there is any other way it can satisfy itself as to their identity.

The chapter also deals with KYC requirements in the context of multipartite relationships, eg, where one firm introduces a customer to another, or where more than one firm is involved in providing the service to the customer. In such cases, a firm may rely on the due diligence conducted by another regulated firm.

Regardless of the type of due diligence conducted at the outset, in all cases the firm must conduct ongoing monitoring of the business relationship, and this is considered next.

3.5 The Money Laundering Reporting Officer (MLRO) and the Nominated Officer

Learning Objective

3.3.6 Understand the approach adopted covered by the Senior Management Arrangements, Systems and Controls Sourcebook [SYSC], in particular, the systems and controls that the FCA and PRA expect firms to have adopted, the role of the Money Laundering Reporting Officer, Nominated Officer and the Compliance function [SYSC 3.2.6, 3.2.6 (A)–(J) (FCA), 3.2.7 (FCA/PRA), 3.2.8, SYSC 6.3 (FCA)]

3.3.9 Understand the importance of ongoing monitoring of business relationships and being able to recognise a suspicious transaction and the requirement for staff to report to the MLRO and for the firm to report to the National Crime Agency (NCA)

Under POCA 2002, it is an offence to fail to disclose a suspicion of ML. Obviously, this requires the staff at financial services firms to be aware of what constitutes a suspicion, and there is a requirement that staff must be trained to recognise and deal with what may be a ML transaction. Firms are also required to ensure that business relationships are understood, and monitored, sufficiently well that their staff will recognise patterns of activity which are not in keeping with the customer's anticipated profile.

The disclosure of suspicions is made, ultimately, to the legal authorities, namely the NCA; however, disclosure goes through two stages. Firstly, the employee with a suspicion should disclose that suspicion within the firm to the MLRO – a required controlled function. It is the MLRO who reviews matters, and decides whether the suspicion should be passed on to the NCA.

It is important to appreciate that, by reporting to the MLRO, the employee with the suspicion has fulfilled their responsibilities under the law – they have disclosed their suspicions. Similarly, by reporting to the NCA, the MLRO has fulfilled their responsibilities under the law.

The main part of the Handbook that relates to the MLRO is the SYSC Sourcebook. As an approved person, the MLRO is subject to the approved persons' regime. The MLRO is primarily responsible for ensuring a firm adequately trains staff in knowing and understanding the regulatory requirements and how to recognise and deal with suspicious transactions.

3.5.1 MLRO or Nominated Officer?

Under the regulators' rules, all firms (except for sole traders, general insurance firms and mortgage intermediaries) must appoint an MLRO with responsibility for oversight of their compliance with the rules on systems and controls against ML.

The Money Laundering Regulations require all affected firms to appoint a **nominated officer** to be responsible for receiving internal ML disclosures from staff members, and to make external reports to the NCA where necessary. The nominated officer is also responsible for receiving internal disclosures under POCA and the Terrorism Act 2000.

Although the obligations of the MLRO under the FCA requirements are different from those of the nominated officer under POCA, the Terrorism Act or the Money Laundering Regulations 2007, in practice the same person tends to carry on both roles – and is usually known as the MLRO.

3.5.2 The FCA's Principles-Based Approach to Money Laundering Prevention

The FCA's approach to supervision (and that of its predecessor the FSA) is primarily an **outcomes-focused** approach. As a consequence, the earlier, relatively prescriptive Sourcebook on ML was abandoned and replaced with higher-level requirements. These are set out in the SYSC Sourcebook.

These high-level requirements place obligations on firms' senior management to ensure that they have systems and controls in place which are appropriate to the business for the prevention of ML and terrorist financing. The JMLSG Guidance aid firms in interpreting and dealing with these obligations in the context of their specific types of business.

In order to determine the arrangements and controls needed by a firm for these purposes, its senior management needs to have carried out a **risk assessment**. This should consider such factors as the:

- nature of the firm's products and services;
- nature of its client base and geographical location; and
- ways in which these may leave the firm open to abuse by criminals.

3.6 Terrorism and Money Laundering

Learning Objective

3.3.10 Know what activities are regarded as 'terrorism' in the UK [Terrorism Act 2000 Part 1] the obligations on regulated firms under the Counter-Terrorism Act 2008 [money laundering of terrorist funds] [Part 5 section 62 and s.7 parts 1–7] and the Anti-Terrorism Crime & Security Act 2001 Schedule 2 Part 3 [Disclosure of Information] and where to find the sanction list for terrorist activities

In light of the **war against terrorism**, legislation in the form of the Terrorism Act 2000 has defined what amounts to terrorism.

Terrorism is the use or threat of action where it:

- involves serious violence against a person or serious damage to property;
- endangers a person's life, other than the person committing the action;
- creates serious risk to the health or safety of the public (or a section of the public);
- is designed to seriously interfere or disrupt an electronic system;
- is designed to influence the government or intimidate the public (or a section of the public);
- is made for the purpose of advancing a political, religious or ideological cause.

Note, if the threat or action involved firearms or explosives it is terrorism, regardless of whether it was designed to influence the government or intimidate the public (or a section of the public).

Many of the requirements of anti-terrorism legislation are similar to the anti-money laundering provisions encountered earlier. A person commits an offence if he enters into, or becomes concerned with, an arrangement that facilitates the retention or control of terrorist property by concealment, removal from the jurisdiction, transfer to nominees or in any other way. The person may have a defence if he can prove that he did not know, and had no reasonable cause to suspect, that the arrangement related to terrorist property.

There is a duty to report suspicions and it is an offence to fail to report if there are reasonable grounds to have a suspicion. The Terrorism Act 2000 and **Anti-Terrorism Crime Security Act 2001** specify that a failure to report is liable to a term of up to five years in jail, plus a fine.

The **Counter-Terrorism Act (CTA)** became law on 26 November 2008, adding further to the Government's armoury of legislation to tackle terrorism. Of particular interest is **Schedule 7,** which gives new powers to the Treasury to issue directions to firms in the financial sector.

In summary, directions can be given to individual firms, to firms that fit a particular description, or to the sector as a whole, concerning individuals or institutions who are doing business or are resident in a particular non-EEA country or regarding the government in that country. Directions can relate to CDD and ongoing monitoring, systematic reporting on transactions and business relationships, and limiting or ceasing business, as follows:

- **CDD and monitoring** – the provisions are broadly similar to the requirements already imposed under the ML Regulations. However, the Treasury is now able, for example, to direct that CDD be undertaken again or completed **before** entering into a business relationship (where it might otherwise have been conducted in parallel), or that enhanced measures be carried out. It may also direct that specific activity monitoring be carried out.
- **Systematic reporting** – until now, reporting orders have only been available to law enforcement agencies and must be obtained through the courts. Under the CTA, the Treasury itself can now require information to be provided concerning business relationships and transactions involving the specified person(s), on a one-off or periodic basis.
- **Limiting or ceasing business** – the Treasury's powers under the present Money Laundering Regulations (Regulation 18) are limited to where the Financial Action Task Force (FATF) has applied countermeasures. The CTA powers are more flexible and allow directions to be imposed in a wider range of situations (see below). Under the CTA, the Treasury may issue directions when one or more of the following are met:
  - the FATF has advised that countermeasures should be applied to a country (as per the Money Laundering Regulations);
  - the Treasury reasonably believes that ML/terrorist financing activities are being carried on in the country, by its government or by persons resident/incorporated there, which pose a significant threat to the UK's national interests;
  - the Treasury reasonably believes that the country is developing or producing nuclear or chemical weapons, or doing anything to facilitate that, and poses a significant threat to the UK's national interests.

While directions to individual firms will be served upon them, it is not yet clear how orders that apply to specified types of firm or the whole sector (which will require secondary legislation each time) will be publicised. It may or may not be via the sanctions mechanism or something similar – this issue is still being clarified with the Treasury.

Meanwhile, the Treasury regularly publishes lists of individual names and countries that have been identified as unacceptable and with whom UK firms may not conduct business.

3.6.1 The Differences Between Money Laundering and Terrorist Financing

Learning Objective

3.3.11 Understand the importance of preventative measures in respect of terrorist financing and the essential differences between laundering the proceeds of crime and the financing of terrorist acts [JMLSG Guidance 2007 paras 1.38 – 1.39, Preface 9 as amended December 2011] and the interaction between the rules of the FCA, the PRA, the Terrorism Act 2000 and the JMLSG Guidance regarding terrorism [JMLSG Guidance 2007 Preface 27, 28, 29 – as amended December 2011]

Because terrorist groups can have links with other criminal activities, there is inevitably some overlap between anti-money laundering provisions and financing terrorist acts. However, there are two major difficulties when terrorist funds are compared to other ML activities:

1. Often, only quite small sums of money are required to commit terrorist acts.
2. If legitimate funds are used to fund terrorist activities, it is difficult to identify when the funds become terrorist property.

Financial services firms need to ensure that their preventative measures take account of the different nature of terrorist financing in order to comply with the regulator's requirements for combating financial crime.

The JMLSG Guidance provides a sound basis for firms to meet their obligations under POCA, the Terrorism Act, the Money Laundering Regulations and the regulator's rules. The extent to which a firm has followed the guidance is a material factor for offences brought before the courts. Similarly, the regulator will have regard to whether a firm has followed the guidance in deciding whether to prosecute a breach of the Money Laundering Regulations, or whether to take action against a firm for a rule breach.

3.7 The Bribery Act

Learning Objective

3.3.12 Know the main purpose of the Bribery Act 2010 and the categories of offences covered in s1–7 Bribery Act 2010

3.7.1 Overview

The Bribery Act 2010 came into force on 1 July 2011, creating four new offences:

- offering, promising or giving a bribe to another person;
- requesting, agreeing to receive or accepting a bribe from another person;
- bribing a foreign public official; and
- a corporate offence of failing to prevent bribery.

The Act abolished the old common law and legislative offences in the UK against bribery and corruption and set new standards in terms of global measures against corruption.

3.7.2 Penalties

The Act carries a maximum penalty of ten years' imprisonment for all new offences, except the corporate offence which carries an unlimited fine.

The relevant sections are:

- **Section 1** covers the crime of bribery which is described as occurring when a person offers, gives or promises to give a 'financial or other advantage' to another individual in exchange for 'improperly' performing a 'relevant function or activity'.
- **Section 2** covers the offence of being bribed, which is defined as requesting, accepting or agreeing to accept such an advantage, in exchange for improperly performing such a function or activity.
- **Section 3** defines 'relevant function or activity' covering *any function of a public nature; any activity connected with a business, trade or profession; any activity performed in the course of a person's employment; or any activity performed by or on behalf of a body of persons whether corporate or unincorporated'*. This applies to both private and public industry, and encompasses activities performed outside the UK, even activities with no link to the country.
- Under **Section 4**, the activity will be considered to be 'improperly' performed when the expectation of good faith or impartiality has been breached, or when the function has been performed in a way not expected of a person in a position of trust.
- **Section 5** provides that the standard in deciding what would be expected is what a reasonable person in the UK might expect of a person in such a position. Where the breach has occurred in a jurisdiction outside the UK, local practices or customs should be disregarded when deciding this, unless they form part of the 'written law' of the jurisdiction; 'written law' is given to mean any constitution, statute or judicial opinion set down in writing.

- **Section 6** covers bribery of foreign public officials. A person will be guilty of this offence if they promise, offer or give a financial or other advantage to a foreign public official, either directly or through a third party, where such an advantage is not legitimately due. A foreign public official is defined, under Section 6(4), as *'an individual holding legislative, administrative or judicial posts or anyone carrying out a public function for a foreign country or the country's public agencies or an official or agent of a public international organisation'*. The inclusion of 'through a third party' is intended to prevent the use of middle men to avoid committing a crime. The offence under Section 6 only applies to the briber, and not to the official who receives or agrees to receive such a bribe.
- **Section 7** creates the 'broad and innovatory offence' of the failure of commercial organisations to prevent bribery on their behalf. This applies to all commercial organisations that have business in the UK and is strict liability with no need to prove any kind of intention or positive action. It is also an offence of vicarious liability, therefore a commercial organisation can be guilty of the offence if the bribery is carried out by an employee, an agent, a subsidiary, or another third party, as found in Section 8.

3.7.3 Hospitality

A 'financial advantage' could include corporate hospitality. The statutory guidance notes that it will not amount to a bribe provided that the hospitality has a legitimate business aim, is reasonable, proportionate and appropriate in the circumstances. Facilitation payments on the other hand are offences unless it is the written law of the country of the foreign public official that allows or requires the official to accept the advantage offered or where payments have been made under threat of violence.

3.7.4 Defence

A firm has a defence to the offence of failing to prevent a bribe if it can show that it has put in place adequate procedures to prevent bribery. The Ministry of Justice has provided guidance, in the form of six principles, on how firms can implement procedures to prevent bribery:

- **Proportionality** – the action you take should be proportionate to the risks you face and to the size of your business. So you might need to do more to prevent bribery if your organisation is large, or if you are operating in an overseas market where bribery is known to be commonplace, compared to what you might do if your organisation is small, or is operating in markets where bribery is not prevalent.
- **Top level commitment** – those at the top of an organisation are in the best position to ensure their organisation conducts business without bribery. If you are running a business, you will want to show that you have been active in making sure that your staff (including any middle management) and the key people who do business with you and for you understand that you do not tolerate bribery. You may also want to get personally involved in taking the necessary proportionate action to address any bribery risks.
- **Risk assessment** – think about the bribery risks you might face. For example, you might want to do some research into the markets you operate in and the people you deal with, especially if you are entering into new business arrangements and new markets overseas.
- **Due diligence** – knowing exactly who you are dealing with can help to protect your organisation from taking on people who might be less than trustworthy. You may therefore want to ask a few questions and do a few checks before engaging others to represent you in business dealings.

- **Communication** – communicating your policies and procedures to staff and to others who will perform services for you enhances awareness and helps to deter bribery by making clear the basis on which your organisation does business. You may, therefore, want to think about whether additional training or awareness-raising would be appropriate or proportionate to the size and type of your business.
- **Monitoring and review** – the risks you face and the effectiveness of your procedures may change over time. You may want, therefore, to keep an eye on the anti-bribery steps you have taken so that they keep pace with any changes in the bribery risks you face when, for example, you enter new markets.

4. The Model Code

Learning Objective

3.4.1   Know the main purpose and provisions of the Model Code on share dealing by directors and other persons discharging managerial responsibilities, including: close periods; undisclosed inside information; chairman's approval; dealings by the chairman; short-term dealing; exceptional circumstances; application and record-keeping

The FCA fulfils the role of the UK Listing Authority (UKLA). This means that it is the authority competent to set the requirements for shares or other securities to be **listed**. Listing allows, for example, a company to have its shares traded on a recognised investment exchange, such as the LSE.

As part of its listing rules, the UKLA has produced the **Model Code**. Listed companies must comply with the Model Code restricting the ability of their senior managers and officers (**restricted persons**) to deal in the company's securities. Equally, the Code sets out how restricted persons may deal in the securities of the company they work for, without falling foul of the insider dealing or market abuse regimes.

Firstly, the Model Code requires restricted persons to seek **clearance** before buying or selling securities. Normally, it is the chairman of the company who gives this clearance. If the chairman himself seeks permission, the clearance will be given by the chief executive officer (CEO); if chairman and CEO are the same person, then the clearance will be given by the board.

Restricted persons who are not directors can seek clearance from the company secretary or a designated director.

A response to a request for clearance must be given within five business days of the request. Once clearance has been given, the person must deal as soon as possible and in any event within two days of receiving clearance.

There are prescribed circumstances when clearance must be refused:

- on **short-term** considerations; investments with a maturity of one year or less are always considered short-term;

- during any period where **inside information** may exist;
- during a **close period**.

A close period is any of the following:

- the 60 days leading up to a preliminary announcement of the company's annual results;
- the 60 days leading up to publication of the company's annual financial report;
- if the company reports on a half-yearly basis, the period from the end of the relevant financial period until the time of publication;
- the 30 days leading up to the publication of quarterly results.

If a person is in severe financial difficulty, or there exists some other exceptional circumstance, clearance may be given to sell (but not buy) when the Code would otherwise have prohibited the sale. The person must not be in possession of inside information, and only a designated director can give clearance. The Code states that the FCA should be consulted over requests to deal in exceptional circumstances. A tax liability is not normally considered an exceptional circumstance (unless the person has no other way of settling the liability); but a court order or some other legal obligation to sell the securities may meet the exceptional test.

The company must keep a record of the response to a request to deal and any clearance given, and provide the restricted person with a copy of the response and the clearance.

5. The Disclosure and Transparency Rules

Learning Objective

3.5.1 Know the purpose of the Disclosure and Transparency rules and the control of information [DTR 2.1.3, 2.6.1]

The Disclosure and Transparency rules (DTR) are part of the Handbook. The Disclosure Rules are made by the FCA in its role as UKLA, and the Transparency Rules give effect in the UK to the Transparency Directive. Both sets of rules apply to issuers of securities listed to trade on certain markets.

The purpose of the **Disclosure Rules**, in accordance with EU provisions for dealing with inside information and preventing market abuse, is to:

- promote prompt and fair disclosure of relevant information to the market;
- set out specific circumstances in which an issuer can delay the public disclosure of inside information; and
- set out requirements to ensure that such information is kept confidential in order to protect investors and prevent insider dealing.

The purpose of the **Transparency Rules** is to implement the requirements of the Transparency Directive and to ensure there is adequate transparency of and access to information in the UK financial markets.

5.1 Control of Inside Information

The Disclosure Rules set out the requirements for the control of inside information, in two respects:

- **Denying access** – an issuer must establish effective arrangements to deny access to inside information to persons other than those who require it for the exercise of their functions within the issuer.
- **Breaches of confidentiality** - an issuer must have measures in place that enable public disclosure to be made via an approved regulatory information service (RIS) as soon as possible, in cases where the issuer is unable to ensure the confidentiality of the inside information. These measures should include a holding announcement to be used if a breach of confidentiality occurs when the issuer is legitimately delaying disclosure of inside information to protect its own interests, in accordance with FCA rules that permit this. The holding announcement must give as much detail as possible, state why a full announcement can't be made, and undertake to announce further details as soon as possible.

6. The Data Protection Act

Learning Objective

3.6.1   Know the eight Data Protection Principles; the need for notification of data controllers with the Information Commissioner; the record-keeping requirements of FCA-regulated firms [DPA Schedule 1, Part 1 & COBS Schedule 1 – record keeping requirements (FCA) and SYSC 3 & 9 (FCA/PRA)]

6.1 Data Protection Principles

The Data Protection Act 1998 provides for the way with which **personal data** must be dealt in order to protect the rights of the persons concerned. Personal data is data which relates to living individuals.

Any firm determining the way personal data is held and processed is known as a **data controller** and is, therefore, responsible for compliance with the Data Protection Act. All data controllers must be registered with the Information Commissioner.

The Data Protection Act lays down **eight principles**, which must be complied with:

1. Personal data shall be processed fairly and lawfully.
2. Personal data shall be obtained for one or more specified and lawful purposes, and shall not be further processed in any manner that is incompatible with those purposes.
3. Personal data shall be adequate, relevant and not excessive in relation to the purpose or purposes for which it is processed.
4. Personal data shall be accurate and, where necessary, kept up-to-date.
5. Personal data shall not be kept for longer than is necessary for its purpose or purposes.
6. Personal data shall be processed in accordance with the rights of the subject under the Act.

7. Appropriate technical and organisational measures shall be taken against unauthorised or unlawful processing of personal data, and against accidental loss or destruction of, or damage to the personal data.

8. Personal data shall not be transferred to a country or territory outside the EEA, unless that country or territory ensures an adequate level of protection in relation to the processing of personal data.

Clearly, these principles of data protection will apply to personal data maintained by financial services firms (who often have a duty to know their customers) and to the personal data maintained by the FCA itself (in relation to its approved persons' regime).

In addition, firms should have regard for the provisions of this Act when considering their record-retention policies. The FCA imposes a number of record-keeping requirements and firms will not be contravening data protection requirements by complying with an FCA rule. Other than this, firms must comply with data protection in not keeping data longer than necessary, and keeping current data accurate, including, for example, in connection with training and competence records for employees).

The Information Commissioner has the authority and power to fine data controllers that do not comply with its requirements in respect of data security.

6.2   Record-Keeping Requirements

The FCA's high-level rules for records maintained by authorised firms are set out in SYSC. Firms must arrange for orderly records to be kept of their business and internal organisation, including all services and transactions undertaken by them. The medium for holding records is not prescribed, but the records should be capable of being reproduced in English and on paper. This includes a requirement to provide a translation if the record is retained in a language other than English. The general principle for retention periods is that they should be retained for as long as relevant to the purpose for which the record was made.

However, in addition to these high-level requirements there are more specific record-keeping rules pertaining to certain types of business. For example, investment firms must retain all records in relation to MiFID business for a period of at least five years, and in relation to non-MiFID business the record-keeping requirement is three years.

Each Handbook module specifies, in Schedule 1 to the module, any detailed record-keeping requirements for that particular module. For example, the Conduct of Business Sourcebook (COBS) has detailed record-keeping requirements relating to specific activities undertaken by firms, such as:

- **COBS 2.3 (Inducements)** – fee, commission or non-monetary benefits received;
- **COBS 3.8 (Client categorisation)** – client classification notice to client, client agreements and the firm's evidence to support the category;
- **COBS 4.11 (Communicating with clients, including financial promotions)** – financial promotion, telemarketing scripts and compliance of financial promotions;
- **COBS 6.2 (Information about the firm)** – scope and range of service for packaged products;
- **COBS 8.1 (Client agreements)** – client agreements;
- **COBS 9.5 (Suitability, including basic advice)** – suitability report, and information supporting the report;

- **COBS 10.7 (Appropriateness for non–advised services)** – appropriateness test and information used in the assessment;
- **COBS 11.5 (Dealing and managing)** – detailed records concerning client orders and decisions to deal in portfolio management;
- **COBS 11.6 (Dealing and managing)** – prior and periodic disclosure on the use of dealing commission;
- **COBS 11.7 (Dealing and managing)** – personal account dealing records;
- **COBS 12.4 (Research recommendations)** – basis of substantiation of research recommendation;
- **COBS 15.3 (Cancellation)** – where the client has exercised the right to cancel;
- **COBS 16 (Reporting information to clients)** – trade confirmation and periodic statements;
- **COBS 19 (Pensions)** – execution-only pension transfer or opt-out; record of why a promotion of a personal pension scheme was justified.

7. Prudential Standards

Learning Objective

3.8.1   Know the purpose of the Capital Adequacy for certain types of investment firms

7.1 Capital Adequacy Requirements

Principle 4 establishes that: *'a firm must maintain adequate financial resources'*. **Financial resources** include both capital resources, and liquidity resources, so that the firm can meet its liabilities as they fall due. The standards differ according to the activities undertaken by the firm and whether the firm's activities also fall within the scope of the Markets in Financial Instruments Directive (MiFID). The standards for investment firms are set out in three Handbook modules:

- **The General Prudential Sourcebook (GENPRU)** – high-level standards, principles and capital adequacy requirements for firms that are subject to the Capital Requirements Directive (CRD).
- **The Prudential Sourcebook for Banks, Building Societies and Investment firms (BIPRU)** – additional provisions for CRD firms, setting out standards for calculating capital to meet specified risks and for maintaining adequate liquidity resources.
- **The Prudential Sourcebook for Investment Firms (IFPRU)** – IFPRU came into force on 1 January 2014 and contains prudential rules applying to investment firms that are subject to CRD IV. The sourcebook is made up of nine chapters:
  - application;
  - supervisory (processes and governance);
  - own funds;
  - credit risk;
  - operational risk;
  - market risk;
  - liquidity;
  - prudential consolidation and large exposures; and
  - public disclosure.

- **Interim Prudential Sourcebook for Investment Businesses (IPRU-INV)** – capital adequacy rules for investment firms that are not subject to the CRD.

The CRD created an EU-wide common framework for financial resources and risk management to minimise the risk of a firm's financial failure. The CRD framework is based on the concept of three pillars:

- **Pillar 1** – minimum capital requirements for credit, market and operational risks.
- **Pillar 2** – firms and supervisors decide whether additional capital should be held to cover risks not covered in Pillar 1.
- **Pillar 3** – disclosure of information about risks, capital and risk management, to improve market discipline.

BIPRU gives additional guidance for assessing risks:

- **credit risk** – the risk of default on loans to which the firm is exposed;
- **operational risk** – the risk of loss resulting from failed processes, people or systems, or from external events including legal risk;
- **market risk** – this is broken down into very specific risks associated with various positions a trading firm may take;
- **group risk consolidation** – risks associated with group arrangements, especially groups containing firms in different sectors (eg, investment, banking and insurance);
- **securitisation risk** – where capital resources held for securitised assets prove inadequate;
- **concentration risk/large exposures** – such as where the firm has made a large loan to a single borrower, or has large exposure to a single counterparty;
- **residual risk** – the risk that techniques the firm uses to mitigate credit risk are less effective than envisaged;
- **insurance risk** – uncertainty as to occurrence, timing and amount of insurance liabilities;
- **business risk** – arising from changes to its business, risk that the firm may not be able to carry out its strategy, risk arising from remuneration policies;
- **interest rate risk** – trading book and non-trading book;
- **pension obligation risk** – arising out of the firm's obligation to make contractual pension contributions or payments;
- **liquidity risk** – the risk that a firm may not be able to meet its liabilities as they fall due without borrowing at excessive cost.

Firms are required to provide detailed reports to the relevant regulator on their capital adequacy; the frequency of reporting depends on the size of the firm and whether it is subject to the CRD or not. Additionally, if at any time a firm knows that its capital resources have fallen below the prescribed minimum, then it must notify the regulator immediately.

Firms subject to the CRD must also comply with provisions relating to the quality of capital that is held. That is, a firm must have regard to the loss absorbency of instruments it wishes to use to meet its capital resource requirements. Capital is broadly split into three types (tiers) for this purpose:

- **Core Tier One capital** – such as permanent share capital, reserves, externally verified interim profits.
- **Tier Two capital** – such as long-term subordinated debt and revaluations reserves.
- **Tier Three capital** – such as short-term subordinated debt and interim trading book profit and loss.

There are restrictions as to how much Tier Two and Tier Three capital may be used to meet the capital resource requirements.

The rules also require firms to stress-test the capital that is, to formulate financial models to assess how well the capital resources stand up against a range of adverse scenarios over specified time periods.

Under the new regulatory structure the PRA is responsible for prudential matters in the most significant firms, deposit-takers and banks. The FCA is responsible for prudential issues for single-regulated firms.

Firms that are not subject to the CRD must adhere to the rules in IPRU-INV. Such firms include:

* authorised professional firms;
* certain types of securities and futures firms not directly subject to MiFID;
* Lloyd's underwriting agents and members' advisers;
* fund managers, including operators of personal pension schemes (SIPP operators);
* exempt Capital Adequacy Directive (CAD) firms or local firms (firms that conduct a limited type of business under MiFID, or are exercising passporting rights);
* service companies;
* personal investment firms that are operating under a MiFID exemption, eg, financial advisory firms;
* credit unions that provide Junior ISAs.

The way that IPRU-INV applies depends on the activity that is conducted by the firm; consequently, if an investment firm's activity changes, this may mean that the firm must comply with different aspects of IPRU-INV (or even GENPRU and BIPRU if the change brings it within the scope of the CRD). Each type of firm has prescribed capital adequacy tests, and all firms must comply with two over-arching requirements:

* firms must at all times have available the amount and type of financial resources required by the regulators' rules;
* firms must notify the relevant regulator immediately they become aware that they are in breach of, or expect shortly to be in breach of, the relevant financial resources rule.

From December 2013 the capital resources tests are changing for personal investment firms that are not subject to the CRD. The test is changing from an 'own funds' test of £10,000 to an expenditure-based test, and the amount of subordinated loan that can be used to meet capital will also be restricted.

The changes have and are being introduced in a staged manner as follows:

* **31 December 2013** – the test became one month's expenditure with a minimum capital floor of £15,000;
* **31 December 2014** – the test is two months' expenditure and subordinated loans will be restricted to 400%;
* **31 December 2015** – the test is three months' expenditure with a minimum capital floor of £20,000, and subordinated loans will be restricted to 200%.

7.2 Basel III

The EU capital adequacy framework has its foundations in the Basel Accord of 1988, agreed by the Basel Committee on Banking Supervision (BCBS). The intention was to strengthen the stability of the international banking system through prescribed capital ratios. The concept of the three pillars of capital adequacy was introduced by Basel II and implemented through the CRD as described in Section 7.1.

The financial crisis of subsequent years has prompted a further strengthening of the framework and CRD II and CRD III have already been implemented within the UK.

Basel III measures include:

- enhancing the quality and quantity of capital;
- increasing the Pillar 1 requirement for counterparty risk and market risk;
- a new leverage ratio as a backstop to risk-based capital;
- two new capital buffers – one for capital conservation and one to act as a counter-cyclical capital buffer;
- an enhanced liquidity regime.

Basel III is a long-term strategy that will be implemented through a CRD IV package. This includes Capital Requirements Regulation (CRR) (Pillar 1 and Pillar 3) and a CRD for Pillar 2, supervisory review and buffers. An EU-wide single rule book for financial services is also being developed.

Both the CRD and CRR Level 1 text has been agreed and published in the Official Journal. They became effective on 1 January 2014.

7.3 Capital Requirements Directive IV (CRD IV)

On 31 July 2013, the FCA published CP13–6 setting out proposed changes to the FCA Handbook required to implement two instruments: the **Capital Requirements Regulation (CRR)** and the **Capital Requirements Directive (CRD)** – together the **Capital Requirements Directive IV (CRD IV)**.

CRD IV is the EU implementation of Basel III which intends to introduce both qualitative and quantitative enhancements to the capital adequacy of banks and investment firms, with rules that were phased in from 1 January 2014.

The legislation had three primary aims:

1. the requirement for banks to hold more and better capital;
2. setting up a new governance framework giving supervisors new powers to monitor banks more closely and take action through possible sanctions; and
3. creating a single rulebook for banking regulation, improving both transparency and enforcement.

The FCA created some new categories of firms that meet certain standards and will not be subject to the full CRD IV. These are known as **BIPRU firms** and the former CRD rules in GENPRU, BIPRU and SYSC will remain. These proposals keep the 'status quo' pending the Commission's review of an appropriate prudential regime by end 2015. It is noteworthy that a BIPRU firm will not be subject to the EU-wide supervisory reporting framework for Financial Reporting (FINREP) and Common Reporting (COREP).

A BIPRU firm is one that is only authorised to carry on one or more of the following MiFID investment activities/services:

a. reception and transmission of orders;
b. execution of orders on behalf of clients;
c. portfolio management;
d. investment advice,

and does not carry out the following:

a. dealing on own account;
b. underwriting and/or placing financial instruments on firm commitment basis;
c. placing of financial instruments without a firm commitment basis;
d. operating an MTF; and
e. ancillary services of safeguarding and administering assets and is not permitted to hold money or securities belonging to their client.

Firms that do not meet the above exclusions are to be known as **IFPRU investment firms**, for which the FCA created a new prudential sourcebook (IFPRU). Depending upon the scope of activities conducted by an IFPRU investment firm, it will be subject to some if not all of the new CRD IV rules pertaining to capital, counterparty credit risk, capital buffers, liquidity adequacy and remuneration requirements (including the new bonus cap). IFPRU firms will also be subject to COREP and possibly FINREP.

At a high level, COREP covers capital requirements, own funds and liquidity, whereas the FINREP pertains to consolidated reporting and will either supplement or supersede the current GABRIEL reports, depending upon the activities of the firm.

A firm that is either a Undertakings for Collective Investment in Transferable Securities (UCITS) management company or alternative investment fund manager under the AIFMD that also conducts the MIFID activity of managing investments (ie, a collective portfolio investment firm (CPMI)) is considered to be an IFPRU Investment firm. Such firms will thus have to adhere to the new definitions on initial capital, own funds and fixed overheads in the CRR and are subject to COREP/FINREP.

The change in definition of investment firm may impact existing 'Exempt CAD' firms. CRD IV prevents such firms from carrying out the ancillary service of safekeeping and administration of assets and related services such as cash/collateral management. An Exempt CAD firm with this permission will be an **IFPRU limited licence firm** under the CRD IV. As such, it would not be subject to any of the capital buffers, the liquidity adequacy rules or large exposures regime but would be subject to variable capital requirements (rather than the flat fixed €50,000), Internal Capital Adequacy Assessment Process (ICAAP) and Pillar 3 obligations as well as COREP/FINREP and, potentially, the Remuneration Code.

8.   Relevant European Regulation

Learning Objective

3.7.1   Know the relevant European Union Directives and the impact on the UK financial services industry in respect of: MiFID – passporting within the EEA and home v's host state regulation; UCITS – selling cross-border collective investment schemes; Prospectus Directive – selling securities cross-border; AIFMD – regulation of AIFMD and the promotion of AIF within the EU; EMIR – requirements placed on EEA established counterparties

As a member of the EU, the UK plays a part in the attempt to create a single market across Europe for financial services. Primarily, the European Parliament issuing directives to the member states, and their subsequent implementation into national legislation, achieves this.

8.1   MiFID – Passporting within the EEA

The Investment Services Directive (ISD) was issued in 1993. Broadly, it specified that, if a firm had been authorised in one member state to provide investment services, this single authorisation enabled the firm to provide those investment services in other member states without requiring any further authorisation. This principle was, and still is, known as the **passport**.

The state providing authorisation is where the firm originates and is commonly referred to as the **home state**. States outside the home state where the firm offers investment services are known as **host states**.

The ISD was repealed and replaced by another EU Directive, the Markets in Financial Instruments Directive (MiFID). MiFID provisions came into force in the UK from 1 November 2007.

One of the key aims of MiFID was to provide investor protection rules across the EEA. Investor protection is ensured, *inter alia*, via the obligation to obtain the best possible result for the client, information disclosure requirements, client-specific rules on suitability and appropriateness and rules on inducements. As a general principle, MiFID places significant importance on the fiduciary duties of firms. That is why MiFID established a general obligation for firms to act in the client's best interest.

MiFID has been designed to support two key policy goals of the EU. These are:

*   extending the scope of the passport to include a wider range of services; and
*   removing a major hurdle to cross-border business, by way of the application of host state rules to incoming passported firms.

Previously, under the ISD, firms had only been able to passport a limited range of investment services into other host states. MiFID widens the range of passportable activities – for example, it now includes:

*   investment advice (which under ISD was only permitted if it was an ancillary service to some other core service being provided – eg, dealing in investments);
*   some underwriting activities;
*   operating an MTF;

- investment activities relating to commodity derivatives, credit derivatives and CFDs, since MiFID has extended the scope of the passport to cover these instruments for the first time;
- investment research, if it is an ancillary service to some other core service.

8.1.1 MiFID Activities and UK-Regulated Activities

While MiFID replaced the ISD, it did not replace any existing UK-regulated activity. If a UK investment firm wishes to exercise passporting rights under MiFID, it must already have Part 4A permission to conduct the equivalent UK-regulated activity as shown in the table above.

MiFID activity	Broadly equivalent to UK-regulated activity
Receipt and transmission of orders in relation to one or more financial instruments	Arranging deals in investments
Execution of orders on behalf of clients	Dealing as principal Dealing as agent
Dealing on own account	Dealing as principal
Portfolio management	Managing investments
Investment advice	Advising on investments
Underwriting of financial instruments and/ or placing of financial instruments on a firm commitment basis	Dealing as principal Dealing as agent
Placing of financial instruments without a firm commitment basis	Dealing as agent Arranging deals in investments
Operation of MTFs	Operating an MTF (formerly known as an alternative trading system)

8.1.2 Ancillary Activities

The same principle applies to MiFID's range of ancillary activities (see table on following page) – UK firms must already have the relevant activity within their Part 4A permission. Additionally, an ancillary activity cannot be passported in its own right – it can only be passported if it is being provided in conjunction with one of the main activities from the table above (see table on the following page).

MiFID ancillary activity	UK-regulated activity
Safekeeping and administration of financial instruments for the account of clients, including custodianship. Also related services such as the management of cash and collateral	Safeguarding and administering investments Sending dematerialised instructions Agreeing to carry on regulated activities
Lending to investors to allow them to effect a transaction in one or more financial instruments when the lender is involved in the transaction	N/A
Advice to undertakings on capital structure, industrial strategy and related matters; also, advice/services relating to mergers and the purchase of undertakings	Dealing as principal Dealing as agent Arranging deals in investments Advising on investments Agreeing to carry on regulated activities
Foreign exchange services (but only if these are connected with the provision of investment services)	Dealing as principal Dealing as agent Arranging deals in investments Advising on investments Agreeing to carry on regulated activities
Investment research and financial analysis, or other forms of general recommendation in relation to transactions in financial instruments	Advising on investments Agreeing to carry on regulated activities
Services in relation to underwriting	Arranging deals in investments Advising on investments Agreeing to carry on regulated activities
Investment services and activities, and ancillary services, related to the underlying assets of certain derivatives when these are connected to the provision of investment or ancillary services	Dealing as principal Dealing as agent Arranging deals in investments Operating an MTF Managing investments Advising on investments Agreeing to carry on regulated activities

8.1.3 Financial Instruments Covered by MiFID

MiFID applies only to activities in relation to a specified list of financial instruments. These are:

- transferable securities;
- money market instruments;
- units in collective investment undertakings;
- derivatives relating to securities, currencies, interest rates or yields, or other financial indices or measures which may be settled physically or in cash;
- commodity derivatives that must be settled in cash or may be settled in cash at the option of one of the parties (other than by default or termination);

- commodity derivatives that can be physically settled provided they are traded on a regulated market and/or an MTF;
- commodity derivatives which can be physically settled, which are not for commercial purposes, and which are similar to other derivatives in certain criteria;
- credit derivatives;
- financial CFDs; and
- derivatives relating to climatic variables, freight rates, emission allowances or inflation rates or other statistics, and certain other derivatives.

Therefore, when exercising passporting rights the firm must also specify the financial instruments that are to be included within the passport. These are broadly equivalent to some (but not all) of the specified investments that are within a UK firm's Part 4A permission.

Financial instruments not covered by MiFID include:

- bank accounts;
- foreign exchange (FX) (unless it relates to the provision of an investment activity or service, eg, buying/selling an option on FX).

8.2   MiFID – Home Versus Host State Regulation

Not all authorised firms are directly subject to the requirements of MiFID: whether they are or not, will depend on the nature of the regulated activities that they have within their Part 4A permission. If the activity is the same as a MiFID activity, then the firm will be caught by MiFID.

Broadly, the range of UK firms which are classified as MiFID firms is as follows:

- investment banks;
- portfolio managers;
- stockbrokers and broker-dealers;
- many futures and options firms;
- firms operating an MTF;
- venture capital firms that meet certain criteria;
- energy market participants, oil market participants and commodity firms which meet certain criteria;
- corporate finance firms which meet certain criteria;
- certain advisers;
- credit institutions which carry on MiFID business; and
- exchanges, UCITS investment firms and some professional firms.

However, there are two important exemptions for investment firms:

Article 3 exemption – this is available for firms that:

- only provide investment advice and receive/transmit orders;
- do not hold client funds or securities;
- only transmit orders to other MiFID firms and certain other institutions.

This exemption is widely used by financial advisory firms. If a firm is relying on the Article 3 exemption and wishes to exercise a MiFID passport, it must first apply to the relevant regulator to vary its UK Part 4A permission to remove the exemption.

Article 2.1(c) incidental exemption – this is available for professional firms if the investment service provided is incidental to the professional practice of their firm.

Firms that do not conduct investment services at all are not within the scope of MiFID. They include insurance undertakings, employee schemes, people administering their own assets, and any firms which do not provide investment services and/or perform investment activities.

As mentioned above, the concept of passporting under MiFID relies on the concept of **home state** and **host state** regulators. In essence, the home state is where the firm carrying on activities is established; the host state is the state in which it is providing services as a **guest**. Firms can either establish a branch in another state, or they can conduct activities from their home state on a cross-border basis.

MiFID requires a high degree of co-operation between regulators to ensure that the investor remains fully protected when activities are conducted on a passported basis. In general terms the home state regulator retains responsibilities for the firm's prudential regulation (financial resources, governance) and the host state regulator applies its rules to the firm's conduct of business in the host state. However, there are some exceptions to this general arrangement.

8.2.1   Regulatory Developments

The following notes are for information only and will not be examined.

The EU is reviewing MiFID, to ensure that it stays relevant in the face of new markets and products. The revisions are being called MiFID II, and the main proposals are:

- extension of the scope, to include commodity firms, data providers and third country firms (institutions based in non-EEA states and authorised by non-EEA competent authorities) operating in EEA states;
- an equivalence decision to be made before third country firms can operate in EEA states, and to require such firms to at least establish branches;
- to include additional financial instruments, such as structured deposits and emissions allowances;
- new requirements for the trading of derivatives, and the introduction of a new venue called organised trading facilities (OTFs), which will require separate permission;
- extension of disclosure requirements and additional transaction reporting;
- enhanced investor protection – a prohibition on commission for independent advisers and portfolio managers; independent firms must know the customer well enough to ensure they match a customer's profile and interests with the products provided; structured UCITS funds will no longer be classed as non-complex instruments, and so will become subject to the non-advised appropriateness test;
- enhanced powers for national regulators to enable them to permanently ban products and to limit a firm's position in certain products, such as commodity derivatives.

The Level 1 text for the Regulation (MiFIR) and the Directive (MiFID II) has been agreed by the European Parliament and Council. It was published in the EU Official Journal in June 2014, and will take effect sometime in 2016.

8.3 UCITS (Undertakings for Collective Investments in Transferable Securities) – Selling Cross-Border Collective Investment Schemes

UCITS stands for Undertakings for Collective Investments in Transferable Securities, and the family of UCITS directives established a set of regulatory standards for open-ended funds across the EU – again, with the aim of facilitating cross-border trade.

Put simply, if a collective fund is set up in accordance with the UCITS rules, it should be able to be sold across the EU, subject only to local tax and marketing laws. So, a UCITS scheme can gain a single authorisation from its home state regulator, and need not apply for further authorisation in other member states before being sold to the public there.

The original UCITS directive was approved in 1985 and adopted by the UK in 1989. It aimed to provide common standards of investor protection for publicly promoted CISs across the EU. However, only a relatively limited range of scheme types could qualify as UCITS and be freely marketed throughout the EU. The requirements which needed to be satisfied included:

- the scheme had to be solely invested in transferable securities;
- no more than 10% of the fund could be in the shares or bonds of a single issuer;
- no more than 5% of the assets of the scheme were allowed to be invested in other CISs;
- the scheme was only able to hold money in bank deposits as ancillary liquid assets and not as a major part of the investment strategy of the scheme;
- the scheme was only able to invest in, or utilise, financial derivatives for efficient portfolio management or hedging purposes.

Demand for a wider variety of funds, marketable throughout the EU, rendered these investment restrictions somewhat out of date. As a result, two new UCITS directives were introduced:

- the **Management Directive** – dealt mainly with the management companies operating UCITS funds – eg, the degree to which they can delegate activities, their capitalisation, internal administration and accounting requirements;
- the **Products Directive** – widened previous investment powers of UCITS schemes, to enable them to invest in money market instruments, other CISs, deposits and financial derivatives. It also allowed certain UCITS to use strategies designed to replicate the performance of stock market indices (index tracker funds).

The most recent UCITS directive – **UCITS IV** – was implemented in the UK on 1 July 2011. UCITS IV repealed previous UCITS directives, and introduced the following changes:

- **Passporting for management companies** – management companies no longer have to be established in the same member state as the fund(s) they operate.

- **Key Investor Information Documents (KIIDs)** – these replaced the simplified prospectus; the KIID is a concise document – not exceeding two sides of A4 – containing standardised product information.
- **Improved cross-border marketing of authorised funds** – a more streamlined process for allowing funds to access the market of another member state without delay.
- **Mergers** – a single framework for cross-border fund mergers, and standardised investor information.
- **Master-feeder structures** – whereby one fund can invest the majority of its assets into another.
- **Improved supervisory co-operation** – between regulators of different member states.

8.4   Prospectus Directive – Selling Securities Cross-Border

The Prospectus Directive is another directive aimed at creating common standards across the EU, this time with the aim of simplifying the issue of a prospectus throughout the EEA.

It was implemented in the UK in July 2005.

The Prospectus Directive sets out common standards in terms of the information that must be provided about the issuer and the securities being issued or admitted for listing. It can be thought of as a single passport for issuers. It means that once a prospectus has been approved by a home state listing authority, it must be accepted for the purpose of listing or public offers throughout the EU. The purpose of the Prospective Directive is therefore to make it easier and cheaper for companies (issuers) to raise capital in Europe.

8.5   Alternative Investment Fund Managers' Directive (AIFMD)

The scope of the AIFMD is broad and, with a few exceptions, covers the management, administration and marketing of alternative investment funds (AIFs). Its focus is on regulating the alternative investment fund manager (AIFM) rather than the AIF.

An AIF is a 'collective investment undertaking' that is not subject to the UCITS regime, and includes hedge funds, private equity funds, retail investment funds, investment companies and real estate funds, among others. The AIFMD establishes an EU-wide harmonised framework for monitoring and supervising risks posed by AIFMs and the AIFs they manage, and for strengthening the internal market in alternative funds. The Directive also includes new requirements for firms acting as a depositary for an AIF.

The FCA implemented the AIFMD from 22 July 2013. The Treasury has afforded some transitional provisions, initially until January 2004, which changed later to 21 July 2014 for firms that are already carrying on the management of AIFs, or are providing services as a depository, custodian or valuer.

Firms that are not yet authorised persons must become authorised with the relevant Part 4A permission before providing services.

The Policy Statement has amended a number of provisions:

- the perimeter guidance manual has been updated to clarify the capital raising processes and how delegates of a non-EEA AIFM should be treated;
- the systems and controls and conduct of business rules, as they apply to full-scope AIFMs and small AIFMs that are not subject to all its requirements;
- prudential rules for AIFMs and UCITS management companies, including a stricter interpretation of the Directive's additional own-funds requirement for self-managed AIFMs;
- the rules have been amended to make them more flexible for UK firms carrying out depositary services for non-EEA AIFs;
- proposed guidance on marketing has been adjusted to accommodate comments from investors and whether listing and trading on a secondary market constitute marketing; this also covers matters related to the notification of cross-border marketing activity;
- lower fee tariffs for small registered AIFMs;
- the rules applying to remuneration of an AIFM's key personnel, although there further work remains to be done;
- the FCA's approach to implementing, at a later date, the prospective EU passport for non-EEA AIFMs and AIFs.

8.6   EMIR (European Markets Infrastructure Regulation)

EMIR is a regulation on OTC derivatives, central counterparties and trade repositories and came into force on 16 August 2012.

EMIR relates to the transparency of the OTC derivative market, and along with elements in CRD IV and MiFID II represents the EU's commitment to the G20 agreement on the reform of OTC derivatives.

EMIR provides rules around reporting of certain derivative contracts to a trade repository, risk mitigation – reconciling contracts with the counterparty and also centrally clearing all derivative contracts.

From 15 September 2013, all EEA counterparties are required to undertake a reconciliation of their outstanding derivative contracts – the frequency ranges from daily, monthly or quarterly for financial counterparties (regulated firms) to quarterly or annual for non-financial counterparties (corporates). In addition firms must agree the process for dispute resolution where they disagree trade details.

From 12 February 2014, all EEA entities were required to start reporting trade details to a trade repository. The difference being that both counterparties must report, unless one entity is a third country entity (Non-EEA). The trade repositories report the trade details to ESMA.

The last piece of EMIR, which has yet to enter into force, is for OTC derivative contracts to be centrally cleared. The first UK central counterparty was authorised under EMIR in March 2014; clearing obligations are due to be phased in from 2015.

End of Chapter Questions

Think of an answer to each question and refer to the appropriate section for confirmation.

1.   Insider dealing is an offence under which act?
      Answer Reference: Section 1.1

2.   What is inside information?
      Answer Reference: Section 1.2

3.   What is the offence of insider dealing?
      Answer Reference: Section 1.3

4.   What financial instruments are caught by insider dealing legislation?
      Answer Reference: Section 1.4

5.   What are the defences against insider dealing?
      Answer Reference: Sections 1.5 & 1.6

6.   What is market abuse?
      Answer Reference: Section 2.1

7.   What are the three types of behaviour that give rise to the offence of market abuse?
      Answer Reference: Section 2.1

8.   How does the FCA provide guidance on what constitutes market abuse?
      Answer Reference: Section 2.2

9.   What behaviours are caught by the FCA's market abuse regime?
      Answer Reference: Section 2.2.1

10.   What is a regular user in the context of market abuse?
      Answer Reference: Section 2.3

11.   What are the penalties for market abuse?
      Answer Reference: Section 2.4

12.   What reporting requirements exist for market abuse?
      Answer Reference: Section 2.5

13.   List three rules that can be used as safe harbours against the charge of market abuse?
      Answer Reference: Section 2.6

14.   What is the link between market abuse and insider dealing?
      Answer Reference: Section 2.7

15.   What is the activity of money laundering?
      Answer Reference: Section 3.1

16.   Name the main sources of rules and regulations governing money laundering.
       Answer Reference: Section 3.1

17.   Describe the three stages of money laundering.
       Answer Reference: Section 3.2

18.   The Money Laundering Regulations 2007 place various requirements on firms. What are they?
       Answer Reference: Section 3.3.1

19.   What defence can be used for the offences under the Proceeds of Crime Act 2002?
       Answer Reference: Section 3.3.2

20.   What three types of customer due diligence requirements are set out in the Joint Money
       Laundering Steering Group Guidance?
       Answer Reference: Section 3.4.3

21.   What are the responsibilities of the MLRO?
       Answer Reference: Section 3.5

22.   What is the definition of terrorism under the Terrorism Act 2000?
       Answer Reference: Section 3.6

23.   What are the main differences between money laundering and terrorist financing activities?
       Answer Reference: Section 3.6.1

24.   What are the main purposes of the Bribery Act 2010?
       Answer Reference: Section 3.7.1

25.   From whom must directors obtain permission before dealing in their own company's shares?
       Answer Reference: Section 4

26.   What is the purpose of the Disclosure and Transparency Rules?
       Answer Reference: Section 5

27.   State the eight principles of good practice under the Data Protection Act 1998.
       Answer Reference: Section 6.1

28.   What is the record-retention period for a firm undertaking MiFID investment business?
       Answer Reference: Section 6.2

29.   What is the purpose of the capital adequacy requirements?
       Answer Reference: Section 7.1

30.   What is passporting?
       Answer Reference: Section 8.1

31.   What responsibilities are imposed by MiFID on home state and host state regulators?
       Answer Reference: Section 8.2

32.   What are the aims of the UCITS Directive?
        Answer Reference: Section 8.3

33.   What is the purpose of the Prospectus Directive?
        Answer Reference: Section 8.4

34.   What is the aim and purpose of EMIR?
        Answer Reference: Section 8.6

Chapter Four

The FCA's Conduct of Business and Client Assets Sourcebooks

This syllabus area will provide approximately 37 of the 75 examination questions

1. Application and General Provisions of COBS

1.1 The Conduct of Business Sourcebook (COBS)

The Conduct of Business Sourcebook (COBS) is contained within the Business Standards block of the Handbook. It came into force on 1 November 2007, replacing the old Conduct of Business rules which were referred to as COB.

The aim of COBS was to move the regulatory approach towards a better focus on outcomes rather than compliance with detailed and prescriptive rules. It also implemented the provisions of MiFID that relate to conduct of business. The provisions of MiFID are high-level, with MiFID setting standards for business conduct but not prescribing how firms should achieve those standards.

COBS contains provisions for investment firms that are not subject to MiFID and also those that are. If the provision is derived from MiFID, the relevant part of MiFID is quoted next to the provision.

1.2 Firms Subject to COBS

Learning Objective

4.1.1 Know the firms subject to the FCA Conduct of Business Sourcebook [COBS 1.1.1–1.1.3, COBS 1 Annex 1 Part 3, Section 3 (FCA/PRA)]

4.1.3 Know the impact of location on firms/activities of the application of the FCA Conduct of Business Sourcebook: permanent place of business in UK [COBS 1.1.1–1.1.3 & Annex 1, Part 2 (FCA/PRA) & Part 3 (1–3) (FCA/PRA 1–2 only)]

The **general application** rule is based on geographical location and states that firms are subject to COBS if they carry on any of a range of activities from an **establishment maintained by them or their appointed representative in the UK**.

Furthermore, COBS generally applies to a firm which carries on business with a client in the UK from an establishment overseas (unless the overseas person meets certain criteria which allow some activities to be excluded from COBS' scope).

There is a special rule (called the **EEA territorial scope rule**) that overrides the general position where this is necessary to be compatible with EU law. This is relevant to a firm that is conducting business subject to MiFID, in circumstances where there is a cross-border element or the firm has established a branch in another EEA state, both of which can be done using passporting rights.

In summary:

- COBS applies to UK firms conducting MiFID business for UK clients within the UK (as for other investment firms);

- COBS applies to UK firms that may have established a branch in another EEA state, but who are conducting MiFID investment business outside of that state's territory (whether this be the UK or another state);
- For an EEA firm that has established a branch in the UK, COBS applies where the business is carried on within the territory of the UK.

There is an exception for investment research and personal account dealing, where the COBS rules apply on a home state basis only. This means that these aspects of COBS apply to UK firms, regardless of where they are conducting business and, in the same vein, an EEA firm conducting MiFID investment business within the UK is not subject to COBS for these rules, but is subject to the equivalent rules of its home state regulator.

1.3 Activities Subject to COBS

Learning Objective

4.1.2 Know the activities which are subject to the FCA Conduct of Business Sourcebook including eligible counterparty business and transactions between regulated market participants [COBS 1.1.1–1.1.3 (FCA/PRA) Annex 1, Part 1(1) & (4) (FCA)]

The activities that are subject to COBS are:

- designated investment business;
- long-term insurance business in relation to life policies;
- accepting deposits – in part, eg, financial promotion rules, and rules on preparing and providing product information.

Certain of the COBS rules are disapplied for specific types of activity. For example, a range of COBS rules are disapplied, in certain cases, for firms carrying on eligible counterparty business (see Section 2.1.3). These include:

- **A large part of COBS 2** – general conduct of business obligations.
- **Much of COBS 4** – communicating with clients (including financial promotions).
- **COBS 6.1** – provision of information about the firm, its services and its remuneration.
- **COBS 8** – client agreements.
- **COBS 10** – appropriateness (for non-advised services).
- **Certain parts of COBS 11** – best execution, client order handling and use of dealing commission.
- **Parts of COBS 12** – labelling of non-independent research.
- **COBS 14.3** – information relating to designated investments.
- **COBS 16** – reporting requirements to clients.

Additionally, members and participants in a regulated market do not have to comply with **COBS 11.4** (client limit orders) in respect of each other, but they must comply when they are executing orders on behalf of clients.

1.4 Appointed Representatives

Learning Objective

4.1.4 Know how the application of the FCA Conduct of Business Sourcebook applies to appointed representatives [COBS 1.1.1 (FCA/PRA)] including financial promotions and firms' responsibilities for appointed representatives [COBS 4.1]

The COBS rules also apply to firms in relation to the relevant activities carried on for them by their appointed representatives.

Appointed representatives are exempt; that is, they can carry out a range of regulated activity under the auspices of their principal firm, which has accepted responsibility for the activity. See Chapter 2 if you need to review the regulated activities that may or may not be conducted by appointed representatives.

Firms must also ensure that their appointed representatives comply with the COBS rules when they communicate financial promotions. Particular mention is made of this in COBS because, technically, a financial promotion communicated by an appointed representative is an exempt promotion and so does not need approval. Therefore, by making particular reference to this matter in COBS, the FCA reminds firms that they are responsible for the content of the financial promotions communicated by their appointed representatives.

1.5 Electronic Media

Learning Objective

4.1.5 Know the provisions of the FCA Conduct of Business Sourcebook regarding electronic media (glossary definitions of durable medium and website conditions)

Increasingly, firms and their customers communicate and transact business electronically. The FCA rules have adapted to reflect this. In particular, where the rules refer to information being transmitted or provided in a **durable medium**, this means:

* paper; or
* any instrument which lets the recipient store the information so that they can access it for future reference, for an appropriate time and on an unchanged basis. It includes storage on a PC but excludes internet sites, unless they meet the requirement for storage and retrieval. So, for example, information conveyed on a web page does not automatically meet the requirements for a durable medium.

With specific reference to website conditions, the FCA requires that:

- if information is provided by means of a website, that provision must be appropriate to the context in which the business between the firm and the client is (or is to be) carried on. That is, there must be evidence that the client has regular access to the internet. Such evidence could, for example, be by way of their providing their email address to carry on that business;
- the client must specifically consent to having information provided to them in that form;
- they must be notified electronically of the website address and the place on it where the information can be accessed;
- the information must be up-to-date; and
- it must be accessible continuously by way of that website for such a period of time as the client may reasonably need to inspect it.

1.6   Recording of Telephone Conversations and Electronic Communications

Learning Objective

4.1.6   Know the recording of voice conversations and electronic communications requirements [COBS 11.8]

Preventing, detecting and deterring market abuse is one of the FCA's key priorities. However, market abuse is one of the most difficult offences to investigate and prosecute. Good quality recordings of voice recordings and of electronic communications (taping) help firms and the FCA to detect and deter inappropriate behaviour.

This is the reason why the regulator developed rules requiring certain firms to record and retain telephone conversations and other electronic communications linked to taking client orders and dealing in financial instruments for a period of six months, and in a medium that allows storage of the information in a way accessible for future reference by the FCA. The rules apply with respect to a firm's activities carried on from an establishment maintained by the firm in the UK.

Electronic communication includes communication made by means of fax, email and instant messaging. The rules also cover telephone conversations made using firm-provided mobile phones but not personal mobile phones.

The rules on the recording of voice conversations and electronic communications apply to a firm which carries out any of the following activities:

- receiving client orders;
- executing client orders;
- arranging for client orders to be executed;
- carrying out transactions on behalf of the firm, or another person in the firm's group, and which are part of the firm's trading activities or of another person in the firm's group;

- executing orders that result from decisions by the firm to deal on behalf of its client;
- placing orders with other entities for execution that result from decisions by the firm to deal on behalf of its client.

The rules apply to the extent that the activities relate to:

- qualifying investments admitted to trading on a prescribed market;
- qualifying investments where a request for admission to trading on such a market has been made; and
- investments which are related to qualifying investments.

However, these rules do not apply to:

- activities carried out between operators, or between operators and depositories, of the same CIS;
- corporate finance business;
- corporate treasury functions;
- a discretionary investment manager, where the telephone call is made with a firm that they believe is subject to the recording obligations [COBS 11.8.5]. Discretionary managers may make a small proportion of calls, infrequently, without recording the call even if they are made to a firm that is not subject to the recording obligations.

For the purpose of the rules, a relevant conversation or communication is any one of the following:

- Between an employee or contractor of the firm with a client, or when acting on behalf of a client, with another person, which concludes an agreement by the firm to carry out the activities referred to above as principal or as agent.
- Between an employee or contractor of the firm with a professional or an eligible counterparty, or, when acting on behalf of a professional client or an eligible counterparty, with another person, which is carried on with a view to the conclusion of an agreement referred to above, and whether or not it is part of the same conversation or communication.

The rules do not include conversations or communications made by investment analysts, retail financial advisers or persons carrying on back office functions, nor to general conversations or communications about market conditions.

A firm must take reasonable steps to prevent an employee from making or receiving calls on privately owned equipment that the firm cannot record or copy.

The recordings must be kept for at least six months from the date they were made in a medium that:

- allows the FCA to have ready access;
- allows for corrections/amendments to be identifiable;
- otherwise cannot be manipulated or altered.

2. Accepting Clients

2.1 Client Categorisation

Learning Objective

4.2.1 Understand client status [PRIN 1.2.1/2/3 (FCA/PRA), Glossary, COBS 3]: definition of client [COBS 3.2]; the application of the rules on client categorisation [COBS 3.1]; retail client [COBS 3.4]; professional client [COBS 3.5] and eligible counterparty [COBS 3.6]

4.2.2 Understand client status [PRIN 1.2.1 (FCA/PRA)/2/3, Glossary, COBS 3]: when a person is acting as agent for another person [COBS 2.4.1–3]; the rule on categorising elective professional clients [COBS 3.5.3–9]; the rule on elective eligible counterparties [COBS 3.6.4–6]; providing clients with a higher level of protection [COBS 3.7]; the requirement to provide notifications of client categorisation [COBS 3.3]

2.1.1 Application of the Client Categorisation Rules

A firm is required to categorise its clients if it is carrying on designated investment business.

MiFID laid down rules as to how client categorisation has to be carried out for MiFID business. For non-MiFID business, the FCA uses the same client categorisation terminology, but the rules on how the categories must be applied are modified in some cases.

If a firm provides a mix of MiFID and non-MiFID services, it must categorise clients in accordance with the MiFID requirements, unless the MiFID business is conducted separately from the non-MiFID business.

So, for example, if a firm were to advise a client on investing in a CIS (advice about which would fall within the scope of MiFID) and also about a life policy (which would not), it should use the MiFID client categorisation.

2.1.2 The Definition of a Client

COBS defines a client as someone to whom a firm provides, intends to provide, or has provided a service in the course of carrying on a regulated activity; and, in the case of MiFID or equivalent third country business, anything which is an ancillary service. The term includes potential clients and people acting as agent for another person (see Section 2.1.4).

In addition, in relation to the financial promotion rules, it includes persons with whom the firm communicates, whether or not they are actually clients.

Clients of a firm's appointed representative or tied agent are regarded as clients of the firm.

2.1.3 The Client Categories

Under COBS, clients may be categorised as:

- a retail client;
- a professional client; or
- an eligible counterparty.

The classification determines the level of protection the client receives, with retail clients being afforded the most protection, and eligible counterparties the least.

A **retail client** is any client who is not a professional client or an eligible counterparty. (Note: the term 'customer' is an umbrella term covering both retail clients and professional clients.)

Professional clients may be either per se professional clients (see below) or elective professional clients (see Section 2.1.5).

Per se professional clients are, generally, those which fall into any of the following categories – unless they are an eligible counterparty, or are categorised differently under other specific provisions.

The categories are:

- An entity required to be authorised or regulated to operate in the financial markets. This includes:
  - a credit institution;
  - an investment firm;
  - any other authorised or regulated financial institution;
  - an insurance company;
  - a CIS or the management company of such a scheme;
  - a pension fund or the management company of a pension fund;
  - a commodity or commodity derivatives dealer;
  - a local;
  - any other institutional investor.
- Large undertakings – companies whose balance sheet, turnover or own funds meet certain levels. Specifically:
  - For MiFID and equivalent third country business, this means undertakings that meeting any two of the following size requirements on a company basis: a balance sheet total of €20 million; a net turnover of €40 million; or own funds of €2 million.
  - For other (non-MiFID) business, large undertakings are:
    - a company whose called up share capital or net assets is, or has at any time in the past two years been, at least £5 million, or currency equivalent (or any company whose holding companies/subsidiaries meet this test);
    - a company which meets (or of which the holding companies/subsidiaries meet) any two of the following criteria: a balance sheet total of €12.5 million; a net turnover of €25 million; an average of 250 employees during the year;
    - a partnership or unincorporated association whose net assets are, or have at any time in the past two years been, at least £5 million, or currency equivalent. In the case of limited partnerships, this should be calculated without deducting any loans owing to the partners;
    - a trustee of a trust (other than certain types of pension scheme dealt with in the next bullet point) which has, or has at any time in the past two years had, assets of at least £10 million;

– a trustee of an occupational pension scheme or a small self-administered scheme, or the trustee/operator of a personal pension or stakeholder pension scheme, where the scheme has, or has at any time in the past two years had, at least 50 members, and assets under management of at least £10 million;
    – a local authority or public authority.

The list of per se professional clients also includes:

- governments, certain public bodies, central banks, international/supranational institutions and similar; and
- institutional investors whose main business is investment in financial instruments.

COBS contains a list with the types of client which can be classified as **eligible counterparties (ECPs)**.

Each of the following is a **per se ECP**, including an entity that is not from an EEA state that is equivalent to any of the following, unless and to the extent it is given a different categorisation under COBS 3:

(The following list is, to a certain extent, identical to the 'per se professional client' listed earlier in this section. However the ECP category is narrower as it does not include large undertakings.)

- a credit institution;
- an investment firm;
- another financial institution authorised or regulated under EU legislation or the national law of an EEA state (that includes regulated institutions in the securities, banking and insurance sectors);
- an insurance company;
- a CIS authorised under the UCITS Directive or its management company;
- a pension fund or its management company;
- a national government or its corresponding office, including a public body that deals with the public debt;
- a supranational organisation;
- a central bank;
- an undertaking exempted from the application of MiFID under either Article 2(1)(k) (certain own account dealers in commodities or commodity derivatives) or Article 2(1)(l) (locals) of that directive;
- a supranational organisation.

A client can only be categorised as an ECP for the following types of business:

- executing orders; and/or
- dealing on own account; and/or
- receiving and transmitting orders;
- ancillary services relating to the above activities;
- arranging.

This means that if the same ECP wants to engage in other types of business, such as investment management or investment advice, for example, it will have to be classified as a per se professional client.

As explained earlier, many of the COBS rules do not apply when the client is an ECP; the result of this is that the ECP will not benefit from the protections afforded by these rules. Having said that, the majority of ECPs are large firms who are very familiar with the financial markets, or are themselves large players in the financial markets and do not need such protections anyway. Some ECPs, however, would rather have more protections by voluntarily asking to opt-down a client category and become a professional client (see Section 2.1.6).

2.1.4   Agents

If a firm knows that someone to whom it is providing services (A) is acting as the agent of another person (B), then the firm should regard A as its client.

The exception is when the firm has agreed in writing with A that it should treat B as its client instead.

There is a further exception if the involvement of A in the arrangement is mainly for the purpose of reducing the firm's duties to B: in this case, B should be treated as the client in any case.

2.1.5   Recategorising Clients and Providing Lower Levels of Protection

Elective Professional Clients

A retail client may be treated as an **elective professional client** when:

- the firm has assessed his (or its) expertise, experience and knowledge and believes he can make his own investment decisions and understands the risks involved (this is called the **qualitative test**); and – additionally – for MiFID business;
- any two of the following are true (this is called the **quantitative test**);
    - the client carried out, on average, ten significantly sized transactions on the relevant market in each of the past four quarters;
    - the size of the client's financial portfolio exceeds €500,000 (defined as including cash deposits and financial instruments);
    - the client works or has worked as a professional in the financial services sector for at least a year on a basis which would require knowledge of the transactions envisaged.

Assuming the client passes the qualitative and, for MiFID business, the quantitative test, the client must put in writing to the firm their wish to be reclassified and the specific services and/or products that this will apply to. The firm has to respond with a clear written warning of the investor protections that will be lost, and the client must state in writing, separately, that they are aware of the consequences of losing such protections.

It is up to the professional client to keep the firm up-to-date with their circumstances and notify the firm of anything that may affect their classification. If a firm becomes aware that a client no longer fulfils the conditions that made for categorisation as an elective professional client, the firm must take appropriate action. If the appropriate action involves recategorising the client as a retail client, the firm must notify that client of its new categorisation.

Elective Eligible Counterparties

A professional client may be treated as an elective ECP if it is a company and it is:

- a per se professional client (other than one which is only a professional client because it is an institutional investor); or
- it asks to be treated as such and is already an elective professional client (but only for the services for which it could be treated as a professional client); and
- it expressly agrees with the firm to be treated as an ECP.

2.1.6 Recategorising Clients and Providing Higher Levels of Protection

Firms must allow professional clients and ECP to request recategorisation, to retail client and professional client respectively, so as to benefit from the higher protections.

In addition, firms can, at their own initiative as well as at the client's request:

- treat per se professional clients as retail clients; and
- treat per se ECP as professional or retail clients.

Recategorisation may be carried out for a client:

- on a general basis; or
- on more specific terms, eg, in relation to a single transaction only.

A firm can classify a client under a different classification for different financial instruments in which they may trade/undertake transactions. However, this would mean complex internal arrangements for firms and this is why most firms will classify a client just once for all financial instruments in which they may undertake transactions.

2.1.7 Notifications of Client Classification

New clients must be notified of how the firm has classified them. They must also, before services are provided, be advised of their rights to request recategorisation and of any limits in their protections that will arise from this.

2.1.8 Policies, Procedures and Records

Firms must implement appropriate written internal policies and procedures to categorise their clients. Firms must make a record of the form or each notice provided and each agreement entered into. This record must be made at the time that standard form is first used and retained for the relevant period after the firm ceases to carry on business with clients who were provided with that form.

2.2   Client Agreements

Learning Objective

4.2.3   Know the requirement for firms to provide client agreements, when a client agreement is required to be signed and when it is acceptable to be provided to clients [COBS 8.1.1–8.1.3]

The requirement to enter into a client agreement applies to designated investment business for a retail client and, to MiFID business and ancillary services or equivalent third country business carried on for a professional client.

It does not apply to insurance firms issuing life policies as principal.

Firms must enter into a written basic agreement with the client, setting out the essential rights and obligations of the firm and the client. The agreement has to be on paper or other durable medium.

However, in good time **before** a retail client is bound by the agreement, or before the provision of investment services, (whichever is earlier) firms must provide the client with:

- the terms of any such agreement; and
- the information about the firm and its services relating to that agreement or those services required by COBS 6.1.4, including authorised communications, conflicts of interest and the firm's authorised status.

A firm may provide the agreement and the information immediately **after** the client is bound by any such agreement if the client requests the use of distance communications and the firm complies with rules on voice telephony communications.

Firms have to notify the client of any material change to terms in the client agreement – again, in good time before the change takes effect, and in a durable medium.

Client agreement records must be maintained for whichever is the longer of:

- five years;
- the duration of the relationship with the client; or
- in the case of a pension transfer, pension opt-outs or freestanding additional voluntary contributions indefinitely.

Firms should also consider other COBS rules, such as fair, clear and not misleading, disclosure of information and distance communications, when considering its approach to client agreements.

2.3   Information Requirements

Learning Objective

4.2.4   Know the requirement to provide information to clients prior to providing services to clients including information relating to the nature and risk of the services and designated investments being offered [COBS 2.2, 6.1.1–4 & 14.3.1–10]

4.2.5   Know the rules on the provision of information in connection with the service of managing investments [COBS 6.1.6]

4.2.6   Know the rules on the provision of information concerning safeguarding of designated investments belonging to clients and client money [COBS 6.1.7]

2.3.1   Information about the Nature and Risks of Investments

COBS 2.2 sets out high level disclosure requirements. Firms carrying on MiFID business, or equivalent third country business, must provide clients with appropriate information in a comprehensible form about:

- the firm and its services;
- designated investments and proposed investment strategies, including appropriate guidance on, and warnings of, risks associated with investments in those designated investments or in respect of particular investment strategies;
- execution venues;
- costs and associated charges;

so that the client is reasonably able to understand the nature and risks of the service and of the specific type of designated investments that are being offered and to take investment decisions on an informed basis.

Firms carrying on non-MiFID business with or for a retail client in relation to derivatives, warrants or stock lending activity must also provide the information quoted above.

These high-level rules are expanded upon in COBS 6.1 in relation to information about the firm, and in COBS 14 in relation to information about products. In general terms, for non-MiFID business the disclosure requirements apply to retail clients and for MiFID business the disclosures must be made to professional clients also.

2.3.2   Information about the Firm

A firm must provide a retail client with the following general information, if relevant:

- The name and address of the firm and contact details necessary to enable the client to communicate effectively with the firm.
- In respect of MiFID business or equivalent third country business, the languages in which the client may communicate with the firm and receive documents and other information from the firm.

- The methods of communication to be used between the firm and the client, including those for the sending and reception of orders.
- A statement of the fact, that the firm is authorised and the name and contact details of the competent authority that has authorised it.
- If the firm is acting through an appointed representative or, where applicable, a tied agent, a statement of this fact specifying in which EEA state the appointed representative or tied agent is registered.
- The nature, frequency and timing of the reports on the performance of the service to be provided by the firm to the client in accordance with the rules on reporting to clients on the provision of services [COBS 16].
- Information about the firm's conflict of interest policy – a summary of the firm's policy, including the manner in which the firm will ensure fair treatment of the client, and that further details are available on request.

2.3.3 Information Requirements Relating to Managing Investment

The firm must provide the retail client with the following information, if applicable:

- Information on the method and frequency of valuation of the investments in the client's portfolio.
- Details of any delegation of the discretionary management of all or part of investments or funds in the client's portfolio.
- Specification of any benchmark against which performance of the portfolio will be compared.
- The types of investment that may be included and the types of transaction that may be carried out, including any limits.
- Objectives, the level of risk to be reflected in the manager's exercise of discretion and any specific constraints on that discretion.

2.3.4 Information on Safeguarding Investments/Money

Firms holding client money or investments for retail clients, subject to the MiFID custody/client money rules (as applicable), also have to provide the following information, as appropriate to the service being provided:

1. That the investments/money may be held by a third party on the firm's behalf.
2. What the firm's responsibility is for any acts/omissions of that third party.
3. What would happen if the third party were to become insolvent.
4. If the investments cannot be separately designated in the country in which they are held by a third party, what this means for the client and what the risks are.
5. That the investments are subject to the laws of a non-EEA jurisdiction and what this means for their rights over them.
6. A summary of the steps the firm has taken to protect the client money/investments, including details of any relevant investor compensation scheme or deposit guarantee scheme.
7. If the money or investments are subject to any security interest, lien or right of set-off, this fact and the terms of it.
8. Full and clear information, in a durable medium, in good time before entering into securities financing transactions using the client's investments, about what the firm's obligations are with regard to those investments and what the risks might be.

Firms holding money or designated investments for **professional clients** must provide them with the information in 6 and 7 above.

2.4   Disclosure of Costs

Learning Objective

4.2.7   Know the rules on disclosure of costs and associated charges, timing of disclosure; medium of disclosure, changes to information provided to the client and compensation information [COBS 6.1.9–6.1.16]

4.2.8   Know the requirements for an adviser to a retail client to be remunerated only by adviser charges in relation to any personal recommendation or related service

Firms must provide their retail clients with information on the costs and charges to which they will be subject, including – where applicable – the following:

- the total price to be paid including all related fees, costs, charges and expenses and any taxes payable via the firm;
- if these cannot be indicated at the time, the basis on which they will be calculated so that the client can verify them;
- the costs charged by the firm, which must be itemised separately in every case;
- if the above are to be paid in foreign currency, what currency is involved and the conversion rates and costs;
- if other costs and taxes not paid or imposed by the firm could be applicable, the fact that this is so;
- how the above items are to be paid/levied;
- information about compensation schemes.

2.4.1   Timing and Medium of Disclosure

Information to clients should be provided in good time before the provision of services. Alternatively, the firm may instead provide the information immediately after the provision of services if:

a.   at the request of the client, the agreement was concluded using a means of distance communication which prevented the firm from providing the information beforehand; and
b.   the firm complies with the rule on voice telephone communications.

The disclosures must be made in a durable medium or, if the website conditions are satisfied, they can be made via the website.

2.4.2   Keeping the Client Up-to-Date

A firm must notify a client in good time about any material change to the information provided which is relevant to a service that the firm is providing to that client. This notification must be in a durable medium if the information to which it relates was given in a durable medium.

2.4.3 Existing Clients

A firm does not need to treat each of several transactions in respect of the same type of financial instrument as a new or different service. This means that it does not need to comply with the disclosure rules in relation to each transaction. The firm should, however, ensure that the client has received all relevant information in relation to a subsequent transaction, such as details of product charges that differ from those disclosed in respect of a previous transaction.

2.4.4 Compensation Information

A firm which carries on a MiFID business must make available to the client who has used or intends to use those services the information necessary for the identification of the compensation scheme or any other investor compensation scheme of which the firm is a member, or any alternative arrangement provided for in accordance with the investor compensation scheme. The information must include the amount and scope of the cover offered by the compensation scheme and any rules laid down by another EEA state, if relevant. If the client so requests, the firm must provide information concerning the conditions governing compensation and the formalities that must be completed to obtain compensation. This information must be provided in a durable medium or via a website if the website conditions are satisfied.

2.4.5 Retail Distribution Review (RDR)

Adviser Charging

In 2009 the then regulator (FSA) published a consultation paper and proposals for implementing the Retail Distribution Review (RDR), which became effective on 1 January 2013. The regulator was seeking to:

- improve the clarity with which firms describe their services to consumers;
- address the potential for adviser remuneration to distort consumer outcomes; and
- increase the professional standards of advisers.

The RDR applies to advised sales for a defined range of retail products, but does not apply to non-advised business – such as execution-only and discretionary management. However, firms that carry out discretionary management, and provide advice as part of that service, will be caught by the RDR.

The Adviser Charging rules in COBS 6.2A (describing advice services) state that a firm must not hold itself out to a retail client as acting independently unless the only personal recommendations in relation to retail investment products it offers to that retail client are based on a comprehensive and fair analysis of the relevant market and are unbiased and unrestricted.

A firm that provides **independent advice** in respect of a relevant market that does not include all retail investment products must include in its disclosure to the retail client an explanation of that market – including the types of retail investment products which constitute that market.

Advisers who are not independent, ie, who do not select instruments from the whole of the market, will be classified as restricted. Where a firm provides **restricted advice**, its disclosure must explain the nature of the restriction. Where a firm provides both independent advice and restricted advice, the disclosure must clearly explain the different nature of the independent advice and restricted advice services.

With regard to charging and the advent of the RDR, advisers can no longer be remunerated from the product provider when making a personal recommendation to a consumer. They must charge the consumer for the advice and service that they are providing and either pay the adviser separately for the services, or the charge for the service can be deducted from the amount that is being invested. It is for the adviser and the consumer to agree the charge, prior to the service being provided by the adviser.

Advisers are also prohibited from receiving trail commission on any new business carried out with consumers, including existing clients. The adviser will, for the time being, be able to receive trail commission on advice provided before 31 December 2012 on legacy business.

A firm must disclose in writing to a retail client, in good time before the provisions of its services in respect of a personal recommendation or basic advice in relation to a retail investment product, whether the advice will be independent advice or restricted advice.

Disclosure must be made in a durable medium or through a website. A firm is able to provide the disclosure by using a 'services and costs disclosure document' or a 'combined initial disclosure document'.

Where a firm provides restricted advice and engages in spoken interaction with a retail client, the firm must disclose orally in good time before the provision of its services in respect of a personal recommendation that it provides restricted advice and the nature of that restriction.

2.5   Reliance on Others

Learning Objective

4.2.9   Know the rules, guidance and evidential provisions regarding reliance on others [COBS 2.4.4/6/7]

If a firm carrying on MiFID business receives an instruction to provide investment or ancillary services for a client through another firm, and that other firm is a MiFID firm or is an investment firm authorised in another EEA state, and subject to equivalent regulations, then the firm can rely on:

- information relayed about the client to it by the third-party firm; and
- recommendations that have been provided by the third-party firm.

The third-party firm retains responsibility for the completeness and accuracy of information, and the appropriateness of recommendations.

The firm takes responsibility for concluding the services or transactions.

When a firm relies on information provided by a third party, this information should be given in writing.

For firms that are not MiFID investment firms, the FCA states that it will generally be reasonable for a firm to rely on information provided to it in writing by an unconnected authorised person, or a professional firm, unless it is aware, or ought reasonably to be aware, of anything that would give it reasonable grounds to question the accuracy of that information. The firm should take reasonable steps to establish that the other person is unconnected and competent to provide the information.

3. Communicating with Clients

3.1 The Application of the Rules on Communicating with Clients and the Financial Promotion Rules

Learning Objective

4.3.1 Know the application of the rules on communication to clients and on fair, clear and not misleading communications and financial promotions [COBS 4.1, 4.2.1–4]

4.3.2 Know the purpose of the financial promotion rules and the relationship with Principles for Businesses 6 and 7 [COBS 4.1]

4.3.3 Know the rule on identifying promotions as such [COBS 4.3]

It is an offence under FSMA for a person to communicate a financial promotion unless:

- the person is an authorised firm;
- the financial promotion has been approved by an authorised firm.

The rules in COBS Chapter 4 apply to firms communicating with clients regarding their designated investment business and communicating or approving a financial promotion other than:

- for qualifying credit, a home purchase plan or a home reversion plan;
- a promotion for a non-investment insurance contract; or
- the promotion of an unregulated CIS which it is not permitted to approve.

They also apply to communications to authorised professional firms in accordance with COBS 18 (Specialist Regimes).

In general, these rules apply to a firm that carries on business with, or communicates a financial promotion to, a client in the UK (including where this is done from an establishment overseas), except that they do not apply to communications made to persons inside the UK by EEA firms. The majority of these rules do not apply when the client is an ECP.

3.1.1 The Purpose of the Rules

The purpose of the financial promotion rules is to ensure that promotions are identified as such, and that they are fair, clear and not misleading.

The financial promotion rules are consistent with Principles 6 and 7 of the Principles for Businesses:

- **Principle 6** – a firm must pay due regard to the interests of its customers and treat them fairly.
- **Principle 7** – a firm must pay due regard to the information needs of its clients and communicate information to them in a way which is clear, fair and not misleading.

The Financial Services Act 2012 provided the FCA with a new power to ban **misleading financial promotions**.

This new power means the FCA can remove promotions immediately from the market, or prevent them being used/launched in the first place, without having to go through its enforcement process.

The process involves the following provisions:

- The FCA will 'give a direction' to an authorised firm to remove its own financial promotion or one it approves on behalf of an authorised firm, setting out the reasons for banning it.
- Firms can make representations to the FCA if they think the wrong decision is being made.
- The FCA will decide whether to confirm, amend or revoke the direction. If it is confirmed, the FCA will publish the direction along with a copy of the promotion and the FCA's reasons behind its decision to ban the promotion.

Fair, Clear and Not Misleading

Firms must ensure that all communications relating to designated investment business, including financial promotions, are fair, clear and not misleading.

The way in which this is achieved should be appropriate and proportionate and take account of the means of communication and what information the communication is intended to convey. So, for example, communications aimed at professional clients may not need to include all the same information as those aimed at retail clients.

In connection with communications that are financial promotions, firms should ensure that:

- those which deal with products or services where a client's capital may be at risk make this clear;
- those quoting yields give a balanced impression of both the short-term and long-term prospects for the investment;
- if an investment product is, or services charges are, complex, or if the firm may receive more than one element of remuneration, this is communicated fairly, clearly and in a manner which is not misleading and which takes into account the information needs of the recipients;
- if the FCA is named as the firm's regulator but the communication also includes matters not regulated by the FCA, that it is made clear that those matters are not regulated by the FCA (NB, a financial promotion **does not** have to include reference to the FCA);
- those relating to packaged or stakeholder products not produced by the firm itself, give a fair, clear and non-misleading impression of the producer or manager of the product.

FCA guidance advises that firms may wish to take account of the *Code of Conduct for the Advertising of Interest-Bearing Accounts*, produced by the British Bankers' Association (BBA) and the Building Societies Association (BSA), when they are drafting financial promotions for deposit accounts.

Identifying Promotions as Such

Firms must ensure that financial promotions that they communicate or approve, and which are addressed to clients, are clearly identifiable as such.

There are some exceptions, for example, if the financial promotion is made to a professional client or ECP.

3.2 Exceptions to the Financial Promotion Rules

Learning Objective

4.3.4 Know the main exceptions to the financial promotion rules in COBS [COBS 4.1, 4.8], the limitations in connection to MiFID business and the existence of the FPO

The financial promotion rules are disapplied in certain cases, notably for excluded communications. These are communications which:

- are exempt under the financial promotion order (FPO – this is a Treasury order which allows unauthorised persons to communicate specified types of promotion, or, in specified circumstances, without the communication having to be approved by an authorised firm); or
- originates outside the UK and cannot have an effect within the UK; or
- an overseas communication that meets criteria for exemption under the FPO; or
- are subject to (or exempted from) the Takeover Code or similar rules in another EEA state; or
- are personal quotes or illustration forms; or
- are one-off promotions that are not cold calls (subject to certain conditions); or
- are promotions about unregulated CISs that are permitted because they fall within one of the exemptions in the FSMA 2000 (Promotion of Collective Investment Schemes) (Exemptions) Order 2001.

However, the exemption for excluded communications will not generally apply in relation to MiFID business.

3.3 Types of Communication

Learning Objective

4.3.5 Know the types and methods of communication addressed by COBS 4

The methods of communication include:

- real time – such as face-to-face, telephone conversations, presentations or other interactive dialogue;
- unsolicited real time – cold calls;
- non-real time – such as emails, letters or website, typically where a record is made;
- direct offer financial promotions. These are promotions that make an offer to any person to enter into an agreement and include a form of response or specify the manner of responding.

3.4 The Rules on Prospectus Advertisements

Learning Objective

4.3.6 Know the rules on prospectus advertisements [PR 3.3]

The section of the COBS rules which deals with communications to clients – COBS 4 – does not apply where the Prospectus Rule PR 3.3 applies instead.

Prospectus Rule PR 3.3 applies to offers, or admission to trading, of transferable securities in respect of which:

- a prospectus is required under s.85 of the FSMA; or
- where an election to produce a prospectus has been made under s.87 of FSMA.

A prospectus advertisement is any type of communication (eg, TV, press, email, letter, text, brochure) that specifically promotes the offer to subscribe or acquire securities.

An advertisement relating to such offers or admissions to trading must not be issued, unless:

1. it states that a prospectus has been (or will be) published, and where investors can obtain it;
2. it is clearly recognisable as an advertisement;
3. the information in it is not inaccurate, or misleading; and
4. it is consistent with the information that is, or is required to be, in the prospectus.

Any written advertisement falling under these rules must also contain a bold and prominent statement to the effect that it is not itself a prospectus, but an advertisement, and that investors should not subscribe for any transferable securities that it refers to, except on the basis of information in the prospectus.

3.5 Communicating with Retail Clients

Learning Objective

4.3.7 Know the general rule in connection with communicating with retail clients [COBS 4.5]

Firms must ensure that where they provide information about designated investment business, or issue/approve a financial promotion that is likely to be received by a retail client, they adhere to certain rules. These rules state that:

- the firm's name is included on the communication;
- the information is accurate and does not emphasise potential benefits without also giving fair and prominent indication of any relevant risks;
- the information is sufficient for, and presented in a way likely to be understood by, the average member of the group at whom it is directed or by whom it is likely to be received;
- the information does not disguise, diminish, or obscure important items, statements or warnings.

Where comparisons are made, they must be meaningful and presented in a fair and balanced way. For MiFID business, the data sources for the comparisons must be cited, as must any key facts and assumptions used.

Where tax treatment is mentioned, firms must explain that this depends on the individual circumstances of each client and that it may be subject to change.

Information included in financial promotions must be consistent with that given in the course of carrying on business.

These rules are disapplied for third-party prospectuses and image advertising. For non-MiFID businesses they are also disapplied for excluded communications.

3.6 Past, Simulated Past and Future Performance

Learning Objective

4.3.8 Know the rules on past, simulated past and future performance [COBS 4.6 excluding 4.6.4–4.6.4B]

3.6.1 Past Performance

Firms must ensure that information including indications of past performance is such that:

- the past performance indication is not the most prominent feature;
- it covers at least the immediately preceding five years (or the whole period that the investment has been offered/the financial index has been established/the service has been provided if this is less than five years); in any event, it must show complete 12-month periods;

- reference periods and sources are clearly shown;
- there is a clear and prominent warning that the data/figures refer to the past and that past performance is not a reliable indicator of future results;
- if the figures are in a currency other than that of the EEA state in which the client is resident, that the currency is stated and there is a warning about the possible effects of currency fluctuations;
- if the performance is cited 'gross', that the effect of commissions, fees and other charges is disclosed.

3.6.2   Simulated Past Performance

When firms give figures based on simulated (ie, notional, not having taken place in reality) past performance because the product or service does not have a track record, a firm must ensure that the simulated past performance figures:

- relate to an investment or financial index;
- are based on the actual past performance of one or more investments/indices which are the same as, or underlie, the investments being simulated;
- meet the rules set out above on past performance (except for the statement that they relate to that investment's past performance, since they do not);
- contain a prominent warning that they relate to simulated past performance and that past performance is not a reliable indicator of future performance.

3.6.3   Future Performance

Firms must ensure that information containing an indication of the possible future performance of relevant business, a relevant investment, a structured deposit or a financial index:

- is not based on, and does not refer to, simulated past performance;
- is based on reasonable assumptions supported by objective data;
- where it is based on gross performance, discloses the effects of commissions, fees or other charges; and
- contains a prominent warning that such forecasts are not reliable indicators of future performance.

3.7   Direct Offers or Invitations

Learning Objective

4.3.9   Know the rule on financial promotions containing offers or invitations [COBS 4.7.1–4]

Direct offer promotions – those making a direct offer or invitation, such as in a newspaper, trade magazine or mailed directly – likely to be received by a retail client must contain:

- prescribed information about the firm and its services;
- where relevant, prescribed information about the management of the client's investments;
- prescribed information about the safekeeping of client investments and money;
- prescribed information about costs and charges;
- prescribed information about the nature and risks of any relevant designated investments, including information about taxation, where relevant;

- where an investment is the subject of a public offer, if any prospectus published in accordance with the Prospectus Directive is available;
- where a designated investment combines two or more investments or services, so as to result in greater risk than the risks associated with the components singly, an adequate description of those components and how that increase in risk arises;
- where a designated investment incorporates a third-party guarantee, enough detail for the client to make a fair assessment of it.

The above need not be included, however, if the client would have to refer to another document containing that information in order to respond to the offer.

The offer should include a statement that the recipient should seek a personal recommendation if they are unsure about the suitability of the investment or service being promoted.

3.8 Unwritten Promotions and Cold Calling

Learning Objective

4.3.10 Know the rules on unwritten promotions [COBS 4.8.3] and the restriction on cold calling [COBS 4.8.2]

3.8.1 Unwritten Promotions

A firm must not initiate an unwritten promotion to a particular person outside its premises, unless the individual doing so:

- does so at an appropriate time of day;
- identifies himself and his firm at the outset and makes the reason for the contact clear;
- gets clarification of whether the client would like to continue with the communication or terminate it (and does so if requested); and
- gives the client a contact point, if he arranges an appointment with him.

3.8.2 Cold Calling

Cold calling is the practice of authorised persons or exempt persons contacting people without a prior appointment with a view to communicating a financial promotion to them.

Firms must not cold call unless:

- the recipient has an existing client relationship with the firm and would envisage receiving such a call; or
- the call relates to a generally marketable packaged product, which is neither a higher-volatility fund, nor a life policy linked to such a fund; or
- it relates to a controlled activity relating to a limited range of investments, including deposits and readily realisable investments other than warrants or generally marketable non-geared packaged products.

3.9　Overseas Persons

Learning Objective

4.3.11　Know the rule on financial promotions for overseas persons [COBS 4.9.3]

Firms are not permitted to communicate or approve financial promotions for overseas firms, unless the promotion sets out which firm has approved/communicated it, and (if relevant) explains:

- that the rules for the protection of investors will not apply;
- the extent that the UK compensation scheme arrangements will be available (and if they will not, that fact); and
- if the communicator wishes to do so, the details of any overseas compensation/deposit protection scheme applicable.

The firm must not communicate/approve the promotion unless it has no doubt that the overseas firm will deal with its UK retail clients honestly and reliably.

3.10　Approval of Financial Promotions

Learning Objective

4.3.12　Know the requirement for approving financial promotions and the circumstances of relying on another firm's confirmation of compliance [COB 4.10 (FCA), SYSC 3 & 4 (FCA/PRA)]

As mentioned above, it is an offence for an unauthorised person to communicate a financial promotion, unless the promotion is exempt (by virtue of the financial promotion order) or an authorised firm has approved it.

Approving a financial promotion is a formal process set out in the FSMA and reflected in COBS 4.10 rules.

The COBS rules on approval of financial promotions complement requirements under the SYSC. SYSC 3 and SYSC 4 require that a firm which:

- communicates with a client, in relation to designated investment business; or
- communicates or approves a financial promotion,

puts in place systems and controls or policies and procedures in order to comply with the rules on financial promotions.

3.10.1 Approving a Financial Promotion

COBS states that, before an authorised firm approves a financial promotion for communication by an unauthorised person, it must confirm that it complies with the financial promotion rules. If, later, it becomes aware that the financial promotion no longer complies, it must withdraw its approval and notify anyone it knows to be relying on that approval as soon as is reasonably practicable. The rules for approving a financial promotion apply in the same way as though the firm was communicating the financial promotion itself.

Firms may not approve real-time financial promotions, that is, financial promotions to be made in the course of personal visits, telephone conversations or other interactive dialogue.

Authorised firms are restricted in the promotion of unregulated collective schemes, and so they may not approve a financial promotion relating to such a scheme unless they would have been able to legitimately promote it for themselves, namely, by way of an exemption or in compliance with certain rules made for this purpose.

If a firm approves a financial promotion for which any of the financial promotion rules are disapplied, it must do so on the terms that its approval is limited to those circumstances. For example, if the approval is for communication to a professional client or ECP, the approval must state this limitation. If an unauthorised person then communicates the promotion outside of the limited approval, they are committing an offence.

3.10.2 Firms Relying on Promotions Approved by Another Party

In relation to non-MiFID business only, a firm is not in breach of the rules if it communicates a financial promotion that has been produced by another party and:

- takes reasonable care to establish that another authorised firm has confirmed that the promotion complies with the rules;
- takes reasonable care that it communicates it only to the type of recipient it was intended for at the time of the confirmation;
- as far as it is (or should be) aware, the promotion is still fair, clear and not misleading, and has not been withdrawn by the other party.

4.   Advising and Selling

4.1   Application of the Rules on Suitability

Learning Objective

4.4.1   Understand the application of the rules on identifying client needs and advising [COBS 9.1.1–9.1.4] and the rules on churning and switching [COBS 9.3.2]

The COBS rules on the suitability requirements apply when firms:

- make personal recommendations relating to designated investments;
- manage investments.

There are specific rules relating to the provision of basic advice (personal recommendations on stakeholder products); firms may, if they choose, apply those rules instead of the more general rules on suitability when advising on stakeholder products.

For non-MiFID business, the rules only apply to:

- retail clients; or
- where the firm is managing the assets of an occupational, stakeholder or personal pension scheme.

4.1.1   Churning and Switching

Churning is the activity of over dealing/trading more frequently for a client in order to generate additional fees/commissions for the firm. It is relevant where, for example, a firm manages a client's portfolio on a discretionary basis. Switching is the activity of selling one investment and replacing it with another.

The FCA's guidance on churning and switching is contained in the COBS rules on suitability. It states that, in the context of assessing suitability, a series of transactions that look suitable in isolation may not be so if the recommendations/trading decisions to make them are so frequent as to be detrimental to the client.

It states also that firms should bear the client's investment strategy in mind when determining how frequently to deal for them, including determining whether or not it is suitable to switch between packaged products.

4.2 Suitability Assessment

4.2.1 The Requirement to Assess Suitability

Learning Objective

4.4.2 Understand the purpose of the suitability rules and the requirement for assessing suitability [COBS 9.2.1–3]

The suitability rules exist to ensure that firms take reasonable steps to ensure that personal recommendations (or decisions to trade) are suitable for their clients' needs.

When a firm makes a personal recommendation or is managing a client's investments, they should obtain the necessary information regarding the client's:

- knowledge and experience in the investment field relevant to the specific type of designated investment business;
- financial situation; and
- investment objectives.

This enables the firm to make the recommendations, or take the decisions, which are suitable for the client.

It is a matter of ongoing concern for the FCA, that, despite the rules, there are persistent failings within firms to ensure that personal recommendations, or decisions to trade, are suitable for their clients. The concerns centre on the failure to assess properly the risk a client is prepared to take, and inappropriate use of risk profiling and asset allocation tools that may not be fit for purpose.

The FCA requires firms to ensure that:

- they have a robust process for assessing the risk a customer is willing and able to take, including:
  - assessing a customer's capacity for loss;
  - identifying customers that are best suited to placing their money in cash deposits because they are unwilling or unable to accept the risk of loss of capital;
  - appropriately interpreting customer responses to questions and not attributing inappropriate weight to certain answers;
- tools, where used, are fit for purpose and any limitations recognised and mitigated;
- any questions and answers that are used to establish the risk a customer is willing and able to take, and descriptions used to check this, are fair, clear and not misleading;
- they have a robust and flexible process for ensuring investment selections are suitable, given a customer's investment objectives and financial situation (including the risk they are willing and able to take) as well as their knowledge and experience;
- they understand the nature and risks of products or assets selected for customers; and
- they engage customers in a suitability assessment process (including risk-profiling) which acts in the best interests of those customers.

4.2.2   The Suitability Report

Learning Objective

4.4.5   Understand the obligation to provide a retail client with a suitability report [COBS 9.4.1–3]

4.4.6   Know the timing and contents of a suitability report [COBS 9.4]

A firm must provide a retail client with a suitability report if it makes a personal recommendation to the client, where the client:

- acquires a holding in, or sells all or part of a holding in:
  - ○ a regulated CIS;
  - ○ an investment trust, where the shares have been or are to be acquired through an investment trust savings scheme;
  - ○ an investment trust where the shares are to be held in an ISA which has been promoted as the means for investing in one or more specific investment trusts; or
- buys, sells, surrenders, converts or cancels rights under, or suspends contributions to, a personal pension scheme or a stakeholder pension scheme; or
- elects to make income withdrawals or purchase a short-term annuity; or
- enters into a pension transfer or pension opt-out.

A firm must also provide a suitability report if it makes a personal recommendation in connection with a life assurance policy.

There are some exceptions to the requirement to provide a suitability report:

- if a firm, acting as investment manager for a retail client, makes a personal recommendation in connection with a regulated CIS;
- if the client is habitually resident outside the EEA and is not present in the UK at the time of acknowledging consent to the proposal form to which the personal recommendation relates;
- if the personal recommendation is made by a friendly society in connection with a small life policy sold by it, with a premium not exceeding £50 a year or (if payable weekly) £1 a week;
- if the personal recommendation is to increase a regular premium to an existing contract; or
- if it is to invest additional single premiums or single contributions to an existing packaged product, to which a single premium or single contribution has previously been paid.

In terms of timing, a suitability report must be provided:

- in connection with a life policy, before the contract is concluded – unless the necessary information is provided orally, or cover is required immediately (in which case the report must be provided in a durable medium immediately after the contract is concluded); or
- in connection with a personal pension scheme or a stakeholder pension, where the cancellation rules apply, within 14 days of concluding the contract; or
- in any other case, when or as soon as possible after the transaction is effected or executed.

The suitability report must, at least, specify the client's demands and needs, explain any possible disadvantages of the transaction for the client and why the firm has concluded that the recommended transaction is suitable for the client – having due regard to the information provided by the client.

If the transaction is the sale of a life policy by telephone, and the only contact between the firm and client before the contract is concluded is by telephone, then the suitability report must:

- comply with the Distance Marketing Directive (DMD) rules;
- be provided immediately after conclusion of the contract; and
- be in a durable medium.

4.2.3   Information Required to Make a Suitability Assessment

Learning Objective

4.4.3   Understand the information which a firm must obtain from a client in order to make a suitability assessment [COBS 9.2.1–7]; and the guidance on assessing suitability [COBS 9.3.1]

In order to make a suitability assessment, a firm should establish, and take account of, the client's:

- knowledge and experience in the investment relevant to the specific type of designated investment or service;
- level of investment risk that they can bear financially and that is consistent with their investment objectives; and
- investment objectives.

In order to do so, a firm should gather enough information from its client to understand the essential facts about them. It must have a reasonable basis to believe that (bearing in mind its nature) the service or transaction:

- meets their investment objectives;
- carries a level of investment risk that they can bear financially; and
- carries risks that the client has the experience and knowledge to understand.

In terms of assessing the client's knowledge and experience, the firm should gather information on:

- the types of service/transaction/investment with which they are familiar;
- the nature, volume, frequency and period of their involvement in such transactions/investments; and
- their level of education, profession or relevant former profession.

Firms must not discourage clients from providing this information (eg, because it would rule a particular transaction out and result in a loss of business to the firm). They are entitled to rely on the information the client provides, unless it is manifestly out of date, inaccurate or incomplete.

If a firm does not obtain the information it needs to assess suitability in this way, it must not make a personal recommendation to the client or take a decision to trade for them.

4.2.4   Assessing Suitability – Professional Clients

Learning Objective

4.4.4   Know the application of the assessing suitability rules for professional clients [COBS 9.2.8]

A firm is entitled to assume that a client classified as a professional client in respect of MiFID or equivalent third-country business, for certain products, transactions or services, has the necessary experience and knowledge in that area and that the client is able financially to bear any related investments risks consistent with their investment objectives.

4.3   The Application of the Rules on Appropriateness (Non-Advised Sales)

Learning Objective

4.4.7   Understand the application and purpose of the rules on non-advised sales [COBS 10.1]

4.4.8   Understand the obligations for assessing appropriateness [COBS 10.2]

4.4.9   Know the circumstances in which it is not necessary to assess appropriateness [COBS 10.4– 10.6]

The rules on non-advised sales apply to a range of MiFID (and some non-MiFID) investment services that do not involve advice or discretionary portfolio management. Specifically, they apply to:

- firms providing MiFID investment services other than the provision of personal recommendations or the managing of investments (because these services are covered by suitability rules);
- firms arranging deals, or dealing, in warrants and derivatives for retail clients, where the firm is, or should be, aware that the client's application or order is in response to a direct offer financial promotion;
- firms which assess appropriateness on behalf of other MiFID firms.

The purpose of the appropriateness test is to provide a degree of protection for non-advised transactions.

4.3.1   The Obligation to Assess Appropriateness (Non-Advised Sales)

When a firm provides one of the above services, it must ask the client for information about their knowledge and experience in the investment field of the specific type of product or service offered or demanded, so that it can assess whether the product/service is appropriate.

In assessing appropriateness, the firm:

- must determine whether the client has the experience and knowledge to understand the risks involved;

- may assume that a client, classified as a professional client for certain services/products, has the necessary knowledge and experience in that field for which it is classified as a professional client.

In terms of a client's knowledge and experience, a firm should obtain information (to the extent appropriate to the circumstances) on:

- the types of service/transaction/investment with which they are familiar;
- the nature, volume, frequency and period of their involvement in such transactions/investments;
- the level of education, profession or relevant former profession.

The firm must not discourage a client from providing this information.

A firm is entitled to rely on information provided by a client unless it is aware that the information is out of date, inaccurate or incomplete. A firm can use information it already has in its possession. A firm may satisfy itself that a client's knowledge alone is sufficient for them to understand the risk involved in a product or service. Where reasonable, a firm may infer knowledge from experience.

4.3.2 The Obligation to Warn Clients

If a firm believes, based on the above assessment, that the product or service contemplated is not appropriate for the client, it must warn them of that fact. It may do so in a standardised format.

Further, if the client declines to provide the information the firm needs to assess appropriateness, the firm must warn them that it will then be unable to assess the product/service's appropriateness for them (and again it may do so in standard format). If the client then asks the firm to proceed regardless, it is up to the firm to decide whether to do so based on the circumstances.

4.3.3 Circumstances when Assessment is Unnecessary

Firms are not required to ask clients to provide information or assess appropriateness if:

- the service is execution-only, or for the receipt and transmission of client orders, in relation to particular financial instruments and is at the client's initiative; and
- the client has been clearly informed that the firm is not required to do so in this particular case and that they will therefore not get the benefit of the protection under the rules on assessing and suitability; and
- the firm complies with its obligations regarding conflicts of interest. (You should remember as well that Principle 8 of the Principles for Businesses states that *a firm must manage conflicts of interest fairly, both between itself and its customers and between a customer and another client'.*)

The particular financial instruments are:

- shares listed on a regulated market or an equivalent third-country market;
- money market instruments, bonds or other forms of securitised debt (provided they do not have embedded derivatives);
- holdings in UCITS funds;
- other investments meeting a definition of non-complex investments.

A financial instrument is non-complex if:

- it is not a derivative;
- there is sufficient liquidity in it;
- it does not involve liability for the client that exceeds the cost of acquiring the investment; and
- it is publicly available and comprehensive information is available on it.

Firms do not need to reassess appropriateness each time if a client is engaged in a series of similar transactions or services, but they must do so before beginning to provide a new service. If a client was engaged in a course of dealings of this type before 1 November 2007, the firm may assume that he has the necessary experience and knowledge to understand the risks. (Note this does not mean, however, that the other criteria may necessarily be deemed to have been met.)

5. Product Disclosure

5.1 The Purpose and Nature of the Rules

Learning Objective

4.5.1 Know the purpose of the rule on the sale of packaged products to retail clients, the rule requiring the provision of key features to retail clients and the main features to be explained in the key features [COBS 13.1.1/3/4, 13.2.1/2/4, 13.3.1/2 (excluding Annex 1R) & 14.1.1, 14.3.1/2]

4.5.3 Know the requirements for a firm making a personal recommendation to be independent or restricted

5.1.1 Key Investor Information Documents (KIIDs)

Authorised fund managers (AFMs) must for each UCITS scheme, that it manages, produce a key investor information document (KIID).

The KIID must be fair, clear and not misleading and be consistent with relevant parts of the prospectus.

It must include appropriate information about the essential characteristics of the UCITS scheme which is to be provided to investors, enabling investors to reasonably understand the nature and risks of the investment product being offered to them and, therefore, make investment decisions on an informed basis.

In addition, it must provide information on the following essential elements in respect of the UCITS scheme:

a. identification of the scheme;
b. a short description of its investment objectives and investment policy;
c. past performance presentation or, where relevant, performance scenarios;

d.   costs and associated charges; and

e.   a risk/reward profile of the investment, including appropriate guidance and warnings in relation to the risks associated with investments in the scheme.

5.1.2   Key Features Documents (KFDs)

The rules on product disclosure requires that a firm prepares a disclosure document, in good time before it needs to, in respect of:

- each package product;
- cash deposit ISA;
- cash deposit child trust fund (CTF); and
- a key features illustration for each packaged product it produces.

KIIDs cover the terms and features of a product in a prescribed level of detail.

The exceptions are:

- where another firm has agreed to prepare such a document;
- KIIDs are not needed for certain types of schemes, or in some cases if the information is already provided in enough detail in another document;
- there are some specific rules for reinsurance and pure protection insurance contracts.

Firms must provide particular information on the nature and risks of designated investments to clients for whom they undertake MiFID business. They must also do so for retail clients in relation to certain other business.

5.1.3   Independent vs Restricted Advice

Firms providing advice on retail investment products to retail clients have needed to describe these services as either 'independent' or 'restricted'.

The new standard for independent advice is intended to ensure that such advice is genuinely free from bias towards particular solutions or any restrictions that would limit the range of solutions that firms can recommend to their clients. In providing independent advice, a firm should not be restricted by product provider, and should also be able to objectively consider all types of retail investment products which are capable of meeting the investment needs and objectives of a retail client.

Independent advice is defined in the Handbook as *'a personal recommendation to a retail client in relation to a retail investment product where the personal recommendation provided meets the requirements of the rule on independent advice' (COBS 6.2A.3R).*

Restricted advice, which is advice that does not meet the standard for independent advice, will come in many different forms. The key FCA requirement is in a firm's disclosure to clients. In its written disclosure, a firm that provides restricted advice must explain the nature of the restriction (COBS 6.2A.6R).

5.2 Cancellation and the Right to Withdraw

Learning Objective

4.5.2 Know the purpose and requirements of the cancellation and withdrawal rights [COBS 15.1.1, 15.2.1, 15.2.3, 15.2.5, 15.3.1, 15.3.2]

The rules on cancellation apply to:

*   most firms providing retail financial products based on designated investments or deposits; and
*   firms entering into distance contracts with consumers, relating to deposits or designated investments.

They are intended to ensure that clients entering into the relevant range of transactions have the opportunity to reconsider, within a certain period of time, and to cancel the transaction. When a consumer does so, the effect is that the contract is terminated.

In summary, the **cancellation periods** are as follows:

*   life and pension products – 30 calendar days;
*   cash deposit Individual Savings Accounts (ISAs) – 14 calendar days;
*   non-life and pensions products (advised, non-distance contracts) – 14 calendar days;
*   non-life and pensions products (distance contracts) – 14 calendar days.

For example, should a client who receives a cancellation notice in respect of an advised purchase of an authorised unit trust (AUT) or OEIC wish to exercise their right to cancel, they must do so within 14 days.

The cancellation period starts either from the day the contract concludes, or from the day the client receives contractual information, if later.

If cancellation rights apply, firms must tell consumers of their rights in good time before (or where that is not possible, immediately after) the consumer is bound by the contract; and they must do so in a durable medium. They must tell the consumer of:

*   the existence of the cancellation/withdrawal right;
*   its duration;
*   the conditions for exercising it (including information on any amount the consumer may have to pay);
*   what happens if he does not exercise it; and
*   practical details of how to exercise it, including the address to which he must send any notification.

A firm need not do this if the consumer is already receiving similar information from it, or another person, under the COBS rules (distance marketing disclosures rules and providing product information).

If a consumer exercises the right to cancel, they must notify the firm; the notification is deemed to have been observed if it is despatched before the deadline expires. The consumer does not need to give any reason for cancelling.

The record-keeping retention period is:

- indefinitely for pension transfers, pension opt-outs or free-standing additional voluntary contributions (FSAVCs);
- at least five years in relation to a life policy, pension contract, personal pension scheme or stakeholder pension scheme;
- at least three years in any other case.

In September 2012, the then regulator, the FSA, published a report on the findings of a thematic review into financial incentives for retail sales staff. The report showed that most firms had incentive schemes that were likely to drive mis-selling, without effective controls in place to manage the risks. The report highlighted areas of concern and provided draft guidance for firms that were finalised in January 2013.

The FCA made it clear that it expected firms to:

- consider if their incentive schemes increased the risk of mis-selling and, if so, how;
- review whether their governance and controls were adequate; and
- take action to address any inadequacies.

The FCA also said that it would undertake follow-up work to assess how firms had responded, leaving open the possibility of strengthening its rules.

The FCA's intervention to date has resulted in significant change, increased awareness and focus on financial incentives.

The majority of the largest UK-based retail banks have either replaced or made significant changes to their incentive schemes to reduce risk to consumers. They have also improved their controls.

Nearly all other firms appear to have considered their guidance and many have made changes or improvements. The level of engagement and change was less at the smallest firms.

However, there is still work to be done. The FCA estimates that around one in ten of the firms with sales teams had higher-risk incentive scheme features where it appeared they were not managing the risk properly at the time of the FCA's assessment.

The FCA identified common areas where firms may need to do more to manage incentive risks effectively, in particular:

- checking for spikes or trends in the sales patterns of individuals to identify areas of increased risk;
- doing more to monitor poor behaviour in face-to-face sales conversations;
- managing the risks in discretionary incentive schemes and balanced scorecards, including the risk that discretion could be misused;
- monitoring non-advised sales to ensure staff who are incentivised to sell do not give personal recommendations;
- improving oversight of incentives used by appointed representatives;
- recognising that remuneration that is effectively 100% variable pay based on sales, increases the risk of mis-selling and managing this risk.

6. Dealing and Managing

6.1 The Application of the Rules on Dealing and Managing

Learning Objective

4.6.1 Know the application of the rules on dealing and managing [COBS 11.1]

The COBS rules on dealing and managing are:

- Best execution (COBS 11.2).
- Client order handling (COBS 11.3).
- Client limit orders (COBS 11.4).
- Record keeping, client orders and transactions (COBS 11.5).
- Use of dealing commission (COBS 11.6).
- Personal account dealing (COBS 11.7).
- Recording telephone conversations and electronic communications (COBS 11.8).

The rules on dealing and managing (aside from those on personal account dealing) apply generally to authorised firms; there are some variations in application, depending on the nature of business and location of the firm.

- Certain provisions (those marked in the Handbook with an EU) apply to non-MiFID firms as if they were rules.
- The rules on the use of dealing commissions (see Section 6.3) apply to a firm that acts as an investment manager.
- The rules on personal account dealing (see Section 6.8) apply to the designated investment business of an authorised firm, in relation to the activities it carries on from an establishment in the UK. These rules:
  - also apply to passported activities carried on by a UK MiFID investment firm from a branch in another EEA state;
  - do not apply to the UK branch of an EEA MiFID firm in relation to its MiFID business.

6.2   Conflicts of Interest

6.2.1   The Principles and Rules on Conflicts of Interest

Learning Objective

4.6.2   Understand the application and purpose of the principles and rules on conflict of interest; the rules on identifying conflicts and types of conflicts; the rules on recording and disclosure of conflicts [PRIN 2.1.1 Principle 8 (FCA/PRA), SYSC 10.1.1–6 + 10.1.8/9 (FCA/PRA)]

4.6.4   Understand the rules on managing conflicts of interest [SYSC 10.1.7 (FCA/PRA)] and how to manage conflicts of interest to ensure the fair treatment of clients [SYSC 10.2 (FCA/PRA)] including: information barriers such as Chinese walls; reporting lines; remuneration structures; segregation of duties; policy of independence

The rules on conflicts of interest are contained in SYSC. They apply to both common platform firms in respect of regulated business and of ancillary services which constitute MiFID business, as well as to non-MiFID firms and business.

They require that firms take all reasonable steps to identify conflicts of interest between:

*   the firm, including its managers, employees, appointed representatives/tied agents and parties connected by way of control and a client of the firm; and
*   one client of the firm and another.

The types of conflicts of interests that may arise include:

*   realising a financial gain, or avoiding a financial loss, at the expense of a client;
*   having an interest in the outcome of a service or transaction that is distinct from the client's interest;
*   having an incentive to favour one client over others;
*   carrying on the same business as the client;
*   receiving inducements from someone other than the client, that are over and above the standard commission or fee.

Firms under these obligations should:

*   maintain and operate effective organisational and administrative arrangements, designed to prevent conflicts of interest from adversely affecting the interests of their clients;
*   for those producing externally facing investment research, have appropriate information controls and barriers to stop information from these research activities from flowing to the rest of the firm's business;
*   if a conflict arises the firm must disclose the interest to the client before undertaking business for the client – the disclosure must be in a durable medium and be in sufficient detail to allow the client to make an informed decision as to the provision of the service. (note that disclosure alone is insufficient to meet the rules; the firm's arrangements should be designed to prevent conflicts arising in the first place);
*   prepare, maintain and implement an effective conflicts policy – see Section 6.2.2;

- provide retail clients and potential retail clients with a description of that policy; and
- keep records of those of its activities where a conflict has arisen.

One type of organisational arrangement for controlling information is to establish **Chinese walls**. This is the term given to arrangements whereby information held by an employee in one part of the business must be withheld from (or, if this is not possible, at least not used by) the people with or for whom he acts in another part of the business.

If a firm establishes and maintains a Chinese wall, it must:

- withhold or not use the information held; and
- for that purpose, permit its employees in one part of the business to withhold the information from those employed in another part of the business;
- but only to the extent that at least one of those parts of the business is carrying on regulated activities, or another activity carried on in connection with a regulated activity.

The requirement to maintain Chinese walls includes taking reasonable steps to ensure that these arrangements remain effective and are adequately monitored.

Example of a Chinese Wall

When a firm establishes and maintains a Chinese wall, it allows the persons on one side of the wall, eg, corporate finance, to withhold information from persons on the other side of the wall, eg, equity research/market-making arm.

The effect of the Chinese wall rule is that the corporate finance department may have plans for a company that will change the valuation of that company's shares. The equity research/market-making arm on the other side of the wall should have no knowledge of these plans; consequently the inability to pass this knowledge on to clients is not seen as a failure of duty to their clients.

A firm will therefore not be guilty of the offences of market manipulation (FSA 2012 s.89-s.92), market abuse (s.118 FSMA) or be liable to a lawsuit under s.138D FSMA when the failure arises from the operation of a Chinese wall.

6.2.2 Conflicts of Interest Policies

Learning Objective

4.6.3 Know the rule requiring a conflicts policy and the contents of the policy [SYSC 10.1.10/11/12 (FCA/PRA)–10.1./13/14/15]

As noted above, affected firms are required to have in place effective arrangements for preventing and managing conflicts of interest. Specifically, the rules require firms to have a written conflicts of interest policy that is appropriate to the scale and nature of the firm's activity.

If a firm is a member of a group, the policy should take into account any potential conflicts arising from the structure/business activities of other members of that group.

Firstly, the policy needs to set out the circumstances that may give rise to a conflict, paying particular attention to circumstances where a person performs two or more roles in relation to (for example) investment research and advice, proprietary trading, portfolio management and corporate finance business.

Secondly, the policy needs to state the procedures for managing such conflicts. These procedures should cover:

- control of information to prevent the exchange of information that may harm the interest of one or more clients;
- separate supervision of persons who are engaged in activities for different clients whose interests may conflict with each other or those of the firm;
- removal of any direct link between remuneration of individuals whose activities may give rise to conflicts;
- measures to prevent or limit one person exercising inappropriate influence over another;
- measures to control an individual's involvement in a series of activities that may give rise to a conflict.

For corporate finance firms who are managing an offering of securities, the policy needs to have particular regard to the offering process (for example, whether the firm might place securities with its investment clients or with its own proprietary book); and it should include specific detail on arrangements for allocation and pricing.

6.2.3   Investment Research and Research Recommendations

Learning Objective

4.6.5   Know the rules on managing conflict in connection with investment research and research recommendations [COBS 12.2.1/3/5/10, 12.3.2/3/4, 12.4.1/4/5/6/7/9/10/15/16/17]]

There are particular conduct of business rules for managing conflicts of interest, when a firm produces **investment research**. Investment research is information recommending or suggesting an investment strategy, including opinion as to the present or future value/price of the investments, and intended for distribution to the public as opposed to just for use within the firm or the firm's group.

It has to be clearly labelled as investment research and presented as an objective or independent explanation of the matters that are the subject of the research. It must not be presented in such a way that it would constitute a personal recommendation to a client of an investment firm.

Measures and Arrangements

If a firm produces investment research, it must implement all the measures for managing conflicts of interest set out in SYSC 10.1.11R in relation to the financial analysts involved in producing research, and other relevant persons, if their interests may conflict with those to whom it is disseminated. The arrangements must be such as to prevent dealing ahead, by ensuring that:

- Financial analysts and other relevant persons, who know the likely timing/content of investment research which is not yet publicly available or available to clients and which cannot be inferred from information that is available, do not undertake personal transactions, or trade for others, until the recipient of the investment research has had a reasonable opportunity to act on it. There are certain exceptions, such as the receipt of an instruction from an execution-only client or a market maker acting in good faith.
- In any event, they do not undertake personal account transactions in the investments to which the research relates, without prior approval from the firm's compliance or legal department and then only in exceptional circumstances.
- The firm and any person involved in the production of research do not accept inducements from those with a material interest in the subject matter of the research.
- They do not promise issuers favourable research coverage.
- If draft investment research includes a recommendation or target price, no-one other than financial analysts may review the draft, other than for the purpose of verifying compliance with the firm's legal obligations.

The firm does not have to comply with the rules on conflict of interest, or with the above arrangements, if it is disseminating investment research on behalf of another person. That is, so long as the following conditions are met:

- that person is not in the same group as the firm;
- the firm does not substantially amend the research;
- the firm does not hold itself out as having produced the research; and
- the firm verifies that the person who has produced the research is subject to the conflicts of interest requirements and the rules on the above arrangements, or has established a policy covering these requirements.

The rules are different if a firm produces **non-independent research**. That is, in summary, research that includes a **research recommendation**; this being a recommended strategy or a particular investment recommendation and the research does not otherwise comply with the conditions to ensure the independence of the research.

In this case, research is treated as a financial promotion and the rules of COBS 4 apply. Additionally, the research must include the following aspects:

- it is clearly identified as a marketing communication; and
- it contains a clear and prominent statement that it has not been prepared in accordance with the requirements for the independence of investment research, and that it is not subject to the prohibitions on dealing ahead that apply to investment research.

There is a high-level requirement to take reasonable steps to identify and manage conflicts of interest that may arise from the production of non-independent research, for example, research that is intended firstly for internal use by the firm and then later publication to clients.

Firms that prepare or disseminate **research recommendations** have to comply with detailed standards for presentation and disclosure of certain information. In summary, these are to:

- ensure that a research recommendation is fairly presented;
- disclose the firm's interests in, or any conflicts of interest concerning, the investments that are the subject of the research recommendation;
- give the name of the firm and its regulator;
- give the identity and job title of the person who prepared the research recommendation;
- ensure that facts are clearly distinguished from interpretation, estimates and opinion;
- ensure that sources are reliable or, if there is any doubt, this should be indicated;
- ensure that projections, forecasts and price targets are clearly labelled and include the main assumptions;
- ensure that the research recommendation can be substantiated as reasonable, if so requested by the FCA.

Fair presentation requires that:

- material sources are indicated, including the issuer (where relevant) and whether the recommendation has been disclosed to the issuer and amended prior to dissemination;
- basis of valuation for setting price targets are adequately summarised;
- the meaning of buy, sell, and hold, including time horizons, should be adequately explained, and include risk warnings and sensitivity analysis of the relevant assumptions;
- reference is made to planned frequency of updates to the research recommendation (if any) or any changes to coverage policy previously announced;
- the date of first release of the research recommendation, and the date and time of any prices, are given;
- any substantive difference between this and a research recommendation issued during the previous 12 months has to be clearly indicated, specifying the change and the date of the change.

The standards for **disclosure of interests** and **conflicts of interest** are:

- all relationships of the firm or affiliated company that may impair the objectivity of the research recommendation, including relationships with, or conflicts of interests with, issuers;
- relationships of legal and natural persons within the firm who were involved in the preparation of the research recommendation, including whether their remuneration is linked to investment banking transactions by the firm or affiliated company;
- any interests that may be accessible, prior to dissemination, by persons producing the research recommendation, or by any other person who could reasonably have had access to the information (other than those responsible for compliance);
- disclosures concerning a firm's (or affiliated company's) shareholdings in excess of 5% in an issuer, and any other financial interests;
- statements indicating (where relevant) that the firm is a market maker, liquidity provider, lead manager; or concerning any investment banking services, or research recommendation services, provided for the issuer;

- disclosure of the firm's arrangements for preventing conflicts of interest, including information barriers;
- if shares are acquired by a person involved in the research recommendation, the price and date of acquisition.

If compliance with the disclosure standards would be disproportionate to the length of the research presentation, the firm can indicate where the information may be found, eg, on a website page.

The following information has to be published **quarterly**, and also disclosed in research recommendations:

- the proportion of research recommendations published during the quarter that are buy hold and sell;
- the proportion of investments, in each category, issued by issuers to which the firm supplied material investment banking services during the previous 12 months.

If the firm disseminates research recommendations produced by a **third party**, it must:

- state the identity of the firm and its regulator;
- ensure that any summaries of third party recommendations are fair, clear and not misleading;
- identify the source research recommendation and identify where the third party's disclosures are accessible;
- ensure that the detailed disclosures above are made as though it had produced the recommendation itself.

If the firm materially **amends a third party recommendation** prior to dissemination, it has to:

- give a description of any alterations made by the firm prior to dissemination if there is a change of direction (eg, buy to sell) or comply with the disclosure rules concerning time horizons as though it had produced the research recommendation;
- maintain a written policy providing for recipients of the information to be directed to where they can access the third party producer, the original recommendation and the third party's disclosures.

6.3 Inducements and the Use of Dealing Commissions

Learning Objective

4.6.6 Know the application of the inducements rules [COBS 2.3.1–2 & 2.3.10–16] and the use of dealing commission, including what benefits can be supplied/obtained under such agreements [COBS 11.6]

6.3.1 Inducements

The inducements rules should be seen as payments rules as they prohibit any payment unless expressly permitted. The rules on inducements apply to firms carrying on designated investment business that is MiFID business as well non-MiFID business. The rules only apply to professional clients and retail clients, therefore, investment firms undertaking ECP business will not be subject to the detailed inducement provisions.

In relation to MiFID business, firms are prohibited from paying or accepting any fees or commissions, or providing or receiving non-money benefits, other than:

- fees, commissions or non-monetary benefits paid to or by the client, or someone on his behalf (such as management fees); or
- proper fees which are necessary for the provision of the service (eg, custody costs, legal fees, settlement fees) and which cannot by their nature give rise to conflicts;
- fees, commissions or non-monetary benefits paid to/by a third party (or someone on their behalf). These are permissible only if:
  - they do not impair compliance with the firm's duty to act in the client's best interests;
  - they are designed to enhance the quality of the service to the client; and
  - they are disclosed in accordance with set standards prior to the provisions of the service to the client.

Packaged product providers must not pay commissions on terms that are linked to the volume of business transacted, or if the recipient has a financial interest in the commission being repaid.

Reasonable non-monetary benefits that may be provided include:

- gifts, hospitality and promotional competition prizes of reasonable value;
- assistance with financial promotion;
- joint marketing exercises – the provision of product literature, Freepost envelopes, articles and news for publication;
- training, seminars and conferences;
- travel and accommodation expenses incurred in training, seminars, conferences;
- technical services and information technology.

In all cases, it is a requirement that the benefit enhances the service for the client, that such benefits are not made available to one firm and not another, and that the value of benefits is reasonable.

Firms can satisfy their disclosure obligations under these rules if they:

- disclose the essential arrangements for such payments/benefits in summary form;
- undertake to their client that further details will be disclosed on request; and
- do, in fact, give such details on request.

Firms must also keep full records of such payments/benefits made to other firms, for all MiFID business.

Since 31 December 2012, providers of retail investment products, and their associated firms, must not have any shareholdings or voting power in advisory firms and must not provide credit to such firms, other than in accordance with specified conditions, in order to prevent conflicts of interest and bias (such as the channelling of business).

6.3.2   The Use of Dealing Commissions

In addition to the general rules on inducements, there are specific rules concerning the use of dealing commission.

When an investment manager executes customer orders that relate to certain designated investments (shares, warrants, certificates representing certain securities, options and rights to, or interests in, investments of shares), it is not permitted to use client-dealing commissions, generated from dealing on behalf of its clients, to purchase goods or services, unless these goods or services relate to **execution services** or the **provision of research**.

These commission agreements are allowed only for goods or services that assist the recipient firm in providing a better service to its customers.

The rules state that an investment manager must not execute its customer orders through a broker or another person and pass the charges on to its customers, unless the investment manager has reasonable grounds to be satisfied that the goods and services in return for the charges are:

1. related to the **execution of trades** on behalf of the investment manager's customers;
2. comprise the **provision of research**; and
3. will reasonably assist the investment manager in providing services to its customers and do not (or are not likely to) impact the investment manager's duty to act in the best interests of its customers.

When the goods or services relate to the **execution of trades**, an investment manager has reasonable grounds to be satisfied that the requirements are met if the goods or services are:

1. linked to the arranging and conclusion of a specific investment transaction, or series of related transactions; and
2. provided between the point at which the investment manager makes an investment or trading decision and the point at which the investment transaction, or series of transactions, is concluded.

When the goods or services relate to the **provision of research**, an investment manager has reasonable grounds to be satisfied that the requirements are met if the research:

1. is capable of adding value to the investment or trading decisions, by providing new insight that informs the investment manager when making such decisions;
2. whatever form its output takes, represents original thought, in the critical and careful consideration and assessment of new and existing facts, and does not merely repeat or repackage what has been presented before;
3. has intellectual rigour and does not merely state what is commonplace or self-evident; and
4. involves analysis or manipulation of data to reach meaningful conclusions.

The FCA indicates that the following goods and services do not meet the requirements:

- valuation or portfolio measurement services;
- computer hardware;
- connectivity services, such as electronic networks and dedicated telephone lines;
- seminar fees;
- subscription for publications;
- travel, accommodation or entertainment costs;
- order and execution management systems;
- office administration software, such as word processing or accounting programmes;
- membership fees to professional associations;
- the purchase or rental of standard office equipment or ancillary facilities;
- employee salaries;
- direct money payments;
- publicly available information; and
- custody services (other than incidental to the execution of trades).

Furthermore, the investment manager should not enter into any arrangements that could compromise its ability to comply with its best execution obligations.

An investment manager that enters into arrangements concerning the receipt of goods or services that relate to the execution of trades or the provision of research must make adequate prior disclosure to customers. This must include the firm's policy, why it feels the need to use dealing commission to purchase goods and services and a description of those received for execution and those for research.

Additionally, investment managers must make the above disclosures periodically, eg, annually, and keep records of all prior and periodic disclosures made. The record needs to be kept for five years.

6.3.3 Providing Credit and Other Benefits to Firms that Advise on Retail Investment Products

To comply with the best interests rules, any stake held, or credit provided, by a retail investment provider in a firm providing personal recommendations to retail clients should be on commercial terms and should not attach arrangements relating to the channelling of business.

The following are considered to be reasonable and capable of enhancing the quality of the service provided to a client and, depending on the circumstances, are capable of being paid or received without breaching the client's best interests rule. However, in each case, it will be a question of fact whether these conditions are satisfied and do not breach the best interest rules.

Reasonable Non-Monetary Benefits

- **Gifts, hospitality and promotional competition prizes** – a retail investment product provider giving and a firm receiving gifts, hospitality and promotional competition prizes of a reasonable value.
- **Promotion** – a retail investment product provider assisting another firm to promote its retail investment products so that the quality of its service to clients is enhanced. Such assistance should not be of a kind or value that is likely to impair the recipient firm's ability to pay due regard to the interests of its clients, and to give advice on, and recommend, retail investment products available from the recipient firm's whole range or ranges.
- **Joint marketing exercises** – a retail investment product provider providing generic product literature (that is, letter heading, leaflets, forms and envelopes) that is suitable for use and distribution by or on behalf of another firm if the literature enhances the quality of the service to the client and is not primarily of promotional benefit to the retail investment product provider and the total costs (for example, packaging, posting, mailing lists) of distributing such literature to its client are borne by the recipient firm.

A retail investment product provider supplying another firm with 'freepost' envelopes, for forwarding such items as completed applications, medical reports or copy client agreements.

A retail investment product provider supplying product specific literature (for example, key features documents, minimum information) to another firm if the literature does not contain the name of any other firm; or if the name of the recipient firm is included, the literature enhances the quality of the service to the client and is not primarily of promotional benefit to the recipient firm.

A retail investment product provider supplying draft articles, news items and financial promotions for publication in another firm's magazine, only if in each case any costs paid by the product provider for placing the articles and financial promotions are not more than market rate, and exclude distribution costs.

- **Seminars and conferences** – a retail investment product provider taking part in a seminar organised by another firm or a third party and paying toward the cost of the seminar, if its participation is for a genuine business purpose, and the contribution is reasonable and proportionate to its participation and by reference to the time and sessions at the seminar when its staff play an active role.
- **Technical services and information technology** – this might include a retail investment product provider supplying a 'freephone' link, supplying another firm with quotations and projections relating to its retail investment products, advice on the completion of forms or other documents, access to data processing facilities, or access to data, that is related to the retail investment product provider's business and software that gives information about the retail investment product provider's retail investment products.
- **Training** – a retail investment product provider providing another firm with training facilities of any kind (for example, lectures, venue, written material and software).

- **Travel and accommodation expenses** – a retail investment product provider reimbursing another firm's reasonable travel and accommodation expenses in instances such as the other firm participating in market research conducted by or for the retail investment product provider, or attending an annual national event of a United Kingdom trade association hosted or co-hosted by the retail investment product provider.

In interpreting the above reasonable non-monetary benefits, retail investment product providers should be aware that where a benefit is made available to one firm and not another, this is more likely to impair compliance with the client's best interests rule.

6.4   Best Execution

6.4.1   The Requirement for Best Execution

Learning Objective

4.6.7   Understand the requirements of providing best execution [COBS 11.2.1–13]

The rules on best execution apply to MiFID and non-MiFID firms and business; however, there is an exemption from the requirements for firms acting in the capacity of an operator of a regulated collective scheme when purchasing or selling units/shares in that scheme.

The **best execution** rules under COBS require firms to execute orders on the terms that are most favourable to their client. Broadly, they apply where a firm owes contractual or agency obligations to its client and is acting on behalf of that client.

Specifically, they require that firms take all reasonable steps to obtain, when executing orders, the best possible result for their clients, taking into account the **execution factors**. These factors are price, costs, speed, likelihood of execution and settlement, size, nature or any other consideration relevant to the execution of an order. The relative importance of each factor will depend on the following criteria and characteristics:

- the client, including how they are categorised;
- the client order;
- the financial instruments involved; and
- the execution venues to which that order can be directed.

Best execution is not merely how to achieve the best price. Any of the other factors mentioned above should be considered and, depending on the criteria or characteristics, could be given precedence. For some transactions, for example, the likelihood of execution could be given precedence over the speed of execution. In other transactions, the direct and/or implicit execution costs of a particular venue could be so high, as to be given precedence over the price of the instrument of this venue.

The obligation to take all reasonable steps to obtain the best possible results for its clients applies to a firm which owes contractual or agency obligations to the client. The obligation to deliver the best possible result when executing client orders applies in relation to all types of financial instruments. However, given the differences in market structures or the structure of financial instruments, it may be difficult to identify and apply a uniform standard of and procedure for best execution that is effective and appropriate for all classes of instrument. Therefore, best execution obligations should be applied in a manner that takes into account all the different circumstances associated with the execution of orders related to particular types of financial instruments.

The Role of Price

For retail clients, firms must take account of the total consideration for the transaction, ie, the price of the financial instrument and the costs relating to execution, including all expenses directly related to it, such as execution venue fees, clearing and settlement fees, and any fees paid to third parties.

Best Execution Where There are Competing Execution Venues

If a firm can execute the client's order on more than one execution venue, the firm must take into account both its own costs and the costs of the relevant venues in assessing which will give the best outcome. Its own commissions should not allow it to discriminate unfairly between execution venues, and a firm should not charge a different commission or spread to clients for execution in different venues, if that difference does not reflect actual differences in the cost to the firm of executing on those venues.

6.4.2   Order Execution Policies

Learning Objective

4.6.8   Understand the requirements for an order execution policy, its disclosure, the requirements for consent and review [COBS 11.2.14–18, 11.2.22–26 & 11.2.28]

4.6.10   Understand the rules on monitoring the effectiveness of execution arrangements and policy; demonstrating compliance with the execution policy; and the duties of portfolio managers and receivers and transmitters to act in a client's best interest [COBS 11.2.27, 11.2.29–34]

Firms are required to establish an order execution policy to enable them to obtain the best possible results for their clients. This must include, for each class of financial instrument in which the firm deals, information about the different execution venues where the firm executes its client orders, and the factors that will affect the choice of venue used.

The policy must include those venues that enable the firm to obtain the best possible result for its clients consistently.

Firms must give their clients appropriate information about their execution policies; this needs to be more detailed for retail clients. Firms must obtain their clients' prior consent to their order execution policies (although this may be tacit).

Firms must review their order execution policies whenever a material event occurs, but at least annually. Firms must notify clients of any material changes to their order execution arrangements or execution policy. However, the FCA does not define the term 'material change'.

Compliance with Policies, and the Obligations on Portfolio Managers and Firms Receiving/Transmitting Orders

Firms must monitor the effectiveness of their execution arrangements and policies, to identify and (if need be) correct any deficiencies. In addition they must be able to demonstrate to their clients, on request, that they have executed their orders in accordance with their execution policy.

Portfolio managers must act in their clients' best interests when placing orders for them, on the basis of the firm's investment decisions.

Firms receiving and transmitting orders for clients must also act in their clients' best interests when transmitting those orders to other parties (eg, brokers) to execute. This means taking account of the execution factors listed in Section 6.4.1 (unless the client has given specific instructions, in which case these must be followed).

Portfolio managers, and receivers/transmitters of orders, must also maintain order execution policies, but need not get client consent to them.

The policy must identify, in respect of each class of instruments, the entities with which the orders are placed or to which they transmit orders for execution. The entities must have execution arrangements that enable the firm to comply with its obligations under the best execution requirements, when it places an order with or transmits an order to that entity for execution.

6.4.3 Specific Client Instructions

Learning Objective

4.6.9   Understand the rules on following specific instructions from a client [COBS 11.2.19–21]

Wherever a firm receives a specific instruction from a client, it must execute the order as instructed. It will be deemed to have satisfied its obligation to obtain the **best possible result** if it follows such specific instructions (even if an alternative means of executing the order would have given a better result).

Firms should not induce clients to instruct an order in a particular way, by expressly indicating or implicitly suggesting the content of the instruction to the client, if they know that any instruction to the client will have the likely effect of preventing them from obtaining the best possible result for the client.

6.5   Client Order Handling

Learning Objective

4.6.11   Understand the rule on client order handling [COBS 11.3.1] and the conditions to be satisfied when carrying out client orders [COBS 11.3.2–6]

Firms must apply procedures and arrangements which provide for the prompt, fair and expeditious execution of client orders, relative to the other orders or trading interests of the firm. (Note, you should see that this rule is also consistent with the need for firms to avoid conflicts of interest, where possible.)

In particular, these should allow comparable client orders to be executed in the order in which they are received.

Firms should ensure that:

- executed client orders are promptly and accurately recorded and allocated;
- comparable orders are executed sequentially and promptly, unless this is impracticable or client interests require otherwise;
- retail clients are informed of any material difficulty in the prompt execution of their order, promptly on the firm becoming aware of this;
- if the firm is responsible for overseeing or arranging settlement, that the assets or money are delivered promptly and correctly.

Firms must not misuse information relating to client orders and must also take steps to prevent its abuse (eg, in order to profit by dealing on its own account).

6.6   Aggregation and Allocation

Learning Objective

4.6.12   Understand the rules on aggregation and allocation of orders [COBS 11.3.7–8]; and the rules on aggregation and allocation of transactions for own account [COBS 11.3.9–13]

Firms must only aggregate their own-account deals with those of a client, or aggregate two or more clients' deals, if:

- this is unlikely to disadvantage any of the aggregated clients;
- the fact that aggregation may work to their disadvantage is disclosed to the clients; and
- an order allocation policy has been established which provides (in sufficiently precise terms) for the fair allocation of transactions. This must cover how volume and price of orders will affect allocation; it must also cover how partial allocations will be dealt with.

If an aggregated order is only partly executed, the firm must then allocate the various trades in order with this allocation policy.

If a firm has their own-account deals in an aggregated order along with those of clients, it must not allocate them in a way which is detrimental to the clients. In particular, it must allocate the client orders in priority over its own, unless it can show that, without the inclusion of its own order, less favourable terms would have been obtained; in these circumstances, it may allocate the deals proportionately.

The firm's order allocation policy must incorporate procedures preventing the reallocation of own-account orders, aggregated with client orders, in a way detrimental to a client. The reallocation shall be considered detrimental to a client if an effect of it is to give unfair preference to the firm or any particular person.

6.7 Client Limit Orders

Learning Objective

4.6.13 Know the rules on client limit orders – the obligation to make unexecuted client limit orders public [COBS 11.4]

Unless the client instructs otherwise, a firm which receives a client limit order for shares listed on a regulated market and which cannot immediately execute it under the prevailing market conditions must make the limit order public (in a manner easily accessible to other market participants) immediately so that it can be executed as soon as possible. (It need not do so, however, for orders over normal market size.) It may do this by:

- transmitting the order to a regulated market or MTF operating an order book trading system; or
- ensuring the order is made public and can be easily executed as soon as market conditions allow.

6.8 Personal Account Dealing

Learning Objective

4.6.14 Understand the purpose and application of the personal account dealing rule and the restrictions on personal account dealing [COBS 11.7.1–3]

4.6.15 Know the arrangements required to comply with the personal account dealing rules including the notification requirements; and exceptions regarding personal account dealing [COBS 11.7.4–7]

6.8.1 The Application and Purpose of the Personal Account Dealing Rules

Firms must have arrangements in place to prevent their employees who are relevant persons (directors, partners of the firm or its appointed representatives, and other personnel involved in regulated activities either directly or via an outsourcing arrangement) from:

1. entering into a personal transaction that is contrary to the MAD; involves misuse or improper disclosure of confidential information; or conflicts with the firm's duties to a customer;
2. improperly advising or procuring that anyone else enters into a transaction that (if it had been done by the employee himself) would have fallen foul of 1. above or of a relevant provision; or
3. improperly disclosing information or opinion, if he knows or should know that the person to whom he has disclosed it is likely to enter into a transaction that (if it had been done by the employee himself) would have fallen foul of 1. above or of a relevant provision, or encouraging someone else to do so.

The relevant provisions are:

*   the rules on personal account transactions undertaken by financial analysts contained elsewhere in COBS (these rules were explained in Section 6.2.3);
*   the rules on the misuse of information relating to pending client orders (which were explained in Section 6.5).

Firms must keep records of all personal transactions notified to them, and of any authorisation or prohibition made in connection with them.

6.8.2 Compliance with, and Exceptions to, the Personal Account Dealing Rules

The arrangements must ensure that the affected employees are aware of the restrictions on personal transactions, and of the firm's procedures in this regard. They must be such that the firm is informed promptly of any such personal transaction, either by notification of it or some other procedure enabling the firm to identify it.

If outsourcing takes place, the arrangements must be such that the outsource maintains a record of personal transactions undertaken by any relevant person and provides it to the firm promptly on request.

The rules on personal account dealing do not apply to:

*   deals under a discretionary management service, if there is no prior communication between the portfolio manager and the relevant person (or any other person for whose account the transaction is being executed) about the deal;
*   deals in units/shares in certain classes of fund, where the relevant person (and any other person for whom the deals are effected) is not involved in the management of the fund;
*   personal transactions in life policies.

Personnel (other than directors or partners of a firm or its appointed representatives) are only subject to the personal account dealing rules to the extent that they are involved in the provision of the firm's investment or portfolio management services.

The restrictions do not apply separately to each transaction in a succession that are being carried out in accordance with a prior instruction, unless the instruction is changed or a new instruction is issued. Nor do they apply if the instruction is withdrawn, so long as the investments that had been acquired are not disposed of at the same time as the instruction is withdrawn.

7.   Reporting to Clients

7.1   Confirmation of Transactions and Periodic Statements

Learning Objective

4.7.1   Know general client reporting and occasional reporting requirements (COBS 16.1–16.2)

4.7.2   Know the rules on periodic reporting to retail and professional clients, the exceptions to the requirements and the record-keeping requirements [COBS 16.3]

7.1.1   Transaction Reporting

Firms are required to ensure that clients receive adequate reports on the services they provide to them. These must include any associated costs.

If a firm (other than one managing investments – see Section 7.1.2 below) carries out an order for a client it must:

- provide the essential information on the execution of the order, promptly and in a durable medium;
- for retail clients only, send the **trade confirmation information** as soon as possible (but no later than on the next business day); if the confirmation is received from a third party, the firm must pass the details on no later than the business day following receipt;
- provide clients with information about the status of their orders on request.

It need not do this if the same details are already being sent to the client by another person.

There are also some exceptions to the above rules eg, for a series of orders executed in funds, where the firm may report all the trades once every six months. Also, for non-MiFID business, eg, if the client has confirmed that confirmations need not be sent, or for transactions in life policies or personal pensions, or if the investment is held within a Junior ISA (JISA).

Trade confirmation information includes:

- the firm's identification;
- name/designation of the client;
- trading day and time;
- type of order;
- venue and instrument identification;
- buy/sell indicator or the nature of the order if not buy/sell;
- quantity, price and total consideration;
- total commission and expenses, including mark-up or mark-down (if relevant);
- rate of exchange (if relevant);
- client's responsibilities for settlement;
- statement that the firm was the client's counterparty (if relevant).

Firms must keep copies of all confirmations sent to clients:

- for MiFID business, for at least five years from the date of despatch;
- for other business, for at least three years from the date of despatch.

For the purpose of calculating the unit price in the trade confirmation information, when the order is executed in tranches, firms may supply clients with the information about the price of each tranche or the average price.

7.1.2 Periodic Reporting

The reporting rules for firms providing investment management services are addressed in the FCA's **periodic reporting** rules. Investment managers must provide retail and professional clients with periodic statements, unless another party provides these.

For retail clients only, the statement must contain prescribed information (periodic information), being:

- the name of the firm;
- the name/designation of the retail client's account;
- the contents and valuation of the portfolio, including each investment and its value, cash balance at the beginning and end of the period, and performance;
- total amount of charges, itemised to show management fees and execution costs, together with a note that a more detailed breakdown can be provided on request;
- a comparison of the firm's performance against the relevant benchmark(s);
- total amount of dividends, interest and other payments received;
- information about corporate actions.

Periodic statements must be sent to the retail client at least six-monthly, with the following exceptions:

- the retail client may request statements three-monthly instead (the firm must advise the client of this right);
- if the client receives deal-by-deal confirmations, and certain higher-risk investments are excluded, the statement may be sent every 12 months;
- if the client has authorised that their portfolio be leveraged, the statement must be provided monthly.

If a retail client elects to receive deal-by-deal confirmation, the investment manager must comply with the transaction reporting rules above for prescribed content and timing of the report.

For professional clients, the firm must promptly provide essential information relating to each deal.

A firm must make and retain a copy of any periodic statement:

- for MiFID business, for a period of at least five years;
- for other business, for a period of at least three years.

There are also exceptions for certain overseas customers and in respect of JISAs.

If firms manage investments for retail clients, or operate certain types of account for them which include uncovered open positions, they must report any losses over a pre-agreed limit to the client. They must do so by the end of the business day on which the limit is breached; if this happens on a non-business day, by the end of the next business day.

8. Client Assets

8.1 The Purpose of the Client Money and Custody Rules

Learning Objective

4.8.1 Understand the purpose of the client money and custody rules in CASS including the requirement for segregation and that it is held in trust [CASS 6.2.1–3; 7.12.1–2; 7.13.2/3/5/12]

The rules relating to the custody and safeguarding of client money and client assets are contained in the Client Assets Sourcebook (CASS). They exist to ensure that firms take adequate steps to protect those client assets for which they are responsible.

CASS, in general, applies to every firm, with some specific exemptions (see Section 8.3). CASS applies directly in respect of activities conducted with or for all categories of client, ie, retail clients, professional clients and ECPs.

CASS 6 contains the custody rules that apply when a firm holds financial instruments of a client in the course of MiFID business and when it is safeguarding and administering investments in the course of non-MiFID business.

CASS 7 (Client Money and Distribution Rules) applies to a MiFID investment firm either:

- when it holds client money in the course of its MiFID business or in respect of any investment agreement entered into, or to be entered into, with or for a client; or
- when, in the course of non-MiFID business, it opts to comply with the MiFID client money rules.

Firms must, when holding safe custody assets belonging to clients, make adequate arrangements, so as to safeguard clients' ownership rights, especially in the event of the firm's insolvency and to prevent the use of safe custody assets belonging to a client on the firm's own account, except with the client's express consent. Firms must also introduce adequate organisational arrangements to minimise the risk of loss or diminution of client's safe custody assets.

The firm must effect correct registration of legal title to the assets in the name of the client, nominee or other authorised person as appropriate to the nature of the service being provided. If a firm owns a nominee, it must accept the same level of responsibility for the nominee as though the firm held the assets.

The firm must have robust organisational arrangements to prevent the misuse or loss of client money.

Within CASS, there is a requirement to segregate client money from any other money held by the firm. This is aimed at ensuring that, if the firm fails, money will not be used to repay its creditors. Usually, this is done by ensuring that it is placed promptly in a separately designated client money account with a bank and ensuring that the bank treats it as separate from the firm's own. This is achieved by the firm holding the client money in trust. The trust is a statutory trust, created by CASS 7.7.2R.

When a client bank account is opened, the firm must send a notice to the bank about the trust, and state that the bank may not combine money in the client account with any other accounts held in the name of the firm. The title of the client account must distinguish it from any other account held by the firm. In the case of client bank accounts in the UK the bank must acknowledge this arrangement within 20 days, otherwise the firm must withdraw the money and deposit it with another bank as soon as possible.

There are a number of circumstances when the client money rules will not apply, for example where money is held in connection with a delivery versus payment (DvP) transaction (unless the DvP does not occur by the close of business on the third business day following the date of payment of a delivery obligation) or where it becomes due and payable to the firm.

The latest proposed enhancement to the Client Assets regime is the recent FCA Consultation Paper (13/5) *'Review of the client assets regime for investment business'*.

This consultation paper is designed to address the need to balance the speedy return of client assets with the need to ensure accurate distribution. The FCA has proposed that upon the failure of a firm, the initial distribution of client assets should be allowed on the basis of the firm's own records, from an initial client money pool, CMP1. Any residual money after initial distribution would go into a second pool, CMP2, which would then be distributed by the firm on the basis of its own claims process.

The consultation paper contains detailed provisions about the day-to-day handling of client money as well as matters concerning insolvency. The proposal includes the treatment of delivery versus payment (DvP) transactions, what can be done with unclaimed client assets, reconciliations and buffers, and record-keeping.

Also provided are two new proforma documents: the client assets disclosure document and the acknowledgement letter for banks.

The FCA has stated that the client assets disclosure document is intended to act as a tool by which clients are reminded of the arrangements in place for the protection of their assets. It is also intended to be a single-source record of the contractual arrangements a firm may have in place which could impact a client's rights to, or interests in, client assets.

Whilst not a new requirement to achieve 'trust' status, the FCA has formally proposed to require firms to obtain an acknowledgement letter for all client bank accounts (not just those located in the UK), and a new requirement to remove the 20 business days grace period for firms to obtain a duly counter-signed acknowledgment letter (in effect, prohibiting the placement of client money into an account until the relevant acknowledgement letter has been signed and returned to the firm).

The FCA has committed (in its 2014 Business Plan) to continue with its review of the client assets regime for investment business and to publish new rules to strengthen existing protections for consumers and enhance the integrity of UK financial markets.

8.2 The Requirement to Reconcile

Learning Objective

4.8.2 Know the requirements for reconciling client assets and client money including the timing and identification of discrepancies [CASS 6.6.11/13/16/17/19/22/24/27/28/34/37/44/54; 7.15.5/20/22/29/31/32/33]

8.2.1 Reconciliation of Safe Custody Assets

Firms must keep such records and accounts as necessary to enable them at any time and without delay to distinguish safe custody assets held for one client from safe custody assets held for any other client, and from the firm's own assets.

CASS 6.5 sets out the obligations of firms to perform internal and external reconciliations on safe custody assets.

Internal reconciliations should be carried out as often as necessary between the records of safe custody assets held for each client and the records of safe custody assets held by the firm and by third parties.

Broadly, external reconciliations should be made as often as necessary to ensure the accuracy of a firm's records and accounts, between its internal accounts and records and those of any third parties by whom those safe custody assets are held. If possible, someone who has not been involved in the production or maintenance of the records being reconciled should do them.

If the reconciliation shows a discrepancy, the firm must make good (or provide the equivalent of) any shortfall for which it is responsible. If another person is responsible, the firm should take reasonable steps to resolve the position with that person.

Firms must inform the FCA without delay of any failure to comply with the reconciliation requirements, including reconciliation discrepancies and making good any such differences.

Firms that hold client assets and money are required to have an external audit and report on the systems and controls. The firm's auditor must conduct this report at least annually and send it to the FCA within four months of the date of the audit.

8.2.2 Reconciliation of Client Money

Firms must keep such records and accounts as necessary to enable them at any time and without delay to distinguish client money held for one client from client money held for any other client, and from their own money.

CASS 7.6 sets out the obligations of firms to perform internal and external reconciliations on client money.

Internal Client Money Reconciliations

As explained in CASS 7.6.6G, in complying with its obligations under CASS 7.6.2R (Records and accounts), and where relevant SYSC 4.1.1R (General organisational requirements) and SYSC 6.1.1R (Compliance), firms should carry out internal reconciliations of records and accounts of client money the firm holds in client bank accounts and client transaction accounts. The FCA considers the following method of reconciliation to be appropriate for these purposes (the standard method of internal client money reconciliation):

- Each business day, a firm that adopts the **normal approach** should check whether its client money resource, being the aggregate balance on the firm's client bank accounts, as at the close of business on the previous business day, was at least equal to the client money requirement as at the close of business on that day.
- Each business day, a firm that adopts the **alternative approach** should ensure that its client money resource, being the aggregate balance on the firm's client bank accounts, as at the close of business on that business day is at least equal to the client money requirement as at the close of business on the previous business day. No excess or shortfall should arise when adopting the alternative approach.

For the purposes of performing its reconciliations of records and accounts, a firm should use the values contained in its accounting records, for example its cash book, rather than values contained in statements received.

If a reconciliation shows a discrepancy, the firm must investigate to identify the reason for the discrepancy and ensure that either any shortfall is paid into the client bank account or any excess is withdrawn from the client bank account by close of business on the day the reconciliation is performed.

A remittance made up of client money and money intended to pay the firm's fees is classified as client money. The FCA has set a method of reconciliation of client money balances called the **standard method of client reconciliation**.

External Reconciliations

This means cross-checking the internal client money accounts against the records of third parties (for example, banks) with whom client money is held. Firms must perform external reconciliations as often as is necessary and as soon as reasonably practicable after the date to which the reconciliation relates.

If there is a discrepancy, the firm must investigate and correct it as soon as possible. If it cannot do so and the firm should be holding a greater amount of client money, it must pay its own money into the client bank account pending resolution of the discrepancy, which it must correct as soon as possible.

If a firm has not complied with these requirements, or is for some reason unable to comply in a material aspect with a particular requirement, it must inform the FCA in writing.

The FCA believes that an adequate method of reconciling client money balances with external records is as follows:

- A reconciliation of a client bank account as recorded by the firm with the statement issued by the bank (or other form of confirmation issued by the bank).
- A reconciliation of the balance on each client transaction account as recorded by the firm, with the balance of that account as set out in the statement (or other form of confirmation) issued by the person with whom the account is held.

8.3   The Exemptions from CASS

Learning Objective

4.8.3   Know the exemptions from the requirements of the CASS rules [CASS 1.2.3–4; 6.1.1–6; 6.2.10/13/14/15; 7.1.1–10 & 7.1.12]

CASS does not apply to:

- ICVCs;
- incoming EEA firms other than insurers, for their passported activities;
- UCITS-qualifying schemes;
- a credit institution (eg, a bank) under the Banking Consolidation Directive (BCD), in relation to deposits held in accounts with themselves;
- coins held for the value of their metal;
- money held in connection with a DvP transaction (unless payment does not occur after three business days);
- money due and payable to the firm;
- if a firm carries on business in its name but on behalf of the client where that is required by the very nature of the transaction and the client is in agreement;
- the custody rules (CASS 6) and the client money rules (CASS 7) do not apply if a client transfers full ownership of a safe custody asset or client money to a firm for the purpose of securing or otherwise covering present or future, actual contingent or prospective obligations.

Specific rules within CASS may be disapplied depending on the nature of a firm's activities; the details are set out within the individual rules.

8.4   Enhancing the Client Money and Assets (CASS) Regime

Several changes have been added to the CASS regime designed to enhance consumer protection by improving governance and oversight in the holding of client money and assets.

- **Prime brokerage – increased rehypothecation disclosure and transparency** – each prime brokerage agreement must include a disclosure annex that summarises contractual re-hypothecation provisions. Prime brokers must also offer clients daily reporting.
- **Restricting the placement of client money deposits within a group** – there is a 20% limit on the amount of client money which can be deposited intra-group.

- **Prohibiting the use of general liens in custodian agreements** – there is a prohibition on general or omnibus liens, the only exceptions being liens relating to charges and liabilities properly incurred as a result of the provision of custody services: intra-day payments, contractual settlement and standing credit lines.
- **CASS classification** – CASS firms are classified according to the amount of client money and assets held. Large CASS firms are firms holding more than £1 billion of client money or more than £100 billion of client assets; medium CASS firms are those holding between £1 million and £1 billion of client money or between £10 million and £100 billion of client assets; and small CASS firms are those holding less than £1 million of client money or less than £10 million of client assets.
- **Client money and assets return (CMAR)** – submitted monthly by large and medium CASS firms. The return includes detailed information on a firm's holding of client money and client assets such as:
  - balances of client money and assets;
  - institutions where the client money and assets are held and amounts;
  - information on internal and external reconciliations;
  - information on outsourcing arrangements;
  - CASS breaches.
- **CASS operational oversight controlled function (CF10A)** – this significant influence function has been established for large and medium CASS firms. This is a required function that can only be held by one person with the firm. This requirement is modified for small CASS firms (see above) and these firms can allocate this responsibility to their existing holder of the oversight function or any significant influence function holder, providing that they make a record of this decision.

A specialist unit within the FCA – the Client Assets Unit (CASS Unit) – has specific responsibility for the supervision of the client assets regime.

On 7 July 2013, the FCA published a consultation paper (CP13/5) on proposed changes to the rules in relation to client money, custody assets and mandates over client money. This paper follows the CP12/22 which was published in September 2012 and was entitled *Client Assets Regime: EMIR, Multiple Pools and the Wider Review*. The FCA's proposals aimed to enhance its client assets regime to achieve better results for consumers and increase confidence in financial markets. These changes would affect firms that are subject to the Client Money and Assets Sourcebook (CASS) of the FCA Handbook.

One of the key proposals relates to changes to the existing client money distribution regime on the insolvency of an investment firm following on from the collapse of Lehman's, MF Global and others.

Following earlier consultation noted above, the FCA significantly revised the UK Client Assets Protection Regime (CASS) when it published Policy Statement 14/9 on 10 June 2014. The revised rules will have a significant impact on banks, brokers and asset managers. It also proposed changes to how ISA managers comply with the CASS regime in Consultation Paper 14/9 on 11 June 2014. The revised CASS rules will come into force in stages. Some rules took effect on 1 July 2014.

On 1 December 2014, rules that require repapering of client documentation came into force. Firms have until 1 June 2015 to implement some of the rules that are likely to require significant IT systems changes.

For ease of reference, the area of greatest change can be grouped in broad categories:

- **Title Transfer Collateral Arrangements (TTCAs)**

  Without major change to the existing provisions, for TTCAs the final rules state that the arrangement must be set out in a written agreement covering *'the client's agreement to the terms of the TTCA, any terms under which ownership of the client's assets or monies may transfer back from the firm to the client, and any terms for the termination of the TTCA or for the overall agreement through which the TTCA was agreed'.*

- **Custody Assets Reconciliations**

  Firms that hold custody assets will be required to undertake an **internal custody record check** being either internal custody reconciliation or an internal systems evaluation. Furthermore, firms are required to undertake a physical assets reconciliation (where applicable) and an external custody reconciliation. The adequacy of such systems will be reported on as part of the client assets report by the CASS auditor.

  To use the **internal custody reconciliation method** firms will need to maintain two sets of internal records:

  - a **client-specific safe custody asset record**; and
  - an **aggregate safe custody asset record**.

- **Client Money Reconciliations**

  The two existing standard methods of internal client money reconciliation have been retained, with a restriction on who can use the **net negative add-back** method. While the 'net negative add-back' method for the internal client money reconciliation has been retained for most asset management firms although the FCA does not appear to consider this a proper method and has indicated that it may consult on removing this in the future.

  Firms may wish to consider how they may be able to develop their systems to use the other standard method **individual client balance**. The 'individual client balance' method the FCA will allow firms to calculate each individual client balance on a product-by-product or business line basis instead of the previous requirement for it to be based on the entire firm's holdings for an individual client, with an appropriate level of reasoning or justification.

  External client money reconciliations will be required at least monthly but for those firms that undertake daily transactions in client money a daily external client money reconciliation is required.

- **DvP Window – Commercial settlement systems**

  In respect of the DvP window for transactions settled through a commercial settlement system the basic requirements have not changed but the new rules now require a firm to ensure each client agrees to the holding of its assets or monies within the DvP window. The agreement needs to be documented in writing and retained.

- **DvP window – Regulated Collective Investment Schemes**

  This window has been reduced from four days to one-day rather than removed completely as was suggested in earlier consultation discussions. The wording of the one day window is different to that of the four-day window and is based largely on when money/assets are received. This also needs to be documented.

- **Unbreakable Term Deposits**

  A 30-day limit for client money on unbreakable term deposits has been introduced.

- **Acknowledgement Letters**

  Trust acknowledgement letters for client money bank accounts will need to be in a standard form and on firm headed paper for both UK and non-UK accounts. All accounts will need to include the term 'client' in their title and be specifically identified in the body of the acknowledgement letter. Firms will have until 1 June 2015 to re-paper existing letters.

A firm will not be able to put client money into a new client money account until a signed acknowledgement letter is received back from the bank concerned. The 20-day grace period for UK accounts and the 'flexibility' on non-UK accounts is no longer valid.

- **CAMPSA**

  For clearing firms in respect of the use of house accounts for mixed payments and receipts. There has been the introduction of 'CAMPSA' – Clearing Arrangement Mandatory Prudent Segregation Amount, which needs to be 'calculated and adjusted' at least quarterly.

- **Cleared Funds**

  The FCA described its approach as *'instead of creating a general restriction on the ability of firms to undertake business for clients with their money until that money has cleared into a client bank account, the final rules set out explicit guidance that states that a firm should ensure its organisational arrangements are adequate to minimise the risk that client money held by the firm may be paid for the account of a client whose money is yet to be received by the firm'*. This allows firms to decide, together with an appropriate supporting policy and documentation of process.

- **Independent Auditor Reports**

  Whilst a report is not required for non-standard client assets reconciliation it is still required for the use of the Alternative Approach to client money segregation including a reconfirm for those that currently use this approach reflecting the impact of new requirements imposed by the policy statement (PS), in particular the Mandatory Prudent Segregation Amount (MPSA). Firms will be required to calculate the MPSA at least every quarter.

- **Record Keeping**

  A number of record keeping requirements have been clarified or amended. As an example, the FCA will expect firms to be able to determine the total amount of client money they should be holding for each client within two business days of having taken a decision to do so, or at the request of the FCA. While some firms will have systems that do this, some organisation may face a challenge in creating what is effectively a 'single customer view'.

- **Client Assets Disclosure Document**

  Some firms will be pleased that the Client Assets Disclosure Document (CADD) has been put on the back burner, at least for the time being (paragraph 9.31). The FCA has not ruled out further consultation on the *'topic of reporting and providing information to clients on client assets'*.

End of Chapter Questions

Think of an answer to each question and refer to the appropriate section for confirmation.

1. What is the impact of location on the application of the COBS rules?
   Answer Reference: Section 1.2

2. What activities are subject to the COBS rules?
   Answer Reference: Section 1.3

3. Which COBS rules are disapplied for firms undertaking ECP business?
   Answer Reference: Section 1.3

4. Do appointed representatives have to comply with the COBS rules?
   Answer Reference: Section 1.4

5. What types of conversations must be recorded?
   Answer Reference: Section 1.6

6. How will a MiFID firm classify its client in relation to non-MiFID business?
   Answer Reference: Section 2.1.1

7. What are the three client categories?

   Answer Reference: Section 2.1.3

8. What are the criteria for reclassifying a retail client as an elective professional client?
   Answer Reference: Section 2.1.5

9. Who are elective eligible counterparties?
   Answer Reference: Section 2.1.5

10. What are the notification requirements to clients on their client categorisation?
    Answer Reference: Section 2.1.7

11. What information must be disclosed prior to providing services?
    Answer Reference: Section 2.3.1

12. When is a firm required to provide a client agreement?
    Answer Reference: Section 2.3.2

13. What is the purpose of the financial promotion rules?
    Answer Reference: Section 3.1.1

14. Which two of the Principles for Businesses are amplified by the financial promotion rules?
    Answer Reference: Section 3.1.1

15. What types of communication are subject to the fair, clear and not misleading communication rule?
    Answer Reference: Section 3.1.1

16. List the main exceptions to the financial promotion rules.
    Answer Reference: Section 3.2

17. When do the prospectus advertisements rules apply?
    Answer Reference: Section 3.4

18. When is a firm permitted to cold call retail clients?
    Answer Reference: Section 3.8.2

19. What are the rules on churning and who they do they apply to?
    Answer Reference: Section 4.1.1

20. What is the purpose of the suitability rules for retail clients?
    Answer Reference: Section 4.2.1

21. What is the appropriateness test?
    Answer Reference: Section 4.3.1

22. What is the purpose of the cancellation rules?
    Answer Reference: Section 5.2

23. State four steps a firm could take to manage conflicts of interest.
    Answer Reference: Section 6.2

24. What is the difference between investment research and research recommendations?
    Answer Reference: Section 6.2.3

25. What payments are permitted under the inducements rules?
    Answer Reference: Section 6.3.1

26. What is the purpose of the best execution requirements?
    Answer Reference: Section 6.4.1

27. What is an order execution policy?
    Answer Reference: Section 6.4.2

28. What is the purpose of the personal account dealing rules?
    Answer Reference: Section 6.8.1

29. What is trade confirmation information?
    Answer Reference: Section 7.1.1

30. How frequently must a periodic statement be sent to a retail client?
    Answer Reference: Section 7.1.2

31.   What is the purpose of the client money segregation and trust rules?
      Answer Reference: Section 8.1

32.   What are the reconciliation requirements for safe custody investments and client money?
      Answer Reference: Section 8.2.1

Chapter Five

Complaints and Redress

This syllabus area will provide approximately 3 of the 75 examination questions

1. Complaints

1.1 The Purpose of the Rules

It is almost inevitable that customers will raise complaints against a firm; sometimes these complaints will be valid and sometimes they will not. The FCA requires authorised firms to deal with all complaints promptly and fairly, and there are additional requirements for handling complaints from persons who are eligible to subsequently take their grievance to the Financial Ombudsman Service (FOS).

1.2 Procedures

Learning Objective

5.1.1   Know the procedures a firm must implement and follow to handle customer complaints [DISP 1.2.1/3, 1.3.3, 1.4.1, 1.6.1/2/5, 1.9.1, 1.10.1]

The FCA requires firms to have appropriate written procedures for handling expressions of dissatisfaction from **eligible complaints** (see Section 1.3). However, a firm is able to apply these procedures to other complainants as well, if it chooses to. These procedures should be followed regardless of whether the complaint is oral or written, and whether the complaint is justified or not, as long as it relates to the firm's provision of (or failure to provide) a financial service.

These internal complaints-handling procedures should provide for:

- the receiving of complaints;
- responding to complaints;
- appropriately investigating complaints; and
- notifying eligible complainants of their right to go to the FOS where relevant. You should remember that we looked at the FOS, and its relationship with the FCA, in Chapter 1.

The complaints-handling rules are contained in the **Disputes Resolution: Complaints Sourcebook (DISP 1)** which is entitled: **Treating Complainants Fairly**. This chapter of DISP contains rules and guidance on how respondents should deal promptly and fairly with complaints in respect of business carried on from establishments in the UK or by branches of UK firms in other EEA states.

In order to aid consumer awareness of the protections offered by the regulatory system, firms must:

- publish appropriate summary details of their internal process for resolving complaints and of the right of eligible complainants to take unresolved complaints to the FOS;
- refer eligible complainants in writing to the availability of these summary details at, or immediately after, the point of sale; and
- provide such summary details in writing on request and when acknowledging a complaint.

These provisions are the **Consumer Awareness Rules (DISP 1.2)**.

The **Complaints Handling Rules** are set out in **DISP 1.3** and require firms to have effective and transparent procedures for the reasonable and prompt handling of all complaints, without charge to a complainant. These procedures should allow complaints to be made by any reasonable means, and recognise the need for resolution. Firms must put in place appropriate management controls and take reasonable steps to ensure that when handling complaints they identify and remedy any recurring of systemic problems, for example, by establishing formal processes for:

- identifying the root causes of complaints and common root causes of complaints about particular products or services;
- analysing how many complaints are resolved within one business day of receipt;
- considering whether root causes may also affect other processes or products, including those not directly complained of: and
- correcting, where reasonable to do so, such root causes and prioritising how they are dealt with;
- providing regular reports to senior personnel on recurring or systemic problems;
- keeping records of analysis, and of senior personnel response to management information on root causes of complaints.

The **Complaints Resolution Rules (DISP 1.4)** state that, once a firm has received a complaint, it must investigate the complaint competently, diligently and impartially, obtaining additional information as necessary. It must assess fairly, consistently and promptly:

- the subject matter of the complaint;
- whether the complaint should be upheld;
- what remedial action or redress (or both) may be appropriate; and
- if appropriate, whether it has reasonable grounds to be satisfied that another firm may be solely or jointly responsible for the matter alleged in the complaint.

The following factors may be relevant when assessing a complaint:

- all the evidence available and the particular circumstances of the complaint;
- similarities with other complaints received by the firm;
- relevant guidance published by the FCA, other relevant regulators or the FOS; and
- analysis of FOS decisions.

The firm must offer redress or remedial action when it decides this is appropriate and explain to the complainant promptly, and in a way that is fair, clear and not misleading, its assessment of the complaint, its decision on it and any offer of remedial action or redress. Finally, it should comply promptly with any offer of remedial action or redress accepted by the complainant.

1.3 Eligible Complainants

Learning Objectives

5.1.1 Know the procedures a firm must implement and follow to handle customer complaints [DISP 1.2.1/3, 1.3.3, 1.4.1, 1.6.1/2/5, 1.9.1, 1.10.1]

5.1.3 Know the criteria for a complainant to be eligible to lodge a complaint [DISP 2.2]

Not all complainants will have the right to subsequently take their grievance to the FOS. Access to the FOS depends on whether the circumstances fall within the FOS jurisdiction (see below) and whether the complainant is an **eligible complainant**.

Eligible complainants are:

- **consumers** – any person using or contemplating using the services of an authorised firm or an appointed representative;
- **micro-enterprises** – any person engaged in economic activity, irrespective of legal form, employing fewer than ten persons and having a turnover or balance sheet not exceeding €2 million at the time the complaint is raised;
- **charities** with an annual income of less than £1 million at the time the complaint is raised; and
- **a trustee of a trust** with a net asset value of less than £1 million at the time the complaint is raised.

A further condition for eligibility is that the complaint must arise out of a business relationship with the firm. For example, they are a customer, or they have a beneficial interest in a pension scheme, or they are a policyholder.

Other authorised firms are generally not eligible complainants, although they may be eligible if the complaint is in respect of an activity for which they do not have permission themselves.

ECPs and professional clients (other than a trustee of a pension scheme) are generally not eligible complainants, but they may be so if the complaint was about an activity other than that for which they are classified.

1.4 Stages and Timings

The FCA sets certain standards which must be observed when a firm receives a complaint. These should be reflected in a firm's internal complaints handling procedures, as follows. On receipt of a complaint, a firm must:

- send the complainant a prompt written acknowledgement that the complaint is being dealt with;
- keep the complainant informed of progress;
- within eight weeks, send a written to response to the complainant. This will either be a **final response** or a holding response.

A **final response** does one of the following:

- accepts the complaint and offers redress or remedial action; or
- offers redress or remedial action without accepting the complaint; or
- rejects the complaint and gives reasons for doing so;

The final response must also:

- inform the complainant that if they are still dissatisfied they may refer the matter to the FOS and they should do this within six months; and
- include a copy of the FOS leaflet.

If the firm is not able to send a final response within eight weeks it must send a written response that:

- explains why the firm is not yet able to make a final response and indicate when this will be provided;
- informs the complainant that they may now refer the matter to FOS;
- includes the FOS leaflet.

1.5   Record-Keeping and Reporting

Records must be kept in relation to complaints, both for FCA monitoring purposes and to enable the firm to co-operate fully with the FOS, if necessary. These should include:

- the name of the complainant;
- the substance of the complaint; and
- the measures taken for the resolution of the complaint.

The records must be retained for a minimum of five years from the date the complaint was received if the complaint relates to MiFID business, and three years for all other complaints.

The FCA requires firms to provide it with twice-yearly reports on the following:

- complaints opened;
- complaints closed within four or eight weeks;
- complaints closed after eight weeks; and
- amounts of redress paid.

Firms receiving 500 or more reportable complaints in a six-month reporting period are obliged to publish specified data. The FCA produces a report based on the firm's published data.

2. The Financial Ombudsman Service (FOS)

Learning Objective

5.1.2 Know the role of the Financial Ombudsman Service (FOS) [DISP Complaints Sourcebook – Dispute Resolution: Complaints: Introduction] and the awards which can be made [DISP 3.7.2/4]

2.1 The Role of the FOS

Under the provisions of FSMA, the FCA has the power to make rules relating to the handling of complaints (outlined in Section 1) and an independent body has been established to administer and operate a dispute resolution scheme. The dispute resolution scheme is known as the Financial Ombudsman Service (FOS), and the body that operates it is the Financial Ombudsman Service Ltd. The FOS is designed to resolve complaints about financial services firms quickly and with minimum formality. Importantly, it is free to complainants, which removes the deterrent effect of anxiety over legal costs. The FOS does not replace the court system, however, and any complainant is entitled to take civil action against a firm regardless of whether or not the complaint has been considered by the FOS.

2.2 Compulsory versus Voluntary Jurisdictions

The FOS comprises two jurisdictions:

1. Its **compulsory jurisdiction (CJ)** extends to complaints from eligible complainants against FCA-authorised firms in relation to their regulated activities (and any ancillary activities) which the firm is unable to resolve to the satisfaction of the complainant within the timescales outlined above. Authorised firms are automatically subject to the compulsory jurisdiction.
2. Its **voluntary jurisdiction (VJ)** covers complaints which are not within the compulsory jurisdiction. Businesses can opt into the VJ by entering into a contractual arrangement with the FOS. In doing so, they become **VJ participants**. The FCA has stated that certain complaints which do not fall within the compulsory jurisdiction can be considered under the VJ.

2.3 FOS Awards

The FOS can require the firm to pay over money as a result of a complaint. This monetary award against the firm will be an amount which the FOS considers to be fair compensation; however, the sum cannot exceed £150,000. If the decision is made to make a monetary award, this can be as compensation for **financial loss, pain and suffering, damage to reputation** and **distress or inconvenience**.

In calculating the maximum amount of award, the FOS excludes interest on the award, costs which were reasonably incurred by the complainant in respect of the complaint, and interest on costs.

When the FOS has adjudicated on complaint and it will write to the complainant asking for confirmation of whether the complainant accepts or rejects the decision. If the decision is accepted, it is final and binding on both parties.

3. The Financial Services Compensation Scheme (FSCS)

Learning Objective

5.1.4   Know the circumstances in which the Financial Services Compensation Scheme will pay compensation [COMP 3.2, 4.2.1/2/3] (FCA/PRA), and the compensation payable in respect of protected deposits and protected investment business [COMP 10.2.1/3] (FCA/PRA)

3.1   Purpose

The Financial Services Compensation Scheme (FSCS) was established to pay compensation to eligible claimants in the event of a default by an authorised person, which is typically the firm's insurance cover becoming exhausted and the firm suffering insolvency. It is essentially an insurance policy that is paid for by all authorised firms and provides protection to valid claims for compensation in the event of a firm collapsing. Eligible claimants are certain persons who have a protected claim against an authorised person who is in default. They include most clients of the defaulting firm, except:

- other authorised firms – but see the note below;
- overseas financial institutions;
- CISs, their trustees and operators;
- some pension and retirement funds – but see the note below;
- supranational institutions, governments and central administrative authorities;
- provincial, regional, local and municipal authorities;
- directors and managers of the firm in default and their relatives (unless the firm is a small mutual association and the directors/managers are not salaried; or unless the firm is a credit union);
- companies in the same group as the firm in default unless that company is also a trustee of certain pension schemes;
- persons holding 5% or more of the defaulting firm's capital, or of any firm in the same group;
- auditors of the firm in default;
- any person who has contributed to the firm's default;
- large companies or large mutual associations;
- large partnerships;
- persons whose claim arises from transactions in connection with which they have been convicted of money laundering;
- persons whose claim arises under the Third Parties (Rights against Insurers) Act 1930.

There are special arrangements for protected insurance claims; generally, all small businesses are eligible claimants. There is an exception, however, for claims arising out of contracts entered into before 30 November 2001, which is that a small business can only be an eligible claimant if it is a partnership can they be eligible claimants.

Note: although generally other authorised firms are not eligible, the following types of authorised firms are eligible if the claim arises from an activity for which they don't have permission:

- sole trader firms;
- credit unions;
- trustees or operators of stakeholder or personal pension scheme;
- small businesses – those with an annual turnover of less than £1 million.

Also, although pension funds are generally excluded, trustees of small self-administered schemes or occupational schemes, where the employer is not a large company, large partnership or large mutual association, are also brought back in as eligible claimants.

The protected claims can relate to money on deposit with a bank (protected deposits); or claims on contracts of insurance (protected contracts of insurance); or in connection with protected investment business, (designated investment business); or any claims against the manager or trustee of an authorised unit trust or the authorised corporate director (ACD) or depository of an ICVC, providing that, in each case, the claim is made by the holder of the units.

For the activities to be protected investment business, they must be carried on within the UK.

It is important to note that, as operating an unregulated CIS is designated investment business, claims against a UK-authorised unregulated scheme operator carrying on business in the UK are eligible under the FSCS. There are similar arrangements under the Investor Compensation Directive to cover claims against a UK MiFID investment firm carrying on investment business via a branch in another EEA state.

In summary, in order to receive compensation, the person making the claim must be an eligible claimant and must have a protected claim against an authorised firm that is in default. The precise amount of compensation that is payable depends upon the amount of money lost by the claimant and the type of protected claim.

3.2   Compensation Payable

There are limits to the amount of compensation that the FSCS will pay to eligible claimants:

- **For protected deposits** – 100% of the first £85,000 of the claim. This is the sterling equivalent of the €100,000 deposit compensation limit applying to deposit takers within the EEA.
- **For protected investment business** – 100% of the first £50,000 of the claim.

4. Super-Complaints and Mass-Detriment References

Learning Objective

5.1.5 Know the framework under which the FCA can be alerted to super-complaints and mass-detriment references

Under the Financial Services Act 2012, certain consumer bodies are allowed to make what are referred to as **super-complaints**. A super-complaint allows the consumer body to raise competition and consumer issues with the FCA where a feature of the UK financial services market is, or appears to be, significantly damaging to the interests of consumers. The consumer bodies allowed to raise these issues must be designated as such by the Treasury.

Furthermore, the FOS and firms themselves are allowed to make **mass-detriment** references. A mass-detriment reference can be made by either the FOS or by a regulated firm if either:

1. It appears that there may have been regular failures by a firm (or firms) to comply with regulatory requirements; and consumers have suffered, or may suffer, loss or damage as a result which could be remedied or relieved by legal proceedings; or
2. It appears that a firm (or firms) has regularly acted in a way that, if a complaint were to be made to the FOS, it is likely that the complaint would be determined in favour of the complainant and an award made.

The FCA is required to publish a response within 90 days of receiving a super-complaint or mass-detriment reference, which the FCA must explain what it intends to do.

End of Chapter Questions

Think of an answer to each question and refer to the appropriate section for confirmation.

1. How must a firm publicise its complaints handling procedures?
    Answer Reference: Section 1.2

2. What procedures should be included within a firm's complaints-handling arrangements?
    Answer Reference: Section 1.2

3. List the types of eligible complainant.
    Answer Reference: Section 1.3

4. What are the record-keeping requirements in relation to complaints-handling?
    Answer Reference: Section 1.5

5. What is the role of the FOS?
    Answer Reference: Section 2.1

6. What is the difference between compulsory jurisdiction and voluntary jurisdiction?
    Answer Reference: Section 2.2

7. In addition to costs, what is the maximum monetary award the Financial Ombudsman can compel a firm to pay to a complainant?
    Answer Reference: Section 2.3

8. What is the role of the FSCS?
    Answer Reference: Section 3.1

9. Who are normally excluded from claiming compensation from the FSCS?
    Answer Reference: Section 3.1

10. What compensation is available under the FSCS for protected deposits?
    Answer Reference: Section 3.2

11. What is the compensation limit for protected investment business?
    Answer Reference: Section 3.2

12. What are super-complaints and mass-detriment references and how quickly must the FCA respond to them?
    Answer Reference: Section 4

Glossary and Abbreviations

Aggregation

Multiple client orders are bulked together and processed as a single order. Customers must be notified of this procedure and its advantages and disadvantages.

Allocation

The division of a single aggregated order between two or more investors' accounts.

Alternative Trading System (ATS)

The term formerly used for a facility provided by authorised firms to allow for multilateral trading, by bringing together buyers and sellers of securities. From 1 November 2007, ATSs were authorised as multilateral trading facilities (MTFs), the term used under the **Markets in Financial Instruments Directive (MiFID)**.

American Depositary Receipt (ADR)

A negotiable instrument representing rights to a block of shares in (generally) a non-US company; the **ADR** is an acknowledgement from a bank or trust company that the block of shares is held by it for the account of its client. ADRs are a common means for non-US companies to have their shares traded in the US.

Ancillary Services

Activities, such as giving advice on **MiFID** instruments, which are passportable only if the firm is already passported in relation to a core investment service or activity (such as dealing), and if that firm is providing those services as ancillary services to that activity.

Appointed Representative

Any type of person, ie, an individual or a company. It must be a party to a contract with an authorised person that allows it/him to carry on certain regulated activities – and the authorised person must have accepted responsibility for the conduct of these regulated activities in writing.

Approved Persons

Individuals who are approved by the **Financial Conduct Authority (FCA)** to undertake controlled functions. These individuals are required to comply with the FCA's Statements of Principle and Code of Practice for **Approved Persons** (APER).

Authorisation

The **Financial Services and Markets Act (FSMA)** requires firms to obtain authorisation prior to conducting investment business. Authorisation is gained by receiving one or more Part 4A permissions from the **Financial Conduct Authority (FCA) and/or the Prudential Regulation Authority (PRA)**.

Bank of England (BoE)

The UK's central bank which acts as the government's banker and determines interest rates via its **Monetary Policy Committee (MPC)**.

Banking Consolidation Directive (BCD) Credit Institution

A credit institution which has its registered office in a **European Economic Area (EEA)** state, excluding any institution to which the BCD does not apply.

Best Execution

Requires that firms take into account not only price factors, but also such issues as other costs, speed, likelihood of execution and settlement, and all these in the light of the size and nature of the deal, in determining the means of obtaining the best outcome for a client when executing his deal.

Base Requirement

Part of the financial resources requirement of an authorised firm.

Capital Adequacy Directive (CAD)

See Capital Requirements Directive.

Capital Requirements Directive (CRD)

A European Union (EU) directive setting out the financial rules for financial firms, formerly known as the Capital Adequacy Directive (CAD). The aim of the CRD is to ensure that firms hold adequate financial resources and have adequate systems and controls to manage the business and the associated risks prudently.

Chinese Walls

Organisational barriers to the flow of information set up in large firms, to prevent the movement of confidential, sensitive information between departments and to manage any potential conflicts of interest.

Churning

Excessive trading by a broker in order to generate commission, regardless of the interests of the customer.

Client

Individuals or firms that conduct business through an authorised person. Clients are categorised as retail, professional or eligible counterparty.

Client Assets

Securities or other assets held by a firm on behalf of its clients. The assets have to be kept separate from the firm's own assets (segregated).

Code of Practice for Approved Persons

A code established by the **Financial Conduct Authority (FCA)** with regard to the behaviour of approved persons (see above).

Collective Investment Schemes (CIS)

A generic term for open-ended funds such as a unit trust and an **open-ended investment company (OEIC)**, also known as an investment company with variable capital (ICVC).

Compulsory Jurisdiction

The term used to describe that range of activities that fall compulsorily within the jurisdiction of the **Financial Ombudsman Service (FOS)**.

Common Platform Firms

Firms subject to either of the **Capital Requirements Directive (CRD)** or the **Markets in Financial Instruments Directive (MiFID)**.

Conduct of Business (COBS) Rules

Rules made by the **Financial Conduct Authority (FCA)** under the **Financial Services and Markets Act 2000 (FSMA)** dealing mainly with the relationship between an authorised firm and its clients.

Contracts of Insurance

Financial products specified by Part III of the **Regulated Activities Order 2001**, with two subdivisions: general and long-term insurance contracts.

Controlled Functions

Certain roles within authorised firms for which the **Financial Conduct Authority (FCA) and the** Prudential Regulation Authority (PRA) requires the job-holder to be approved (see approved persons).

Counterparty Risk Requirement (CRR)

Part of the financial resources requirement for authorised firms, requiring that timely provision is made in case of bad debts/non-deliveries.

Criminal Justice Act 1993

A substantial Act which includes provisions relating to **insider dealing**, including a definition of that offence.

Customer Function

The **controlled function** conducted by persons who interact with a firm's customers, such as an investment manager or an investment adviser.

Data Protection Act 1998

Legislation governing how personal data should be held and the rights of access to it.

Debt Securities

Securities whereby the issuer acknowledges a loan made to it. The term includes instruments such as bonds, certificates of deposit (CDs) and commercial paper.

Dematerialised

The term used to describe stock which is held in electronic form rather than having ownership evidenced by way of paper certificates.

Depositary Receipts

Bearer instruments evidencing rights over a block of shares which are held with a depositary – usually a bank or trust company. **American Depositary Receipts (ADRs)** are a good example. Depositary receipts are specified investment instruments under the **Financial Services and Markets Act (FSMA)**.

Designated Investment Exchange (DIE)

An overseas exchange designated by the **Financial Conduct Authority (FCA)** as meeting certain standards of investor protection, in terms of such criteria as market efficiency, transparency and liquidity.

Designated Professional Body (DPB)

Professional bodies whose members are able to carry on limited financial services business without the need for authorisation from the **Financial Conduct Authority (FCA)**, providing that the limited financial services offered to clients are incidental to their main business. These are the professional bodies for lawyers, accountants, chartered surveyors, licensed conveyancers and actuaries.

Directors' Model Code

The Model Code for directors of a listed company. This sets out standards of conduct for these people, adherence to which should avoid their falling foul of insider dealing legislation. For example, it stipulates that a company director should not deal in his own company's shares without permission, and may only do so at certain times.

Disclosure and Transparency Rules

Contained in the **Financial Conduct Authority (FCA)** DTR Sourcebook. The rules apply to issuers of securities on certain markets and aim to ensure that information is properly handled.

Durable Medium

Paper or any instrument which enables the recipient to store information addressed personally to them in a way accessible for future reference, for a period of time adequate for the purposes of the information.

European Central Counterparty Ltd (EuroCCP)

EuroCCP is a UK-incorporated **recognised clearing house (RCH)** regulated by the **Financial Conduct Authority (FCA)**.

Euroclear UK & Ireland

A recognised clearing house, Euroclear UK & Ireland is the organisation in the UK that operates the **CREST** clearing and settlement system.

European Union (EU) Directives

Legislation issued by the European Union to its member states requiring them to enact and implement local legislation.

European Union (EU) Regulation

Legislation issued by the European Union to member states which does not require members states to implement - rather it has a direct effect within each member state. The European Commission is increasing the use of regulations, as there have been instances of member states implementing directives and interpreting them differently.

European Economic Area (EEA)

The member states of the European Union, plus Iceland, Liechtenstein, Norway and Croatia.

Exempt Persons

Firms exempt from the need to be authorised to carry on regulated activities. The term includes bodies such as **recognised investment exchanges** and **recognised clearing houses**.

FCA Handbook

The document containing the **Financial Conduct Authority** rules, guidance and other provisions, with which authorised firms must comply. The Handbook is divided into a number of separate Sourcebooks and Manuals covering different subjects.

Financial Conduct Authority (FCA)

The Financial Conduct Authority replaced the **Financial Services Authority** as the body responsible for regulating conduct in retail and wholesale markets', supervising the trading infrastructure that supports those markets and for the prudential regulation of firms not prudentially regulated by the Prudential Regulation Authority (PRA).

Financial Ombudsman Service (FOS)

The body established to investigate and determine the outcome of complaints made by eligible complainants. The FOS can make awards where appropriate, up to a maximum of £150,000 plus costs.

Financial Policy Committee (FPC)

The Financial Policy Committee (formed in early 2011) is effectively the UK's risk regulator with responsibility and powers to reduce systemic risk. As an official committee of the Bank of England it focuses on the macro-economic and financial issues that may threaten long-term growth prospects, holding powers of direction and recommendation over the PRA.

Financial Resources Requirement (FRR)

The requirements as to the specific financial resources held by an authorised firm.

Financial Services and Markets Act 2000 (FSMA)

The legislation that established the **Financial Services Authority**, and empowered it to regulate the financial services industry. The Act has subsequently been amended by the Financial Services Act of 2012 to create the twin peaks of regulation in the form of the Financial Conduct Authority (FCA) and the Prudential Regulation Authority (PRA).

Financial Services Act 2012

The Act of Parliament that altered the regulatory framework in the UK by abolishing the Financial Services Authority (FSA) and introducing the Prudential Regulation Authority (PRA), the Financial Conduct Authority (FCA) and the Financial Policy Committee (FPC).

Financial Services Authority (FSA)

The agency created by the **Financial Services and Markets Act 2000 (FSMA)** to be the single financial regulator in the UK was replaced by the Financial Conduct Authority (FCA) and the Prudential Regulation Authority (PRA) on 1 April 2013.

Financial Services Compensation Scheme (FSCS)

The scheme created to provide a safety net for customers in the case of firms which cannot meet their obligations in respect of valid claims.

Fit and Proper

Under the **Financial Services and Markets Act 2000 (FSMA)** every firm conducting investment business must be fit and proper, and ensure that its affairs are conducted soundly and prudently. This is also the minimum standard for becoming and remaining an approved person.

Future

A futures contract is a legally binding arrangement by which parties commit to buy/sell a standard quantity and (if applicable) quality of an asset from another party on a specified date in the future, but at a price agreed today. Because the price is agreed at the outset, the seller is protected from a fall in the price of the underlying asset in the intervening time period (and vice versa).

Her Majesty's Revenue & Customs (HMRC)

The government department responsible for the administration and collection of tax in the UK, and the guidance notes on **HM Treasury's** rules for individual savings accounts (ISAs). HMRC is the result of the merger of two formerly separate departments, HM Customs & Excise and the Inland Revenue.

HM Treasury

The government department that is responsible for formulating and implementing the government's financial and economic policies. Among other things this means that it is responsible for financial services regulation in the UK.

Home State

The term used for the European Union (EU) country where a financial services firm conducting cross-border business is based.

Host State

The term used for an European Union (EU) country in which a financial services firm is doing business from elsewhere.

Inside Information

Information relating to a security, or an issuer, which is not publicly known and which would affect the price of the security if it were made public.

Insider Dealing

One of several offences created under the **Criminal Justice Act 1993** which may be committed by an insider in possession of unpublished price-sensitive information if he attempts to deal in affected securities, encourages others to deal, or passes the information on.

Integration

The third stage of **money laundering**; integration is the stage at which the laundered funds appear to be of legitimate provenance.

Investment Company With Variable Capital (ICVC)

See **Open-Ended Investment Company (OEIC)**.

Joint Money Laundering Steering Group (JMLSG)

A group whose membership is made up of trade bodies in the financial services industry. The JMLSG has published guidance notes which set out how firms should interpret and implement the Money Laundering Regulations. This guidance is not binding but, where there is a breach, compliance with the guidance is relevant to an enforcement court.

Key Investor Information Document (KIID)

A KIID is a document that must be provided to anyone who invests in a fund covered by UCITS IV before they invest. It has a standard layout, with sections describing what the fund does, the investment risks, charges and performance, thus making it easier to compare funds from different providers. KIIDs replaced Simplified Prospectuses in July 2012.

Know Your Customer (KYC)

The **Money Laundering Regulations 2007** and the FCA Rules requiring firms to undertake sufficient due diligence, before taking on a client, to satisfy themselves of the identity of that client.

Layering

The second stage of **money laundering**, in which money or assets are typically passed through a series of transactions to obscure their origin.

London Stock Exchange (LSE)

The dominant UK market for trading in securities, especially shares and bonds. The LSE is a **recognised investment exchange**.

Market Abuse

A set of offences introduced under the **Financial Services and Markets Act 2000 (FSMA)**, judged on what a regular user would view as a failure to observe required market standards. The offences include abuse of information, misleading the market, and distortion of the market.

Market Maker

A firm which quotes bid and offer prices for a named list of securities in the market. Such a firm is normally under an obligation to make a price in any security for which it is market maker, at all times.

Markets in Financial Instruments Directive (MiFID)

A European Union (EU) directive that took effect in the UK on 1 November 2007. It allows firms authorised in one member state to provide/offer investment services to customers in another member state, without requiring further authorisation.

Misleading Statement

The term used for false information given about an investment, in order to (or with the effect of) affecting its value – a criminal act under Section 397 of the **Financial Services and Markets Act 2000 (FSMA)** and a potential form of **market abuse**.

Monetary Policy Committee (MPC)

The committee chaired by the Governor of the **Bank of England** which sets sterling interest rates.

Money Laundering

The process whereby criminals attempt to conceal the true origins of the proceeds of their criminal activities, and to give them the appearance of legitimacy by introducing them into the mainstream financial system.

Money Laundering Regulations 2007

The regulations under which authorised firms, and some other businesses, are required to comply with certain administrative obligations in order to prevent **money laundering**. The obligations include record-keeping, identification of clients, appointment of a **nominated officer** to receive suspicion reports, and staff training. Failure to comply may result in a fine and/or imprisonment.

Money Laundering Reporting Officer (MLRO)

A senior employee who is responsible for a firm's arrangements for the prevention of financial crime, for assessing internal suspicion reports, and, where these appear justified, for reporting those suspicions to the **National Crime Agency (NCA)**.

Multilateral Trading Facilities (MTFs)

A system operated by authorised firms which brings together multiple buyers and sellers of securities, but which is not an exchange. Prior to 1 November 2007, when the **Markets in Financial Instruments Directive (MiFID)** provisions came into force, most MTFs were operated as **alternative trading systems (ATSs)**.

National Crime Agency (NCA)

The law enforcement agency to which suspicions of money laundering must be reported by a firm's money laundering reporting officer (MLRO).

Nominated Officer

A term for the officer who is required to receive a firm's internal suspicion reports under the Proceeds of Crime Act (POCA), the Terrorism Act and the **Money Laundering Regulations**; in practice, usually the same individual as the **money laundering reporting officer (MLRO)**.

Nominee

The party which, under a legal arrangement, holds assets in its own name on behalf of the true beneficial owner.

Open-Ended Investment Company (OEIC)

A **collective investment scheme (CIS)** constituted as an open-ended company. This means that its share capital can expand or contract to meet investor supply and demand. It is also referred to as an **investment company with variable capital (ICVC)**.

Option

Gives the holder the right (but not the obligation) to buy or sell a fixed quantity of an underlying asset on, or before, a specified date in the **future**. There are two basic types of option – puts and calls. The holder of a call option has the right to buy the underlying asset at a given price. The holder of a put option has the right to sell the underlying asset at a given price.

Prudential Regulation Authority (PRA)

The Prudential Regulation Authority (PRA), which is a subsidiary of the Bank of England, is responsible for the prudential regulation of financial firms, including banks, investment banks, building societies and insurance companies.

Part 4A Permission

The term used where persons are granted authorised status by the **Financial Conduct Authority (FCA)** under Part 4A of the **Financial Services and Markets Act 2000 (FSMA)**.

Passporting

The method by which firms authorised in one European Union (EU) member state are – under **Markets in Financial Instruments Directive (MiFID)** – permitted to carry on regulated financial services activities in another state without the need to become fully authorised in that other state.

Placement

The first stage of **money laundering**, in which money is introduced into the financial system.

Principles for Businesses

Eleven key principles established by the **Financial Conduct Authority (FCA)** which must be observed by authorised firms. These Principles are detailed in the Handbook.

Proceeds of Crime Act 2002 (POCA)

Legislation which contains, among other things, anti-money laundering provisions.

Prohibition Order

An order which may be exercised by the **Financial Conduct Authority (FCA)** under powers given to it under Section 56 of the **Financial Services and Markets Act 2000 (FSMA)**. Such an order prohibits the individual in connection with whom it is granted from carrying out particular **controlled functions** on the grounds that they are not fit and proper.

Prudential Regulation

The aspect of financial services regulation which deals with firms' financial resources and governance. The Prudential Regulation Authority (PRA) and the **Financial Conduct Authority (FCA)** are responsible for ensuring the financial soundness of their respective authorised firms.

Prudential Regulation Authority (PRA) Handbook

The document containing the Prudential Regulation Authority (PRA) rules, guidance and other provisions, with which PRA-authorised firms must comply. The Handbook is divided into a number of separate Sourcebooks and Manuals covering different subjects.

Public Interest Disclosure Act 1998

Among other things, provides protection for employees who, in good faith, disclose suspicions of wrongdoing within an organisation.

Recognised Clearing House (RCH)

A term used to denote those clearing houses recognised by the **Financial Conduct Authority (FCA)** as providing appropriate standards of protection in the provision of clearing and settlement facilities to certain markets. **LCH. Clearnet** and **Euroclear UK & Ireland** are the two organisations granted this status.

Recognised Investment Exchange (RIE)

A term used to denote those UK exchanges which operate markets in investments, meeting certain standards set by the **Financial Conduct Authority (FCA)**.

Recognised Overseas Investment Exchange (ROIE)

An overseas exchange offering membership or providing facilities within the UK, and having been recognised by the **Financial Conduct Authority (FCA)** as meeting appropriate standards of investor protection.

Regular User

A hypothetical person regularly using a particular market. It is through the eyes of the regular user that behaviour is assessed for determining whether it meets the standards required under the legacy offences of the **market abuse** regime.

Regulated Activities

Activities for which authorisation (or exemption from the need for that authorisation) is required. Regulated activities are defined in relation both to the activities themselves, and to the investments to which they relate.

Regulated Activities Order 2001 (as amended)

The statutory instrument which defines the range of **regulated activities** and specified investments.

Regulatory Decisions Committee (RDC)

The committee of the **Financial Conduct Authority (FCA)** which is responsible for disciplinary decisions.

Significant Influence Functions

Certain functions carried out by directors and other senior personnel. In the approved persons regime, these comprise the governing functions, the required functions, the systems and control functions and the significant management functions.

Stabilisation

The activity of supporting the price of a new issue of securities or bonds in order to minimise the volatility that can sometimes arise with new issues.

Statements of Principle for Approved Persons

A set of principles established by the **Financial Conduct Authority (FCA)** with which **approved persons** are required to comply at all times.

Tax and Chancery Chamber of the Upper Tribunal (Upper Tribunal)

The Upper Tribunal hears appeals against the regulators' decisions. It is independent of the **Financial Conduct Authority (FCA)** and the Prudential Regulation Authority (PRA) and is appointed by the Government's Ministry of Justice (formerly the Department of Constitutional Affairs).

Threshold Conditions

The conditions which a firm must meet before the **Financial Conduct Authority (FCA)** or the Prudential Regulation Authority (PRA) will authorise it.

Tipping Off

An offence established under various pieces of anti-money laundering and terrorist financing legislation. It involves disclosing the fact that an investigation is, or is likely to be, under way, if that disclosure may imperil any such investigation.

Training and Competence Sourcebook

It sets out **Financial Conduct Authority's** requirements in connection with all staff, and with additional requirements for some specified activities. The Sourcebook includes rules relating to training and competence, and specifies which qualifications are required for certain activities.

Trustee

A person or organisation who is the legal owner of assets held in trust for someone else. The trustee is responsible for safeguarding the assets, complying with the trust deed and (where the trust is a unit trust) overseeing the activities of the unit trust's manager.

UK Listing Authority (UKLA)

Under European Union (EU) regulations each member state must appoint a competent authority for the purpose of listing securities. The competent authority for listing in the UK is the **Financial Conduct Authority (FCA)**; in this capacity, it is called the UK Listing Authority.

Undertakings for Collective Investment in Transferable Securities (UCITS)

Collective investment schemes established under the UCITS Directives. These directives aim to harmonise European Union (EU) member states' laws so as to allow for the operation and marketing of UCITS schemes across EU borders.

Warrant

An investment instrument giving the holder the right to buy a set number of the underlying equities at a predetermined price on specified dates, or at any time, up to the end of a predetermined time period. Warrants are usually issued by companies or by securities houses.

Whistleblowing

The term used when an individual raises concerns over potential wrongdoing. The **Public Interest Disclosure Act 1998** provides some statutory protections for whistleblowers.

ABI
Association of British Insurers

ACD
Authorised Corporate Director

ADR
American Depositary Receipt

AFM
Authorised Fund Manager

AIFM
Alternative Investment Fund Manager

AIFMD
Alternative Investment Fund Managers' Directive

APER
Statements of Principle and Code of Practice for Approved Persons

APR
Approved Persons Regime

ARM
Approved Reporting Mechanism

AUT
Authorised Unit Trust

BBA
British Bankers' Association

BCBS
Basel Committee on Banking Supervision

BCD
Banking Consolidation Directive

BIPRU
Banks, Building Societies and Investment firms Prudential handbook

BMSA
Business Model and Strategy Analysis

BoE
Bank of England

BSA
Building Societies Association

CAD
Capital Adequacy Directive

CADD
Client Assets Disclosure Document

CAMPSA
Clearing Arrangement Mandatory Prudent Segregation Amount

CASS
Client Assets Sourcebook

CC
Competition Commission

CDD
Customer Due Diligence

CEO
Chief Executive Officer

CF
Controlled Function

CFD
Contracts for Difference

CIS
Collective Investment Scheme

CISI
Chartered Institute for Securities & Investment

CJ
Compulsory Jurisdiction

CJA
Criminal Justice Act

CMAR
Client Money and Assets Return

CML
Council of Mortgage Lenders

CMP
Client Money Pool

COB
Conduct of Business Rules

COBS
Conduct of Business Sourcebook

COMP
Compensation Sourcebook

COND
Threshold Conditions

COREP
Common Reporting

CP
Consultation Paper

CPD
Continuing Professional Development

CPMI
Collective Portfolio Investment Firm

CRD
Capital Requirements Directive

CRD IV
Capital Requirements Directive IV

CRR
Capital Requirements Regulation

CTA
Counter-Terrorism Act

CTF
Child Trust Fund

DEPP
Decisions Procedure and Penalties Manual

DISP
Dispute Resolution: Complaints

DMD
Distance Marketing Directive

DPA
Data Protection Act

DPB
Designated Professional Body

DTR
Disclosure and Transparency Rules

DvP
Delivery versus Payment

EBA
European Banking Authority

EC
European Community

ECB
European Central Bank

ECP
Eligible Counterparty

EEA
European Economic Area

EG
Enforcement Guide

EIB
European Investment Bank

EIOPA

European Insurance and Occupational Pension Authority

EMIR

European Markets Infrastructure Regulation

ESA

European Supervisory Authority

ESFS

European System of Financial Supervision

ESMA

European Securities and Markets Authority

ESRB

European Systemic Risk Board

EU

European Union

FATF

Financial Action Task Force

FCA

Financial Conduct Authority

FINREP

Financial Reporting

FIT

Fit and Proper Test for Approved Persons

FOS

Financial Ombudsman Service

FPC

Financial Policy Committee

FPO

Financial Promotion Order

FSA

Financial Services Authority

FSAVC

Free-Standing Additional Voluntary Contribution

FSCS

Financial Services Compensation Scheme

FSF

Firm Systematic Framework

FSMA

Financial Services and Markets Act (2000)

FSR

Financial Stability Report

FX

Foreign Exchange

GDR

Global Depositary Receipt

GENPRU

The General Prudential Sourcebook

HMRC

Her Majesty's Revenue & Customs

ICAAP

Internal Capital Adequacy Assessment Process

ICAEW

Institute of Chartered Accountants in England and Wales

ICO

Information Commissioner's Office

ICVC

Investment Company with Variable Capital

IFPRU

The Prudential Sourcebook for Investment Firms

IMF

International Monetary Fund

IPRU
Interim Prudential Sourcebooks

ISA
Individual Savings Account

ISD
Investment Services Directive

IT
Information Technology

JISA
Junior Individual Savings Account

JMLSG
Joint Money Laundering Steering Group

KFD
Key Features Document

KIID
Key Investor Information Document

KYC
Know Your Customer

LIBOR
London Interbank Offered Rate

LSE
London Stock Exchange

MAD
Market Abuse Directive

MAR
Market Conduct Sourcebook

MiFID
Markets in Financial Instruments Directive

MiFIR
Markets in Financial Instruments Regulation

ML
Money Laundering

MLRO
Money Laundering Reporting Officer

MOU
Memorandum Of Understanding

MPC
Monetary Policy Committee

MPSA
Mandatory Prudent Segregation Amount

MTF
Multilateral Trading Facility

NCA
National Crime Agency

NO
Nominated Officer

NS&I
National Savings and Investments

OEIC
Open-Ended Investment Company

OFT
Office of Fair Trading

OTC
Over-the-Counter

OTF
Organised Trading Facility

PCBS
Parliamentary Commission on Banking Standards

PEP
Politically Exposed Person

PERG
Perimeter Guidance Manual

PIDA
Public Interest Disclosure Act (1998)

plc
Public Limited Company

PPI
Payment Protection Insurance

POCA
Proceeds of Crime Act (2002)

PPF
Pension Protection Fund

PRA
Prudential Regulation Authority

PRIN
Principles for Businesses

PS
Policy Statement

RAO
Regulated Activities Order

RCH
Recognised Clearing House

RDC
Regulatory Decisions Committee

RDR
Retail Distribution Review

RIE
Recognised Investment Exchange

RIS
Regulatory Information Service

RNS
Regulatory News Service

SIF
Significant Influence Function

SIPP
Self-Invested Personal Pension

SMR
Senior Managers Regime

SOCPA
Serious and Organised Crime Police Act 2005

SPS
Statement of Professional Standing

SRA
Sector Risk Assessment

SUP
Supervision Manual

SYSC
Senior Management Arrangements, Systems and Controls Sourcebook

TC
- Training and Competence Sourcebook
- Threshold Condition

TCF
Treating Customers Fairly

TTCAs
Title Transfer Collateral Arrangements

UCITS
Undertakings for Collective Investment in Transferable Securities

UKLA
United Kingdom Listing Authority

VJ
Voluntary Jurisdiction

Multiple Choice
Questions

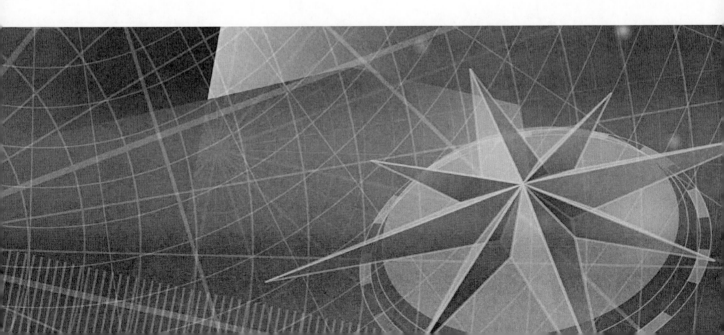

The following multiple choice questions have been compiled to reflect, as closely as possible, the standard that you will experience in your examination. Please note, however, that they are not actual CISI examination questions.

1. Which of the following is one of the FCA's operational objectives?

   A. To ensure retail clients are not over-charged for financial products

   B. To prevent authorised firms from going into default

   C. To secure an appropriate degree of protection for consumers

   D. To ensure authorised firms have adequate financial resources

2. Appeals against FCA decisions are normally considered by which body?

   A. Advisory, Conciliation and Arbitration Service

   B. Financial Ombudsman Service

   C. Office of Fair Trading

   D. Upper Tribunal

3. All of the following are operational objectives given to the FCA under the Financial Services Act 2012, EXCEPT:

   A. Securing an appropriate degree of protection for consumers

   B. Protecting and enhancing the integrity of the UK financial system

   C. Promoting effective competition in the markets for financial services

   D. Ensuring that the relevant markets function well

4. The 'management and control' Principle for Businesses requires firms to have adequate systems in place specifically relating to:

   A. Customer fairness

   B. Cash flow resources

   C. Risk management

   D. Staff training

5. Which of the following is a statutory consequence of contravening the general prohibition?

   A. Approved persons lose their approved status

   B. A firm may not conduct any business within the UK

   C. Civil proceedings may commence

   D. Financial services agreements are likely to be unenforceable

6. Which of the following must be DIRECTLY authorised under the FSMA to carry on regulated activities?

    A. Recognised investment exchange

    B. Hedge fund manager

    C. Recognised clearing house

    D. Appointed representative

7. Which of the following is an excluded activity and, hence, does not require authorisation under FSMA?

    A. Safeguarding and administering investments

    B. Dealing on an agency basis

    C. Dealing as principal in connection with an employee share scheme

    D. Accepting deposits

8. Which of the following is a specified investment under the Regulated Activities Order?

    A. NS&I certificates

    B. Building society bank accounts

    C. Commodity futures for commercial purposes

    D. OEIC shares

9. Which of the following may conduct a limited range of regulated activity under the Part 20 (Provision of Financial Services by Members of the Professions) regime, without the need for authorisation?

    A. Accountants

    B. Independent financial advisers

    C. Market makers dealing in principal

    D. Home finance advisers

10. In order to satisfy the suitability threshold conditions for authorisation, firms are specifically required to:

    A. commission an external assessment

    B. appoint a standards officer

    C. prove that they are fit and proper

    D. provide an acceptability declaration

11. A director of a firm, who is responsible for compliance, MUST apply for which of the following controlled functions?

    A. Director function

    B. Non-executive director function

    C. Customer function

    D. Director function and compliance oversight function

12. What is the FCA's general approach to the supervision of authorised firms?

    A. Precedent-based

    B. Advisory-based

    C. Risk-based

    D. Experience-based

13. Which of the following are statutory notices?

    A. Warning, decision and supervisory notices

    B. Warning, decision and final decision notices

    C. Warning, decision and discontinuance notices

    D. Supervisory, discontinuance and final decision notices

14. If someone deposits criminally obtained banknotes in a building society account, what stage of the money laundering process is this normally known as?

    A. Integration

    B. Layering

    C. Phasing

    D. Placement

15. What action should a Money Laundering Reporting Officer take if a member of staff has identified a suspicious transaction?

    A. Make a notification to HM Treasury

    B. Make a notification to the Financial Conduct Authority

    C. Contact the Serious Fraud Office for advice

    D. Make a report to the National Crime Agency

16. Which of the following instruments are caught under the insider dealing legislation?

    A. Debt securities

    B. Commodities

    C. Foreign exchange

    D. Open-ended investment companies

17. Which of the following is an inside deal?

    A. An investment manager buys shares in his brother's company knowing that is about to be taken over

    B. An investment manager sells units in a collective investment scheme held jointly with his wife

    C. A director encourages an employee to purchase units in a collective investment scheme

    D. A director makes a loan to his own company

18. Which of the following is a special defence against the charge of insider dealing under the Criminal Justice Act?

    A. An individual is providing information in the role of a journalist

    B. An individual is acting on behalf of a friend or relative

    C. A market maker is acting in good faith in the course of his business as a market maker

    D. A market maker is providing data purely for information purposes

19. An individual has acquired inside information and has encouraged a friend to deal in the affected securities. Which of the following statements is TRUE?

    A. This is a perfectly legitimate action

    B. The individual is likely to have committed an offence

    C. Only the friend will be guilty of an offence

    D. Any deal will be automatically void

20. To satisfy the definition of 'market abuse', an individual's behaviour must:

    A. be based on generally available information

    B. be likely to distort the market

    C. constitute a breach of the Criminal Justice Act 1993

    D. constitute a breach of the Money Laundering Regulations 2007

21. The guidance provided by the Joint Money Laundering Steering Group:

    A. has been approved by the FCA and forms part of the Handbook

    B. is mandatory for all investment firms

    C. has been approved by the EU Commission and derives from the Money Laundering Directive

    D. highlights best practice and has been approved by the Treasury

22. Which of the following is a safe harbour against a charge of market abuse under FSMA?

    A. Adherence to the conflicts of interest rules

    B. Price support activities carried out in accordance with the price stabilisation rules

    C. Transactions carried out on a recognised investment exchange with an FCA-authorised and approved firm

    D. Information is available on a subscription service and thought to be widely available

23. Which of the following is TRUE of the market abuse regime under FSMA?

    A. The offence is considered a criminal act

    B. The FCA is not permitted to impose a fine on offenders

    C. The FCA can withdraw approval and authorisation of anyone found guilty of this offence

    D. Offenders can be fined up to a maximum of £100,000

24. Which of the following is a MiFID financial instrument?

    A. Bank account

    B. Contracts for differences on sporting events

    C. Foreign exchange

    D. Credit derivatives

25. If a firm is carrying on activity on an eligible counterparty basis, which of the following rules applies to them?

    A. Provision of information about the firm

    B. Client order handling

    C. Conflicts of interest

    D. Use of dealing commission

26. Under the COBS rules, which financial promotions communicated by their appointed representatives are firms responsible for?

    A. Only those promoting MiFID financial instruments

    B. Those which are published in the consumer press

    C. Those which relate to high-risk investments

    D. All types of financial promotions

27. Why is a commodity derivatives dealer classified as a per se professional client?

    A. Commodity derivatives are MiFID financial instruments

    B. The activity is conducted by way of business

    C. The dealer is an investment firm

    D. The dealer is unable to qualify as a retail client

28. In relation to non-MiFID business, which of the following retail clients may be suitable for reclassification as an elective professional client?

    A. A newly-appointed trustee of a trust exceeding €500,000

    B. A client to whom the firm regularly sends financial promotions for non-mainstream investment opportunities

    C. A client who has recently inherited a sizeable portfolio

    D. The spouse of one of the firm's investment managers

29. Which of the following is a retail investment product?

    A. Home income plan

    B. Occupational pension scheme

    C. Unit trust

    D. Commodity derivative

30. Which of the following statements is TRUE about a client that is an eligible counterparty for executing orders?

    A. If the client requires investment advice they will be classified as a per se professional client for that service

    B. The eligible counterparty status provides the client with regulatory protection for the execution of orders

    C. The firm must conduct both qualitative and quantitative assessments on the client before executing orders

    D. The firm is only required to conduct a qualitative assessment on the client before executing orders

31. Which of the following is TRUE of the client categorisation requirements in the FCA Handbook?

    A. Customers are classed as either retail clients or private clients

    B. Retail clients cannot be opted up to be professional clients

    C. Professional clients can be either elective or per se professional clients

    D. The client classification rules do not apply to non-MiFID business

32. Firms carrying on MiFID business must provide clients with appropriate information on which of the following?

    A. Compliance officer's name

    B. The firm's major shareholders

    C. Where the firm's shares are listed

    D. Costs and associated charges

33. Client agreements must be provided for designated investment business carried out for:

    A. Eligible counterparties (in respect of non-MiFID business)

    B. Professional clients (in respect of non-MiFID business)

    C. Professional clients (in respect of MiFID business)

    D. Eligible counterparties (in respect of MiFID business)

34. Which of the following is TRUE in relation to the rules on disclosure of costs and associated charges?

    A. Applies to retail and professional clients

    B. Commissions do not have to be shown separately

    C. All fees, commissions and charges must be disclosed by the firm

    D. A firm does not have to disclose any taxes payable via the firm

35. Unless a retail client has agreed otherwise with the firm, what is the frequency that an investment manager must send a periodic statement?

    A. Weekly

    B. Quarterly

    C. Six-monthly

    D. Annually

36. In which of the following circumstances does a firm have to send a suitability report?

    A. If the recommendation is to increase a regular premium to an existing life insurance contract

    B. If the recommendation is for a client to undertake a pension transfer

    C. If the firm is acting as an investment manager for a retail client and recommends a regulated collective investment scheme

    D. If the recommendation is to make a further investment into an existing packaged product

37. In which of the following circumstances do the rules on appropriateness apply?

    A. Personal recommendation to a retail client to purchase a UK-authorised collective investment scheme

    B. Retail client responding to a direct offer financial promotion to deal in warrants

    C. Discretionary portfolio management for a retail client

    D. Personal recommendation to a professional client to invest in a hedge fund

38. In which of the following circumstances is a suitability assessment NOT required?

    A. Portfolio manager making a discretionary decision to deal

    B. Financial adviser who advises a client to invest in an UK-authorised collective investment scheme

    C. Private wealth manager who advises a professional client to invest in a hedge fund

    D. A firm transmitting an execution-only order in a security admitted to trading on a recognised investment exchange

39. Why must a suitability report be issued within 14 days of concluding a personal pension scheme?

    A. To allow the client the opportunity to consider the recommendations before the end of the 14-day cancellation period

    B. To allow the pension scheme provider to establish the scheme

    C. To enable the client to compare the costs of the scheme with others

    D. Because this is a MiFID requirement

40. The three categories of products for which Key Features Documents must be provided to clients are packaged products, cash-based ISAs and:

    A. Deposit accounts

    B. Cash-based JISAs

    C. Conventional annuities

    D. Wrap accounts

41. Which of the following is EXEMPT from the financial promotion rules?

    A. A promotion to a professional client

    B. The promotion of non-MiFID business to a retail client

    C. The promotion of packaged products to a UK-domiciled retail client

    D. One-off promotions of non-MiFID business that are not cold calls

42. The rules requiring charges to be included in a direct offer promotion to retail clients can be waived if:

    A. the product is considered to be low-risk

    B. the product has previously been promoted

    C. the charges are included in another document that the client needs to refer to in order to respond to the offer

    D. the charges are below a threshold level which is assessed each year in line with the retail price index

43. What action might a firm take to ensure investment research staff do not pass price-sensitive information to other departments?

    A. Make this a condition of employment for all staff

    B. Establish a Chinese wall policy

    C. Conduct appropriate supervision

    D. Establish a training and competence scheme

44. MiFID firms may accept payments or non-monetary benefits from a third party only if:

    A. the client is a professional client

    B. the amount is below that specified in the firm's conflicts of interest policy

    C. the payment is recorded and details provided to the client on request

    D. the payment enhances the quality of service and is disclosed to the client

45. Which of the following is permitted to be paid from client-dealing commissions?

    A. Order and execution management systems

    B. Research that involves analysis or data manipulation to reach meaningful conclusions

    C. Subscription for publications and journals which directly or indirectly relate to the services provided

    D. Seminar and conference fees

46. The best execution rules under COBS require firms to:

    A. execute orders on the terms that are most favourable to their client

    B. execute orders that achieve the best price first

    C. execute orders that usually achieve the best price and cost for the client

    D. execute orders that achieve the best price and speed of execution for the client

47. What is the MAIN purpose of the client money rules?

    A. To compensate clients if an authorised firm becomes insolvent

    B. To ensure client money benefits from the best possible rate of returns

    C. To segregate and protect client money from a firm's own money

    D. To prevent clients from encashing client money before the due date

48. How often must a firm internally reconcile client assets?

    A. Every day

    B. Monthly

    C. As often as is necessary

    D. At whatever frequency is requested by the client

49. A firm must hold client money accounts in trust with a bank to ensure that:

    A. the firm cannot use client money to repay its own creditors
    B. the bank is able to maintain its regulatory status as designated trustee
    C. no loss will be borne by the client money accounts should the bank become insolvent
    D. the bank is able to retain the client money should the firm become insolvent.

50. What is the MAXIMUM amount of monetary award against an authorised firm that the Financial Ombudsman Service can make?

    A. £35,000
    B. £50,000
    C. £100,000
    D. £150,000

51. Why does the Money Laundering Reporting Officer (MLRO) have responsibility for the training of staff in relation to identifying money laundering activity?

    A. Compliance officers require MLROs to undertake this function
    B. It is required by the Joint Money Laundering Steering Group
    C. It is required by the Financial Conduct Authority
    D. It is required by the Proceeds of Crime Act

52. Which of the following does NOT summarise any of the Chartered Institute for Securities and Investment Principles?

    A. To act honestly and fairly at all times when dealing with clients
    B. To ensure that staff for whom you are responsible maintain relevant standards of competence
    C. To observe standards of market integrity
    D. To identify and manage conflicts of interest to the best of your ability

53. When a firm gives permission to an employee to undertake a personal account transaction it must:

    A. promptly notify the FCA
    B. promptly notify the employee
    C. receive prompt notification that the transaction has been conducted
    D. obtain permission from the FCA

54. For how long must MiFID firms retain copies of confirmations of transactions carried out for retail clients?

    A. Indefinitely

    B. Three years

    C. Five years

    D. Six years

55. Who deals with unresolved disputes between an authorised firm and complainants?

    A. Financial Ombudsman Service

    B. Upper Tribunal

    C. Financial Services Compensation Scheme

    D. FCA's Regulatory Decisions Committee

56. The Proceeds of Crime Act 2002 includes provisions relating to which of the following?

    A. The offence of market abuse

    B. The offence of making false and misleading statements

    C. The protection of persons who inform authorities of their concerns

    D. The requirement to disclose suspicious money laundering transactions

57. Dealing on the basis of inside information on which of the following investments constitutes an offence under the Criminal Justice Act?

    A. Commodity futures

    B. Energy futures

    C. Options on gold

    D. Options on shares

58. When must a firm normally send a written confirmation after carrying out an order for a retail client?

    A. The same business day

    B. The next business day

    C. Within three business days

    D. Within five business days

59. Which of the following bodies is established to provide a safety net for customers of financial services firms that become insolvent?

    A. Financial Services Compensation Scheme

    B. Financial Conduct Authority

    C. Financial Ombudsman Service

    D. Upper Tribunal

60. Which type of statutory notice can be issued by the FCA only with the consent of the recipient?

    A. Final Decision Notice

    B. Further Decision Notice

    C. Notice of Discontinuance

    D. Supervisory Notice

61. With whom must the firm register a data controller under the Data Protection Act?

    A. The UK Department for Business, Innovation and Skills

    B. The FCA

    C. The Information Commissioner

    D. HM Treasury

62. In relation to the FCA's complaints handling requirements, which of the following is TRUE?

    A. The complaint must be dealt with at the firm by an individual involved in the original matter

    B. The firms is not obliged to advise the complainant of their rights to take the complaint to the FOS

    C. The firm's procedures for the receiving of eligible complaints apply to complaints received by both oral and written notification

    D. the firm must maintain a document on its internal procedures for dealing with complaints. However it is only required to provide this to clients/complainants when requested to do so

63. The Financial Services Compensation Scheme can make awards to:

    A. eligible complainants

    B. eligible counterparties

    C. eligible claimants

    D. approved persons

64. Which of the following is TRUE in connection with a MiFID firm communicating with retail clients?

    A. The firm's name must be included in the communication

    B. The information can highlight benefits without having to highlight risks

    C. Financial promotions must name the FCA or PRA as the firm's regulator

    D. Where comparisons are made, the source of the information does not have to be identified

65. The rules on personal account dealing do not apply to which of the following?

    A. Options

    B. Overseas markets

    C. Life policies

    D. IPOs

66. Which of the following is an excluded person in the conduct of regulated activity?

    A. A member of the Society of Lloyds

    B. A firm dealing as principal

    C. The London Stock Exchange

    D. An appointed representative

67. ADRs are included in which category of specified investment?

    A. Certificates representing securities

    B. Contracts for difference

    C. Lloyd's investments

    D. Warrants

68. Overseas persons are excluded from the need for authorisation when conducting business after a legitimate approach from a UK client for which of the following activities?

    A. Accepting deposits

    B. Carrying out insurance contracts

    C. Dealing in investments as principal

    D. Establishing stakeholder pension schemes

69. Best execution requires a firm to:

    A. achieve the fastest result for the order

    B. execute orders on the most favourable terms for the client

    C. obtain consistent rules by using the same venue for the majority of orders

    D. select venues based on commissions' receivable

70. A firm is permitted to deal for itself prior to the publication of a research recommendation under which of the following circumstances?

    A. It anticipates customer demand

    B. It is a market maker acting in good faith

    C. The market price is likely to be unaffected by publication

    D. The firm's documentation states that it may deal ahead of publication

71. In relation to an eligible complaint that reaches the Financial Ombudsman, which of the following is TRUE?

    A. It is resolved between the firm and the complainant under supervision

    B. It is resolved by the Ombudsman

    C. It is resolved by an FCA inspector

    D. It is funded by the Ombudsman and considered in a court of law

72. Which of the following is a regulated activity?

    A. Discussing term assurance generally

    B. Explaining different types of investments

    C. Advising on shares

    D. Advising on bank deposit accounts

73. Which of the following types of client is entitled to the most protection?

    A. Professional

    B. Institutional

    C. Eligible counterparty

    D. Retail

74. What is the close period in the context of the model code for directors in relation to quarterly results announcements?

    A. 15 days

    B. 30 days

    C. 45 days

    D. 60 days

75. Which of the following is a type of MiFID financial instrument?

    A. Bank deposit accounts

    B. Financial contracts for difference

    C. Residential mortgages

    D. Contracts of insurance

Answers to Multiple Choice Questions

Q1.　　　Answer: C　　Ref: Chapter 1, Section 2.1 (LO 1.1.7)

The FCA does not operate a no-fail regime for authorised firms, therefore option B is incorrect. The FCA is not a price regulator and does not specify the cost/charges that authorised firms can charge on financial products, therefore option A is incorrect. The FCA does specify the amount of financial resource some authorised firms must have, but this is not one their statutory objectives, therefore option D is incorrect.

The correct answer is option C. One of the FCA's statutory operational objectives is to ensure that there is appropriate protection for consumers; one example of this is the client money rules where cash managed/held by a firm is held in client money bank accounts and not in the name of the firm.

Q2.　　　Answer: D　　Ref: Chapter 1, Section 6.7 (LO 1.2.3)

The Upper Tribunal operates the appeals procedure for FCA disciplinary decisions.

Q3.　　　Answer: D　　Ref: Chapter 1, Section 2.1 (LO 1.1.1)

Ensuring that the relevant markets function well is the strategic objective of the FCA rather than one of its operational objectives.

Q4.　　　Answer: C　　Ref: Chapter 1, Section 3.1 (LO 1.1.2)

The third principle requires firms to have adequate risk management systems.

Q5.　　　Answer: D　　Ref: Chapter 1, Section 1.1 (LO 1.2.1)

Option D is a statutory consequence; other statutory consequences are imprisonment and/or an unlimited fine.

Q6.　　　Answer: B　　Ref: Chapter 2, Sections 1.1 (LO 2.4.1)

A hedge fund manager needs to be authorised when it undertakes the activity of portfolio management. The others are exempt from the FSMA when carrying on specific regulated activities. For instance, an appointed representative will have a contract with an authorised firm, which allows them to carry on regulated activities, with the authorised firm accepting responsibility for the appointed representative's conduct in respect of the regulated activities undertaken.

Q7.　　　Answer: C　　Ref: Chapter 2, Section 1.3.1 (LO 2.4.2)

Dealing as principal in connection with an employee share scheme is an excluded activity and so does not require authorisation.

Q8.　　　Answer: D　　Ref: Chapter 2, Section 1.2.1 (LO 2.4.3)

Commodity futures for commercial purposes, NS&I products and building society bank accounts are specifically excluded from the RAO, whereas OEIC shares are included.

Q9.   **Answer: A   Ref: Chapter 2, Section 2.3.2 (LO 2.1.1)**

The correct answer is A – accountants do not need authorisation under FSMA when they carry on a limited range of regulated activity which is incidental to their main business. In addition they must operate within a set of rules laid down by the Institute of Chartered Accountants in England and Wales, which is their designated professional body. In these circumstances, the accountant is operating within FSMA Part 20 regime.

Q10.   **Answer: C   Ref: Chapter 2, Section 3.3.2 (LO 2.4.4)**

The suitability condition requires firms to prove themselves fit and proper to be granted Part 4A permission, namely that their affairs will be conducted soundly and prudently.

Q11.   **Answer: D   Ref: Chapter 2, Section 5.3 (LO 2.4.7)**

Compliance oversight function is a required function; the person performing this function has to be separately approved to do so, even if they are also approved for a governing function such as director function.

Q12.   **Answer: C   Ref: Chapter 2, Section 4 (LO 2.4.5)**

The FCA adopts a risk-based approach to supervision. This means that it focuses its resources on mitigating those risks which pose a threat to the achievement of its statutory objectives and that it has regard to the efficient and economic use of its resources.

Q13.   **Answer: A   Ref: Chapter 2, Section 8.2 (LO 2.2.2)**

The FCA publishes statutory notices on its website that comprise warning, decision and supervisory notices. Notices of discontinuance and final notices are deemed non-statutory for the purposes of the DEPP part of the FCA Handbook and are not published on the FCA website.

Q14.   **Answer: D   Ref: Chapter 3, Section 3.2 (LO 3.3.4)**

The placement stage of the money laundering process is the first stage and involves placing criminally obtained cash with a financial institution.

Q15.   **Answer: D   Ref: Chapter 3, Section 3.5 (LO 3.3.9)**

A firm's MLRO must report suspicious activity to the National Crime Agency.

Q16.   **Answer: A   Ref: Chapter 3, Section 1.4 (LO 3.1.1)**

Debt securities are caught under the insider dealing legislation; however, the other three options are not.

Q17.   **Answer: A   Ref: Chapter 3, Section 1.2 (LO 3.1.1)**

Units in collective investment schemes and loans are not securities for the purpose of insider dealing legislation.

Q18.   **Answer: C**   **Ref: Chapter 3, Section 1.6 (LO 3.1.3)**

One of the special defences is where a market maker acts in good faith carrying out its roles as a market maker. The other three options are all general defences under the CJA.

Q19.   **Answer: B**   **Ref: Chapter 3, Section 1.3 (LO 3.1.1)**

Someone commits the offence of insider dealing if they encourage someone else to deal inprice-affected securities when in possession of inside information.

Q20.   **Answer: B**   **Ref: Chapter 3, Section 2.1 (LO 3.2.1)**

The definition of market abuse behaviour includes the requirement that it must be likely to distort the market in the investment.

Q21.   **Answer: D**   **Ref: Chapter 3, Sections 3.1 (LO 3.3.2)**

Option D is correct. Guidance provided by the JMLSG is not approved by the FCA, nor has it been approved by the EU Commission nor forms part of the Money Laundering Directives. The JMLSG guidance is not mandatory; it is industry guidance provided on best practices within the financial services industry.

Q22.   **Answer: B**   **Ref: Chapter 3, Section 2.6 (LO 3.2.6)**

Option B is correct. Compliance with the conflicts of interest rules is not specified as a safe harbour. Nor is Option C. Widely available information does not amount to a safe harbour.

Q23.   **Answer: C**   **Ref: Chapter 3, Sections 2.1, 2.4 (LO 3.2.1)**

Option C is correct. The offence of market abuse is civil rather than criminal, unlike insider dealing which is a criminal offence. The FCA is permitted to impose an unlimited fine (there is no maximum) as well as withdrawing approval/authorisation of anyone found guilty of market abuse.

Q24.   **Answer: D**   **Ref: Chapter 3, Section 8.1.3 (LO 3.7.1)**

The correct option is D, as credit derivatives are a MiFID instrument. Neither bank accounts (A) nor foreign exchange (C) are classed as MiFID instruments. Contracts for difference (CFD) on non-financial instruments (eg, sporting events) are not a MiFID instrument, whereas a CFD on a financial instrument, such as a security.

Q25.   **Answer: C**   **Ref: Chapter 4, Section 1.3 (LO 4.1.2)**

Options A, B and D are disapplied for eligible counterparties (COBS 1 – Annex 1) business. The conflicts of interest rules (SYSC 10) are applicable to all authorised/regulated firms.

Q26.   **Answer: D**   **Ref: Chapter 4, Section 1.4 (LO 4.1.4)**

Firms are responsible for ensuring that appointed representatives comply with the COBS 4 rules when communicating all types of financial promotions.

Q27. **Answer: C** **Ref: Chapter 4, Section 2.1.3 (LO 4.2.1)**

Clients that are investment firms are, by default, classified as per se professional clients. The dealer does not have to 'qualify' for re-classification to retail client; they could request this in order to obtain greater regulatory protection.

Q28. **Answer: B** **Ref: Chapter 4, Section 2.1.5 (LO 4.2.2)**

For non-MiFID business, clients whom the firm assesses as capable of making their own investment decisions can be reclassified as elective professional clients. If a firm considers a client sufficiently sophisticated that the firm is able to promote non-mainstream investments to them, that client is likely to satisfy the qualitative assessment for elective professional client. The other examples do not give any indication of investment expertise.

Q29. **Answer: C** **Ref: Chapter 4, Section 4.2.2 (LO 4.4.5)**

A unit in any type of collective investment scheme, whether or not the scheme is regulated, is classed as a retail investment product.

Q30. **Answer: A** **Ref: Chapter 4, Section 2.1.3 (LO 4.2.1)**

An eligible counterparty only has that classification in relation to eligible counterparty business, such as the execution of orders. If the client requires another service such as investment advice, they will be classified as a per se professional client for that service. Eligible counterparties have little or no protection under the regulatory system. Options C and D are only relevant for retail client reclassification.

Q31. **Answer: C** **Ref: Chapter 4, Section 2.1.3 and 2.1.5 (LO 4.2.2)**

The term 'customers' applies to either retail clients or professional clients (not private clients). Retail clients can be opted up to professional client status providing that they meet certain criteria. The client classification requirements apply to both MiFID and non-MiFID firms and business.

Q32. **Answer: D** **Ref: Chapter 4, Section 2.3.1 (LO 4.2.4)**

Firms carrying on MiFID must provide their clients with appropriate information, in a comprehensible form, about themselves and their service, the investments and strategies to be used, the execution venues on which these may be dealt and any costs and associated charges.

Q33. **Answer: C** **Ref: Chapter 4, Section 2.2 (LO 4.2.3)**

Client agreements are required for business carried out for retail clients and (for MiFID business) professional clients.

Q34. **Answer: C** **Ref: Chapter 4, Section 2.4 (LO 4.2.7)**

The disclosure of costs and charges only has to be disclosed to retail clients. Commission charges/costs must be itemised separately. A firm has to disclose all related fees, commissions, charges and expenses and any taxes payable via the firm.

Q35.   **Answer: C**   **Ref: Chapter 4, Section 7.1.2 (LO 4.7.2)**

Option C is correct. For retail clients the firm must send a statement to them on at least a six-monthly basis, although the retail client can request a quarterly statement from the firm. For leveraged portfolios, the firm must send monthly statements to the client.

Q36.   **Answer: B**   **Ref: Chapter 4, Section 4.2.2 (LO 4.4.5)**

Option B is correct; the other options are all exempt from the requirement to send a suitability report.

Q37.   **Answer: B**   **Ref: Chapter 4, Section 4.3 (LO 4.4.8)**

The rules on non-advised sales (appropriateness) apply to a range of MiFID and non-MiFID investment services which do not involve advice or discretionary portfolio management.

Options A, C and D are covered by the suitability rules, therefore they are incorrect. Option B is correct.

Q38.   **Answer: D**   **Ref: Chapter 4, Section 4 (LO 4.4.2)**

A suitability assessment is not required if the firm is acting on specific instructions from the client.

Q39.   **Answer: A**   **Ref: Chapter 4, Section 4.2.2 (LO 4.4.6)**

The 14-day rule for the issue of suitability reports applies to personal and stakeholder pension schemes, because here the cancellation rules apply.

(The requirement to provide a suitability report within 14 days should not be confused with the actual statutory cooling off period afforded to life and pension products, which is 30 days. Candidates should familiarise themselves with LO 4.5.2 in this regard.)

Q40.   **Answer: B**   **Ref: Chapter 4, Section 5.1.2 (LO 4.5.1)**

A Key Features Document (KFD) is required for packaged products, cash ISAs and cash JISAs.

Q41.   **Answer: D**   **Ref: Chapter 4, Section 3.2 (LO 4.3.4)**

The financial promotions rules are disapplied in certain cases, notably excluded communications. One such rule is a one-off promotion that is not a cold call, if related to non-MiFID business.

All the other options are covered by the financial promotion rules.

Q42.   **Answer: C**   **Ref: Chapter 4, Section 3.7 (LO 4.3.9)**

The mandatory data need not be included if the client has to refer to another document containing that information in order to respond to the offer.

Q43.   **Answer: B**   **Ref: Chapter 4, Section 6.2 (LO 4.6.4)**

The Chinese walls approach prevents information from one part of the firm flowing to another, as part of a firm's arrangements to mitigate against conflicts of interest.

Q44.   **Answer: D**   **Ref: Chapter 4, Section 6.3.1 (LO 4.6.6)**

The inducements rules apply to both retail and professional clients, and apply regardless of a firm's conflicts of interest policy.

For a third-party payment to be acceptable it must satisfy all of the following criteria:

- Disclosed to the client prior to the provision of the service.
- Enhances the quality of the service that the firm is providing to the client.
- Does not impair compliance with the firm's duty to act in the best interest of the client.

Q45.   **Answer: B**   **Ref: Chapter 4, Section 6.3.2 (LO 4.6.6)**

Options A, C and D are incorrect because they do not fall into the criteria for permitted payments – execution or research, as defined in COBS 11.6.

Q46.   **Answer: A**   **Ref: Chapter 4, Section 6.4.1 (LO 4.6.7)**

A is the correct answer. Whilst price, cost and speed of execution are all relevant execution factors to consider, there are other relevant factors that need to be considered for a firm to achieve best execution for a client. These factors are price, costs, speed, likelihood of execution and settlement, size, nature or any other consideration relevant to the execution of an order.

Q47.   **Answer: C**   **Ref: Chapter 4, Section 8.1 (LO 4.8.1)**

The purpose of the client money rules is to protect the client money by requiring segregation away from the firm's own money.

Q48.   **Answer: C**   **Ref: Chapter 4, Section 8.2.1 (LO 4.8.2)**

It is up to a firm to decide the necessary frequency of completing reconciliations of MiFID client money accounts.

Q49.   **Answer: A**   **Ref: Chapter 4, Section 8.1 (LO 4.8.1)**

The purpose of holding the client money in trust is to protect the client money against the firm using it for its own needs, such as repaying creditors.

Q50.   **Answer: D**   **Ref: Chapter 5, Section 2.3 (LO 5.1.2)**

The maximum monetary amount that the FOS can award against a firm is £150,000.

Q51.   **Answer: C**   **Ref: Chapter 3, Section 3.5 (LO 3.3.6)**

The MLRO is a required controlled function.

Q52.   **Answer: B**   **Ref: Chapter 1, Section 8.1 (LO 1.2.5)**

The CISI principles are directed at individual members of the institute.

Q53. **Answer: C** **Ref: Chapter 4, Section 6.8.2 (LO 4.6.15)**

Personal account dealing rules require details of the transactions undertaken to be notified to the firm promptly so that it keeps record of these personal transactions.

Q54. **Answer: C** **Ref: Chapter 4, Section 7.1 (LO 4.7.2)**

The MiFID record keeping requirement is invariably five years.

Q55. **Answer: A** **Ref: Chapter 5, Section 2.1 (LO 5.1.2)**

The FOS is an independent body set up to handle disputes between firms and customers. The FOS will adjudicate on disputes where the customer has tried to resolve the issue/claim directly with the firm.

Q56. **Answer: D** **Ref: Chapter 3, Section 3.1 (LO 3.3.2)**

POCA is concerned with laundering the proceeds of criminal activities.

Q57. **Answer: D** **Ref: Chapter 3, Section 1.4 (LO 3.1.1)**

The insider dealing legislation embraces derivatives on securities and not commodities.

Q58. **Answer: B** **Ref: Chapter 4, Section 7.1.1 (LO 4.7.1)**

For retail clients, the trade confirmation must be sent as soon as possible and no later than the next business day.

Q59. **Answer: A** **Ref: Chapter 5, Section 3.1 (LO 5.1.4)**

The FSCS was established to provide a safety net for customers of financial services firms that become unable to repay them.

Q60. **Answer: B** **Ref: Chapter 2, Section 8.2 (LO 2.2.2)**

A further decision notice can only be issued with the consent of the recipient.

Q61. **Answer: C** **Ref: Chapter 3, Section 6 (LO 3.6.1)**

Under the Data Protection Act, all data controllers must be registered with the Information Commissioner.

Q62. **Answer: C** **Ref: Chapter 5, Section 1.2 (LO 5.1.1)**

Customer complaints procedures apply to complaints received orally or in writing.

Q63. **Answer: C** **Ref: Chapter 5, Section 3.1 (LO 5.1.4)**

The FSCS uses the term eligible claimants for those that can access the scheme.

Q64. **Answer: A** **Ref: Chapter 4, Section 3.5 (LO 4.3.7)**

The firm's name must be included in communications.

Q65. **Answer: C** **Ref: Chapter 4, Section 6.8.2 (LO 4.6.15)**

The rules on personal account dealing do not apply to personal transactions in life policies.

Q66. **Answer: D** **Ref: Chapter 2, Section 2.1 (LO 2.1.1)**

In relation to regulated activities, the legal responsibility for appointed representatives is taken by the authorised firm and the appointed representative is deemed to be exempt.

Q67. **Answer: A** **Ref: Chapter 2, Section 1.2.1 (LO 2.4.3)**

ADRs and GDRs are certificates that represent underlying securities.

Q68. **Answer: C** **Ref: Chapter 2, Section 1.3.5 (LO 2.4.2)**

Overseas persons are not excluded if a legitimate approach relates to deposits, insurance contracts or stakeholder pension schemes.

Q69. **Answer: B** **Ref: Chapter 4, Section 6.4 (LO 4.6.7)**

Best execution is all about getting the best possible outcome for the client.

Q70. **Answer: B** **Ref: Chapter 4, Section 6.2.3 (LO 4.6.5)**

Exceptions to the restriction on trading ahead of the publication of research include execution only client orders and market makers acting in good faith.

Q71. **Answer: B** **Ref: Chapter 5, Section 2.3 (LO 5.1.2)**

FOS decisions accepted by the complainant are binding on both parties.

Q72. **Answer: C** **Ref: Chapter 2, Section 1.2.2 (LO 2.4.1)**

Advising on investments is a regulated activity but does not extend to advice on deposits, nor generic advice or facts.

Q73. **Answer: D** **Ref: Chapter 4, Section 2.1.3 (LO 4.2.1)**

The least sophisticated retail clients are entitled to the most protection.

Q74. **Answer: B** **Ref: Chapter 3, Section 4 (LO 3.4.1)**

The close period is the 30 days before quarterly results and the 60 days before the annual results.

Q75. **Answer: B** **Ref: Chapter 3, Section 8.1.3 (LO 3.7.1)**

MiFID does not consider deposit accounts, mortgages or insurance contracts as financial instruments.

Syllabus Learning Map

Syllabus Unit/ Element		Chapter/ Section
Element 1	**The Regulatory Environment**	**Chapter 1**
1.1	**The Role of the FCA and PRA** On completion, the candidate should:	
1.1.1	know FCA's and PRA's statutory objectives and rule-making powers in respect of authorisation, supervision, enforcement, sanctions and disciplinary action [FSMA]	2
1.1.2	understand the Principles for Businesses [PRIN 1.1.2 (FCA), 1.1.7, 2.1.1 (FCA/PRA)] and the requirement to act honestly, fairly and professionally and to treat customers fairly [COBS 2.1]	3
1.1.3	know the Statements of Principle 1 to 4 and Code of Practice for approved persons for all approved persons functions [APER 1.1A.1, 1.2.3, 2.1A.2, 2.1A.3, 3.1.1A, 4.1, 4.2, 4.3.1 & 4.3.3]	4
1.1.4	know the requirements of the FCA & PRA individual accountability in banking [SMR C–CON 1.1.2, SYSC 5.2.1, Set of Conduct Rules C-CON 2.1/2 (FCA). SMF 2/3/4/5/6, 63E, 64 C, 137G (PRA)]	5.9
1.1.5	know the Statements of Principle 5 to 7 and Code of Practice for approved persons in respect of significant influence functions [APER 2.1A.3, 3.3.1, 4.5.1A/12/13/14 + 4.6.1A/2/3/5/6/8 & 4.7.1A/2/12/13]	4.3
1.1.6	understand the rules and guidance regarding senior management arrangements, systems and controls for both MiFID and non-MiFID investment firms [SYSC 1.2.1, 3.1.1, 4.1.1/2]	5
1.1.7	know the FCA's and the PRA's supervisory approach to regulation including outcome based, early intervention and conduct risk	2
1.2	**Understand the wider structure of UK financial regulation including the responsibilities of the main regulating bodies and the relationship between them:** On completion, the candidate should:	
1.2.1	Market regulators: The Financial Conduct Authority and the Prudential Regulation Authority	1, 6
1.2.2	Other regulators: The UK Competition Commission, The Information Commissioner and The Pensions Regulator	6
1.2.3	The relationships and coordination between the following: • The Financial Conduct Authority • The Prudential Regulation Authority • HMRC • The Financial Ombudsman Scheme (FOS) • The Financial Services Compensation Scheme (FSCS) • The Financial Policy Committee • The Upper Tribunal (Tax and Chancery) • The Bank of England • HM Treasury	6

Syllabus Unit/ Element		Chapter/ Section
1.2.4	know the six types of provisions used by the FCA and PRA in their Handbooks and the status of their approved industry guidance	7
1.2.5	know the Chartered Institute for Securities & Investment's Code of Conduct	8
1.2.6	understand the direct applications of EU legislation and guidance [EC & ESAs]	2.3

Element 2	The Financial Services and Markets Act 2000 and Financial Services Act 2012	Chapter 2
2.1	**Regulated and Prohibited Activities** On completion, the candidate should:	
2.1.1	know the regulated and prohibited activities [Part II/III of FSMA 2000, Regulated Activities Order 2001 and the under-noted guidance in the Perimeter Guidance Manual (PERG)]: • authorised persons [PERG 2.2.3] • exempt persons [PERG 2.10] and FSMA [Exemption Order 2001 (SI 2001/1201)] • offences under the Act [PERG 2.2.1/2] • enforceability of agreements entered into with an unauthorised business [PERG 2.2.2] • defences available under the Act [PERG 2.2.1]	1, 2
2.1.2	understand the regulator's actions in respect of prohibition orders and actions for damages and how private clients can sue for damages when a firm is declared in breach [(FSMA 2000, s.56, 59, 71) (FSA 2012 s.138D)]	1.1.1
2.2	**Performance of Regulated Activities** On completion, the candidate should:	
2.2.1	know the role of the FCA and PRA enforcement divisions, the power of the FCA and PRA to make decisions by executive procedures and the role, scope and consequences of the Regulatory Decisions Committee's responsibility for decision making [DEPP 3.1–3.4, 4.1]	8
2.2.2	know the outcomes of the FCA's and PRA's statutory notices [DEPP 1.2], the regulatory enforcement processes: warning, decision, supervisory and final notices [DEPP 2.2 + 2.3] and the firm's right to refer to the tribunal [DEPP 2.3.2/3]	8.2–8.4
2.2.3	know the FCA's powers of intervention (products and financial promotions)	8.5
2.3	**Information Gathering and Investigations** On completion, the candidate should:	
2.3.1	know the regulator's power to require information and to appoint persons to carry out investigations [FSMA 2000 s.165/7/8]	9
2.4	**Regulated Activities** On completion, the candidate should:	
2.4.1	know the activities specified in Part II of the Regulated Activities Order	1.2.2

Syllabus Unit/ Element		Chapter/ Section
2.4.2	know the main exclusions from the need for authorisation under the FSMA 2000 [Regulated Activities Order] • dealing as principal [PERG 2.8.4] • advice in newspapers [PERG 2.8.12 & 7.1.2] • trustees, nominees and personal representatives [PERG 2.9.3] • employee share schemes [PERG 2.9.13] • overseas persons [PERG 2.9.15]	1.3
2.4.3	know the investments specified in Part III of the Regulated Activities Order	1.2.1
2.4.4	know the authorisation procedures for firms: • the need for authorisation [FSMA s.19. PERG 2.3, Annex 1 & 2, 2.10.9 – 16] • the threshold conditions for authorisation [FSMA Sch 6. COND 2]	3
2.4.5	know the supervisory process: • purpose of supervision arrangements [SUP 1A.2/3] • focus on a firm's senior management [SUP 1A.1.4, SYSC 1.2.1(1)/4.2.1/4.3.1] • tools for supervision [SUP 1A.4.1/2/4/5] • transaction reporting regime [SUP 17.1.4]	4
2.4.6	know the approval processes for approved persons: • the application process [SUP 10A.13.1/2/3] • the criteria for approval as an Approved Person [FIT 1.3, 2.1, 2.2, 2.3]	5
2.4.7	understand FCA's and PRA's controlled functions: the five functional areas, the required functions, the four areas of significant influence functions, the requirement for FCA or PRA approval prior to performing the function [SUP 10A.4/5/6/7/8/9/10/13] and the types of functions listed under Table 10.4.5. FSMA s.59]	5.3
2.4.8	know the Training and Competence regime: • the application of the systems and control responsibilities in relation to the competence of employees [SYSC 3.2.13/14/5.1.1 (FCA/PRA)] • the application of T&C for retail activities [TC 1.1.1/3] and the need for a Statement of Professional Standing • assessing and maintaining competence [TC 2.1.1(1), 2.1.2], the examination requirements before starting activities [TC 2.1.6/7(1)], firms must assess at the outset and at regular intervals the training needs of its employees [TC 2.1.11], maintaining competence [TC 2.1.12/13] • activities to which the T&C rules apply [TC Appendix 1]	6
2.4.9	know the legal and regulatory basis for whistle blowing [SYSC 18.1.2, 18.2.3]	7

Syllabus Unit/ Element		Chapter/ Section
2.5	**Miscellaneous Offences under FSA 2012** On completion, the candidate should:	
2.5.1	know the purpose, provisions, offences and defences of FSA 2012 s.89 –s.92 – misleading statements and practices	10

Element 3	Associated Legislation and Regulation	Chapter 3
3.1	**Insider Dealing** On completion, the candidate should:	
3.1.1	understand the meaning of inside information and insider; the offences and the instruments covered by the legislation [CJA 1993 s.52/56/57/58 + Schedule 2]	1.2–1.4
3.1.2	know the general defences available with regard to insider dealing [CJA 1993 s.53]	1.5
3.1.3	know the special defences: market makers acting in good faith, market information and price stabilisation [CJA 1993 s. 53 and Schedule 1 paras 1–5]	1.6
3.1.4	know the FCA's powers to prosecute insider dealing [FSMA s.402, EG 12.7-10]	1.7
3.2	**Market Abuse** On completion, the candidate should:	
3.2.1	understand the statutory offence of market abuse [FSMA 2000 s.118(1-8)]	2.1
3.2.2	know the status of the FCA's Code of Market Conduct [FSMA 2000 s.119(1) – (3)]; the territorial scope of the legislation and regulation [FSMA 2000 s.118]	2.2
3.2.3	know the offences outlined in the Code of Market Conduct [MAR 1.2.2/7, 1.3.1, 1.4.1, 1.5.1, 1.6.1, 1.7.1, 1.8.1, 1.9.1, 1.2.22]	2.2
3.2.4	know the concept of effect rather than intention [MAR 1.2.3]; the concept of a reasonable regular user [MAR 1.2.20/21] and accepted market practices [MAR 1 Annex 2]	2.3
3.2.5	understand the enforcement regime for market abuse [MAR 1.1.3] and a firm's duty to report suspicious transactions [SUP 15.10.2]	2.4–2.5
3.2.6	know the statutory exceptions (safe harbours) to market abuse [MAR 1.10.1-4 (excl. table 1.10.5)]	2.6
3.2.7	understand the distinction between offences under market abuse, insider dealing [CJA] and under FSA 2012 s.89–s.92 misleading statements	2.7
3.3	**Money Laundering** On completion, the candidate should:	
3.3.1	understand the terms money laundering, criminal conduct and criminal property and the application of money laundering to all crimes [Proceeds of Crime Act 2002 s.340] and the power of the Secretary of State to determine what is relevant criminal conduct	3

Syllabus Unit/ Element		Chapter/ Section
3.3.2	understand that the UK legislation on money laundering is found in the Proceeds of Crime Act 2002 [POCA], as amended by the Serious Organised Crime and Police Act 2005 [SOCPA], the Money Laundering Regulations 2007, the Senior Management Arrangements, Systems and Controls Sourcebook [SYSC] and that guidance to these provisions is found in the Joint Money Laundering Steering Group Guidance and Financial Crime Guide and understand the interaction between them	3
3.3.3	understand the main offence set out in the Money Laundering Regulations (internal controls), which includes obligations on firms for adequate training of individuals on money laundering	3.3.1
3.3.4	understand the three stages of money laundering	3.2
3.3.5	understand the main offences set out in POCA Part 7 Sections 327, 328, 329, 330, 333A, 342 [Assistance ie, concealing, arrangements, acquisition use and possession; failure to disclose; tipping off in the regulated sector] and the implications of Part 7 regarding the objective test in relation to reporting suspicious transactions; that appropriate disclosure [internal for staff and to the National Crime Agency for the firm] is a defence	3.3.2
3.3.6	understand the approach adopted covered by the Senior Management Arrangements, Systems and Controls Sourcebook [SYSC], in particular, the systems and controls that the FCA and PRA expect firms to have adopted, the role of the Money Laundering Reporting Officer, Nominated Officer and the compliance function [SYSC 3.2.6, 3.2.6 (A)-(J) (FCA), 3.2.7 (FCA/PRA), 3.2.8, SYSC 6.3 (FCA)]	3.4.1, 3.5
3.3.7	understand the standards expected by the JMLSG Guidance particularly in relation to: • Risk-based approach • Requirements for directors and senior managers to be responsible for money laundering precautions • Need for risk assessment • Need for enhanced due diligence in relation to politically exposed persons [JMLSG 5.5.1–5.5.29] • Need for high level policy statement • Detailed procedures implementing the firm's risk based approach [JMLSG 1.20, 1.27, 1.40–1.43, 4.17–4.18] • Financial Sanctions regime [JMLSG Part III 4.1–4.10]	3.4.2
3.3.8	understand the money laundering aspects of know your customer (Joint Money Laundering Steering Groups' Guidance for the financial sector [Para 5.1.1 - 5.1.14]	3.4.3
3.3.9	understand the importance of ongoing monitoring of business relationships and being able to recognise a suspicious transaction and the requirement for staff to report to the MLRO and for the firm to report to the National Crime Agency	3.5

Syllabus Unit/ Element		Chapter/ Section
3.3.10	know what activities are regarded as 'terrorism' in the UK [Terrorism Act 2000 Part 1], the obligations on regulated firms under the Counter-Terrorism Act 2008 [money laundering of terrorist funds] [part 5 section 62 and s.7 part 1-7] and the Anti-Terrorism Crime & Security Act 2001 Schedule 2 Part 3 [Disclosure of Information] and where to find the sanction list for terrorist activities	3.6
3.3.11	understand the importance of preventative measures in respect of terrorist financing and the essential differences between laundering the proceeds of crime and the financing of terrorist acts [JMLSG Guidance 2007 paras 1.38 – 1.39, Preface 9 as amended December 2011] and the interaction between the rules of the FCA, the PRA, the Terrorism Act 2000 and the JMLSG Guidance regarding terrorism [JMLSG Guidance 2007 Preface 27, 28, 29 as amended December 2011]	3.6.1
3.3.12	know the main purpose of Bribery Act 2010 and the categories of offences covered in s.1–7 Bribery Act 2010	3
3.4	**Model Code** On completion, the candidate should:	
3.4.1	know the main purpose and provisions of the Model Code on share dealing by directors and other persons discharging managerial responsibilities, including: • close periods • undisclosed inside information • chairman's approval • dealings by the chairman • short-term dealing • exceptional circumstances • application and record keeping	4
3.5	**Disclosure and Transparency Rules** On completion, the candidate should:	
3.5.1	know the purpose of the Disclosure and Transparency Rules and the control of information [DTR 2.1.3, 2.6.1]	5
3.6	**Data Protection Act 1998** On completion, the candidate should:	
3.6.1	know the eight Data Protection Principles; the need for notification of data controllers with the Information Commissioner; the record-keeping requirements of FCA-regulated firms [DPA Schedule 1, Part 1 & COBS Schedule 1 – record keeping requirements (FCA) and SYSC 3 & 9 (FCA/PRA)]	6

Syllabus Unit/ Element		Chapter/ Section
3.7	**Relevant European Regulation** On completion, the candidate should:	
3.7.1	know the relevant European Union Directives and the impact on the UK financial services industry in respect of: • MiFID – passporting within the EEA (and home v's host state regulation) • UCITS – selling cross-border collective investment schemes; • Prospectus Directive – selling securities cross-border • AIFMD – regulation of AIFMD and the promotion of AIF within the EU • EMIR – requirements placed on EEA established counterparties	8
3.8	**Prudential Standards** On completion, the candidate should:	
3.8.1	know the purpose of the Capital Adequacy for certain types of investment firms	7

Element 4	The FCA Conduct of Business Sourcebook/Client Assets	Chapter 4
4.1	**The Application and General Provisions of the FCA Conduct of Business Sourcebook** On completion, the candidate should:	
	The Firms Subject to the Conduct of Business Sourcebook COBS 1	
4.1.1	know the firms subject to the FCA Conduct of Business Sourcebook [COBS 1.1.1-1.1.3, COBS 1 Annex 1 Part 3, section 3 (FCA/PRA)]	1.2
	Activities Subject to the Conduct of Business Sourcebook COBS 1	
4.1.2	know the activities which are subject to the FCA Conduct of Business Sourcebook including eligible counterparty business and transactions between regulated market participants [COBS 1.1.1–1.1.3, Annex 1, Part 1(1) (FCA/PRA) & (4) (FCA)]	1.3
	Impact of Location COBS 1	
4.1.3	know the impact of location on firms/activities of the application of the FCA Conduct of Business Sourcebook: permanent place of business in UK [COBS 1.1.1–1.1.3 & Annex 1, Part 2 (FCA/PRA) & Part 3 (1–3) (FCA/PRA 1–2 only)]	1.2
	Appointed Representatives COBS 1	
4.1.4	know how the application of the FCA Conduct of Business Sourcebook applies to appointed representatives [COBS 1.1.1 (FCA/PRA)] including financial promotions and firm's responsibilities for appointed representatives [COBS 4.1]	1.4
	Electronic Media	
4.1.5	know the provisions of the FCA Conduct of Business Sourcebook regarding electronic media (glossary definitions of durable medium and website conditions)	1.5

Syllabus Unit/ Element		Chapter/ Section
	Telephone & Electronic Communications COBS 11.8	
4.1.6	know the recording of voice conversations and electronic communications requirements [COBS 11.8]	1.6
4.2	**Accepting Clients** On completion, the candidate should:	
	Client Categorisation COBS 3	
4.2.1	understand [PRIN 1.2.1 (FCA/PRA)/2/3, Glossary, COBS 3]: • definition of client [COBS 3.2] • the application of the rules on client categorisation [COBS 3.1] • retail client [COBS 3.4]; professional client [COBS 3.5] and eligible counterparty [COBS 3.6]	2.1
4.2.2	understand client status [PRIN 1.2.1 (FCA/PRA)/2/3, Glossary, COBS 3]: • when a person is acting as agent for another person [COBS 2.4.1–3] • the rule on categorising elective professional clients [COBS 3.5.3–9] • the rule on elective eligible counterparties [COBS 3.6.4 – 6] • providing clients with a higher level of protection [COBS 3.7] • the requirement to provide notifications of client categorisation [COBS 3.3]	2.1
	Client Agreements and Information Provision COBS 2, 6, 7, 8 & 14	
4.2.3	know the requirement for firms to provide client agreements, when a client agreement is required to be signed and when it is acceptable to be provided to clients [COBS 8.1.1 – 8.1.3]	2.2
4.2.4	know the requirement to provide information to clients prior to providing services to clients including information relating to the nature and risk of the services and designated investments being offered [COBS 2.2, 6.1.1–4 & 14.3.1–10]	2.3
4.2.5	know the rules on the provision of information in connection with the service of managing investments [COBS 6.1.6]	2.3
4.2.6	know the rules on the provision of information concerning safeguarding of designated investments belonging to clients and client money [COBS 6.1.7]	2.3
4.2.7	know the rules on disclosure of costs and associated charges, timing of disclosure; medium of disclosure, changes to information provided to the client and compensation information [COBS 6.1.9–6.1.16]	2.4
4.2.8	know the requirements for an adviser to a retail client to be remunerated only by adviser charges in relation to any personal recommendation or related service	2.4
	Reliance on Others COBS 2.4	
4.2.9	know the rules, guidance and evidential provisions regarding reliance on others [COBS 2.4.4/6/7]	2.5

Syllabus Unit/ Element		Chapter/ Section
4.3	**Communicating with Clients, Including Financial Promotions** On completion, the candidate should:	
	Application of the Rules on Communication with Clients, including Financial Promotions COBS 4.1	
4.3.1	know the application of the rules on communication to clients and on fair, clear and not misleading communications and financial promotions [COBS 4.1, 4.2.1–4]	3.1
	The Rule on Fair, Clear and Not Misleading Communications and Identifying Financial Promotions As Such COBS 4.1, 4.2 & 4.3	
4.3.2	know the purpose and application of the financial promotion rules and the relationship with Principles for Businesses 6 and 7 [COBS 4.1]	3.1
4.3.3	know the rule on identifying promotions as such [COBS 4.3]	3.1
	The Main Exceptions (Financial Promotions Order ('FPO'), COBS 4.1 & 4.8 and Glossary Definition of 'Excluded Communications')	
4.3.4	know the main exceptions to the financial promotion rules in COBS [COBS 4.1, 4.8], the limitations in connection to MiFID business and the existence of the FPO	3.2
	Types of Communication COBS 4	
4.3.5	know the types and methods of communication addressed by COBS 4	3.3
4.3.6	know the rules on prospectus advertisements [PR 3.3]	3.4
	Communicating with Retail Clients COBS 4.5	
4.3.7	know the general rule in connection with communicating with retail clients [COBS 4.5]	3.5
	Past, Simulated Past and Future Performance COBS 4.6	
4.3.8	know the rules on past, simulated past and future performance [COBS 4.6 excluding 4.6.4–4.6.4B]	3.6
	Financial Promotions Containing Offers or Invitations COBS 4.7	
4.3.9	know the rule on financial promotions containing offers or invitations [COBS 4.7.1 - 4]	3.7
	Cold Calls and Other Promotions that are Not in Writing COBS 4.8 & 4.9	
4.3.10	know the rules on unwritten promotions [COBS 4.8.3] and the restriction on cold calling [COBS 4.8.2]	3.8
4.3.11	know the rule on financial promotions for overseas persons [COBS 4.9.3]	3.9
	Systems and Controls and Approving and Communicating Financial Promotions COBS 4.10 and SYSC 3 & 4	
4.3.12	know the requirement for approving financial promotions and the circumstances of relying on an another firm's confirmation of compliance [COB 4.10 (FCA), SYSC 3 & 4 (FCA/PRA)]	3.10

Syllabus Unit/ Element		Chapter/ Section
4.4	**Suitability** On completion, the candidate should:	
	Suitability (including basic advice) COBS 9.1	
4.4.1	understand the application of the rules on identifying client needs and advising [COBS 9.1.1-9.1.4] and the rules on churning and switching [COBS 9.3.2]	4.1
	Assessing Suitability COBS 9.2, 9.3 & 9.4	
4.4.2	understand the purpose of the suitability rules and the requirement for assessing suitability [COBS 9.2.1–3]	4.2.1
4.4.3	understand the information which a firm must obtain from a client in order to make a suitability assessment [COBS 9.2.1–7]; and the guidance on assessing suitability [COBS 9.3.1]	4.2.3
4.4.4	know the application of the assessing suitability rules for professional clients [COBS 9.2.8]	4.2.4
4.4.5	understand the obligation to provide a retail client with a suitability report [COBS 9.4.1–3]	4.2.2
4.4.6	know the timing and contents of a suitability report [COBS 9.4]	4.2.2
	Appropriateness (Non-Advised Services) COBS 10	
4.4.7	understand the application and purpose of the rules on non-advised sales [COBS 10.1]	4.3
4.4.8	understand the obligations for assessing appropriateness [COBS 10.2]	4.3
4.4.9	know the circumstances in which it is not necessary to assess appropriateness [COBS 10.4–10.6]	4.3
4.5	**Product Disclosure and the Client's Right to Cancel** On completion, the candidate should:	
	Product disclosure COBS 13, 14 & 15	
4.5.1	know the purpose of the rules on the sale of packaged products to retail clients, the rules requiring the provision of key features to retail clients and the main features to be explained in the key features [COBS 13.1.1/3/4, 13.2.1/2/4, 13.3.1/2 (excluding Annex 1R) & 14.1.1, 14.3.1/2]	5.1
4.5.2	know the purpose and requirements of the cancellation and withdrawal rights [COBS 15.1.1, 15.2.1, 15.2.3, 15.2.5, 15.3.1, 15.3.2]	5.2
4.5.3	Know the requirements for a firm making a personal recommendation to be independent or restricted	5.1
4.6	**Dealing and Managing** On completion, the candidate should:	
	Application of the Rules on Dealing and Managing COBS 11.1	
4.6.1	know the application of the rules on dealing and managing [COBS 11.1]	6.1

Syllabus Unit/ Element		Chapter/ Section
	Conflicts of Interest COBS 12, SYSC 10 and PRIN 2.1	
4.6.2	understand the application and purpose of the principles and rules on conflict of interest; the rules on identifying conflicts and types of conflicts; the rules on recording and disclosure of conflicts [PRIN 2.1.1 Principle 8 (FCA/PRA), SYSC 10.1.1–6 + 10.1.8/9 (FCA/PRA)]	6.2.1
4.6.3	know the rule requiring a conflicts policy and the contents of the policy [SYSC 10.1.10/11/12 (FCA/PRA)–10.1/13/14/15]	6.2.2
4.6.4	understand the rule on managing conflicts of interest (SYSC 10.1.7 (FCA/PRA)) and how to manage conflicts of interest to ensure the fair treatment of clients (SYSC 10.2 (FCA/PRA)) including: information barriers such as Chinese walls; reporting lines; remuneration structures; segregation of duties; policy of independence	6.2.1
4.6.5	know the rules on managing conflict in connection with investment research and research recommendations [COBS 12.2.1/3/5/10, 12.3.2/3/4, 12.4.1/4/5/6/7/9/10/15/16/17]	6.2.3
	Inducements and Use of Dealing Commission COBS 2.3 & 12.6	
4.6.6	know the application of the inducements rules [COBS 2.3.1–2 & 2.3.10–16] and the use of dealing commission, including what benefits can be supplied/obtained under such agreements [COBS 11.6]	6.3
	Best Execution COBS 11	
4.6.7	understand the requirements of providing best execution [COBS 11.2.1–13]	6.4.1
4.6.8	understand the requirements for an order execution policy, its disclosure, the requirements for consent and review [COBS 11.2.14–18, 11.2.22-26 & 11.2.28]	6.4.2
4.6.9	understand the rules on following specific instructions from a client [COBS 11.2.19–21]	6.4.3
4.6.10	understand the rules on monitoring the effectiveness of execution arrangements and policy; demonstrating compliance with the execution policy; and the duties of portfolio managers and receivers and transmitters to act in a client's best interest [COBS 11.2.27, 11.2.29–34]	6.4.2
	Client Order Handling COBS 11.3	
4.6.11	understand the rule on client order handling [COBS 11.3.1] and the conditions to be satisfied when carrying out client orders [COBS 11.3.2–6]	6.5
	Aggregation and Allocation COBS 11.3	
4.6.12	understand the rules on aggregation and allocation of orders [COBS 11.3.7-8] and the rules on aggregation and allocation of transactions for own account [COBS 11.3.9-13]	6.6
	Client Limit Orders COBS 11.4	
4.6.13	know the rules on client limit orders – the obligation to make unexecuted client limit orders public [COBS 11.4]	6.7

Syllabus Unit/ Element		Chapter/ Section
	Personal Account Dealing COBS 11.7	
4.6.14	understand the purpose and application of the personal account dealing rule and the restrictions on personal account dealing [COBS 11.7.1–3]	6.8
4.6.15	know the arrangements required to comply with the personal account dealing rules including the notification requirements; and exceptions regarding personal account dealing [COBS 11.7.4–7]	6.8
4.7	**Reporting to Clients** On completion, the candidate should:	
	Confirmation of Transactions and Periodic Statements COBS 16.1, 16.2, 16.3	
4.7.1	know the general client reporting and occasional reporting requirements [COBS 16.1–16.2]	7.1
4.7.2	know the rules on periodic reporting to retail and professional clients, the exceptions to the requirements and the record-keeping requirements (COBS 16.3)	7.1
4.8	**Client Assets**	
	On completion, the candidate should:	
4.8.1	understand the purpose of the client money and custody rules in CASS including the requirement for segregation and that it is held in trust [CASS 6.2.1-3; 7.12.1-2; 7.13.2/3/5/12]	8.1
4.8.2	know the requirements for reconciling client assets and client money including the timing and identification of discrepancies [CASS 6.6.1 1/13/16/17/19/22/24/27/28/34/37/44/54; 7.15.5/20/22/29/31/32/33]	8.2
4.8.3	know the exemptions from the requirements of the CASS rules [CASS 1.2.3-4; 6.1.1-6; 6.2.10/13/14/15; 7.1.1-10 & 7.1.12]	8.3

Element 5	Complaints and Redress	Chapter 5
5.1	**Customer Complaints** On completion, the candidate should:	
5.1.1	know the procedures a firm must implement and follow to handle customer complaints [DISP 1.2.1/3, 1.3.3, 1.4.1, 1.6.1/2/5, 1.9.1, 1.10.1]	1.2, 1.3
5.1.2	know the role of the Financial Ombudsman Service (FOS) [DISP Complaints Sourcebook – Dispute Resolution: Complaints: Introduction] and the awards which can be made [DISP 3.7.2/4]	2
5.1.3	know the criteria for a complainant to be eligible to lodge a complaint [DISP 2.2]	1.3
5.1.4	know the circumstances in which the Financial Services Compensation Scheme will pay compensation [COMP 3.2 (FCA/PRA), 4.2.1/2/3 (FCA/PRA)] and the compensation payable in respect of protected deposits and protected investment business [COMP 10.2.1/3 (FCA/PRA)]	3
5.1.5	know the framework under which the FCA can be alerted to super-complaints and mass-detriment references	4

Examination Specification

Each examination paper is constructed from a specification that determines the weightings that will be given to each element. The specification is given below.

It is important to note that the numbers quoted may vary slightly from examination to examination as there is some flexibility to ensure that each examination has a consistent level of difficulty. However, the number of questions tested in each element should not change by more than plus or minus 2.

Element Number	Element	Questions
1	The Regulatory Environment	7
2	The Financial Services and Markets Act 2000	10
3	Associated Legislation and Regulation	18
4	The FCA Conduct of Business Sourcebook/Client Assets	37
5	Complaints and Redress	3
Total		**75**

CISI Associate (ACSI) Membership can work for you...

Studying for a CISI qualification is hard work and we're sure you're putting in plenty of hours, but don't lose sight of your goal!

This is just the first step in your career; there is much more to achieve!

The securities and investments industry attracts ambitious and driven individuals. You're probably one yourself and that's great, but on the other hand you're almost certainly surrounded by lots of other people with similar ambitions.

So how can you stay one step ahead during these uncertain times?

Entry Criteria:

Pass in either:

* Investment Operations Certificate (IOC), IFQ, ICWIM, Capital Markets in, eg, Securities, Derivatives, Advanced Certificates; or
* one CISI Diploma/Masters in Wealth Management paper

Joining Fee: £25 or free if applying via prefilled application form   **Annual Subscription (pro rata):** £125

Using your new CISI qualification* to become an Associate (ACSI) member of the Chartered Institute for Securities & Investment could well be the next important career move you make this year, and help you maintain your competence.

Join our global network of over 40,000 financial services professionals and start enjoying both the professional and personal benefits that CISI membership offers. Once you become a member you can use the prestigious ACSI designation after your name and even work towards becoming personally chartered.

* ie, Investment Operations Certificate (IOC), IFQ, ICWIM, Capital Markets

Benefits in Summary...

* Use of the CISI CPD Scheme
* Unlimited free CPD seminars, webcasts, podcasts and online training tools
* Highly recognised designatory letters
* Unlimited free attendance at CISI Professional Forums
* CISI publications including *S&I Review* and *Change – The Regulatory Update*
* 20% discount on all CISI conferences and training courses
* Invitation to CISI Annual Lecture
* Select Benefits – our exclusive personal benefits portfolio

The ACSI designation will provide you with access to a range of member benefits, including Professional Refresher where there are currently over 60 modules available on subjects including Behavioural Finance, Cybercrime and Conduct Risk. CISI TV is also available to members, allowing you to catch up on the latest CISI events, whilst earning valuable CPD hours.

Plus many other networking opportunities which could be invaluable for your career.

Professional Refresher

Self-testing elearning modules to refresh your knowledge, meet regulatory and firm requirements, and earn CPD hours.

Professional Refresher is a training solution to help you remain up-to-date with industry developments, maintain regulatory compliance and demonstrate continuing learning.

This popular online learning tool allows self-administered refresher testing on a variety of topics, including the latest regulatory changes.

There are currently over 60 modules available which address UK and international issues. Modules are reviewed by practitioners frequently and new topics are added to the suite on a regular basis.

Benefits to firms:
- Learning and tests can form part of business T&C programme
- Learning and tests kept up-to-date and accurate by the CISI
- Relevant and useful – devised by industry practitioners
- Access to individual results available as part of management overview facility, 'Super User'
- Records of staff training can be produced for internal use and external audits
- Cost-effective – no additional charge for CISI members
- Available to non-members

Benefits to individuals:
- Comprehensive selection of topics across industry sectors
- Modules are frequently reviewed and updated by industry experts
- New topics introduced regularly
- Free for members
- Successfully passed modules are recorded in your CPD log as Active Learning
- Counts as structured learning for RDR purposes
- On completion of a module, a certificate can be printed out for your own records

The full suite of Professional Refresher modules is free to CISI members or £250 for non-members. Modules are also available individually. To view a full list of Professional Refresher modules visit:

cisi.org/refresher

If you or your firm would like to find out more contact our Client Relationship Management team:

+ 44 20 7645 0670
crm@cisi.org

For more information on our elearning products, contact our Customer Support Centre on +44 20 7645 0777, or visit our website at cisi.org/study

Professional Refresher

Top 5

Integrity & Ethics

- High Level View
- Ethical Behaviour
- An Ethical Approach
- Compliance vs Ethics

Anti-Money Laundering

- Introduction to Money Laundering
- UK Legislation and Regulation
- Money Laundering Regulations 2007
- Proceeds of Crime Act 2002
- Terrorist Financing
- Suspicious Activity Reporting
- Money Laundering Reporting Officer
- Sanctions

Financial Crime

- What is Financial Crime?
- Insider Dealing and Market Abuse Introduction, Legislation, Offences and Rules
- Money Laundering Legislation, Regulations, Financial Sanctions and Reporting Requirements
- Money Laundering and the Role of the MLRO

Information Security and Data Protection

- Information Security: The Key Issues
- Latest Cybercrime Developments
- The Lessons From High-Profile Cases
- Key Identity Issues: Know Your Customer
- Implementing the Data Protection Act 1998
- The Next Decade: Predictions For The Future

UK Bribery Act

- Background to the Act
- The Offences
- What the Offences Cover
- When Has an Offence Been Committed
- The Defences Against Charges of Bribery
- The Penalties

Compliance

Behavioural Finance

- Background to Behavioural Finance
- Biases and Heuristics
- The Regulator's Perspective
- Implications of Behavioural Finance

Conduct Risk

- What is Conduct Risk?
- Regulatory Powers
- Managing Conduct Risk
- Treating Customers Fairly
- Practical Application of Conduct Risk

Conflicts of Interest

- Introduction
- Examples of Conflicts of Interest
- Examples of Enforcement Action
- Policies and Procedures
- Tools to Manage Conflicts of Interest
- Conflict Management Process
- Good Practice

Risk (an overview)

- Definition of Risk
- Key Risk Categories
- Risk Management Process
- Risk Appetite
- Business Continuity
- Fraud and Theft
- Information Security

T&C Supervision Essentials

- Who Expects What From Supervisors?
- Techniques for Effective Routine Supervision
- Practical Skills of Guiding and Coaching
- Developing and Assessing New Advisers
- Techniques for Resolving Poor Performance

Operations

Best Execution

- What Is Best Execution?
- Achieving Best Execution
- Order Execution Policies
- Information to Clients & Client Consent
- Monitoring, the Rules, and Instructions
- Client Order Handling

Central Clearing

- Background to Central Clearing
- The Risks CCPs Mitigate
- The Events of 2007/08
- Target 2 Securities

Corporate Actions

- Corporate Structure and Finance
- Life Cycle of an Event
- Mandatory Events
- Voluntary Events

Wealth

Client Assets and Client Money

- Protecting Client Assets and Client Money
- Ring-Fencing Client Assets and Client Money
- Due Diligence of Custodians
- Reconciliations
- Records and Accounts
- CASS Oversight

Investment Principles and Risk

- Diversification
- Factfind and Risk Profiling
- Investment Management
- Modern Portfolio Theory and Investing Styles
- Direct and Indirect Investments
- Socially Responsible Investment
- Collective Investments
- Investment Trusts
- Dealing in Debt Securities and Equities

Principles of RDR

- Professionalism – Qualifications
- Professionalism – SPS
- Description of Advice – Part 1
- Description of Advice – Part 2
- Adviser Charging

Suitability of Client Investments

- Assessing Suitability
- Risk Profiling and Establishing Risk
- Obtaining Customer Information
- Suitable Questions and Answers
- Making Suitable Investment Selections
- Guidance, Reports and Record Keeping

International

Dodd-Frank Act

- Background and Purpose
- Creation of New Regulatory Bodies
- Too Big to Fail and the Volcker Rule
- Regulation of Derivatives
- Securitisation
- Credit Rating Agencies

Foreign Account Tax Compliance Act (FATCA)

- Reporting by US Taxpayers
- Reporting by Foreign Financial Institutions
- Implementation Timeline

Sovereign Wealth Funds

- Definition and History
- The Major SWFs
- Transparency Issues
- The Future
- Sources

cisi.org/refresher

Feedback to the CISI

Have you found this workbook to be a valuable aid to your studies? We would like your views, so please email us at learningresources@cisi.org with any thoughts, ideas or comments.

Accredited Training Providers

Support for examination students studying for the Chartered Institute for Securities & Investment (CISI) Qualifications is provided by several Accredited Training Providers (ATPs), including Fitch Learning and BPP. The CISI's ATPs offer a range of face-to-face training courses, distance learning programmes, their own learning resources and study packs which have been accredited by the CISI. The CISI works in close collaboration with its ATPs to ensure they are kept informed of changes to CISI examinations so they can build them into their own courses and study packs.

CISI Workbook Specialists Wanted

Workbook Authors

Experienced freelance authors with finance experience, and who have published work in their area of specialism, are sought. Responsibilities include:

- Updating workbooks in line with new syllabuses and any industry developments
- Ensuring that the syllabus is fully covered

Workbook Reviewers

Individuals with a high-level knowledge of the subject area are sought. Responsibilities include:

- Highlighting any inconsistencies against the syllabus
- Assessing the author's interpretation of the workbook

Workbook Technical Reviewers

Technical reviewers provide a detailed review of the workbook and bring the review comments to the panel. Responsibilities include:

- Cross-checking the workbook against the syllabus
- Ensuring sufficient coverage of each learning objective

Workbook Proofreaders

Proofreaders are needed to proof workbooks both grammatically and also in terms of the format and layout. Responsibilities include:

- Checking for spelling and grammar mistakes
- Checking for formatting inconsistencies

If you are interested in becoming a CISI external specialist call:

+44 20 7645 0609

or email:

externalspecialists@cisi.org

For bookings, orders, membership and general enquiries please contact our Customer Support Centre on +44 20 7645 0777, or visit our website at cisi.org